On This, We Agree!

Library of Congress Control Number: 2024942529

ISBN (paperback): 978-1-963271-25-6
ISBN (Ebook): 978-1-963271-26-3

Armin Lear Press, Inc.
215 W Riverside Drive, #4362
Estes Park, CO 80517

On This, We Agree!

The Basis for US Consensus and How
We Can Solve Urgent Problems Today

Carlos D. Torres, PhD

ARMINLEAR

In this age, in this country, public sentiment is everything. With it, nothing can fail; against it, nothing can succeed. Whoever molds public sentiment goes deeper than he who enacts statutes, or pronounces judicial decisions.[1]

—Abraham Lincoln

Contents

Preface

One of the unintentional positives of being an adjunct professor constantly in search of work has been that I have had the experience of teaching at different colleges and universities and in multiple departments. I have spent an inordinate amount of time stretching beyond the boundaries of my field into US economics, politics, and environmental studies, for example. In comparing first-person testimonies with larger societal data for a course at Sonoma State University, I began to see what I believed to be disjunctures between how our differences in the United States are represented in politics and media versus how much accord actually exists among ordinary Americans. There were a few reasons for this: Polarization and drama make headlines, and consensus and solidarity do not, for one. As an anthropologist, I also knew that cognitively, it is much easier to recognize differences in others and harder to reconcile where similarities exist. But as I looked closer at the research and the projected views of our political differences, I began to see evidence that the maintenance of polarization in the United States was profitable to some of the most powerful individuals and corporations in society, that polarization was a strategy of distraction, and I became frustrated by the prevalence of this tactic.

This book, then, was born of an anthropologist's frustrations, realizations, and aspirations. The strategy of infusing the public sphere with polarization and false urgencies leads the American electorate down conspiracy rabbit holes. Polarization and political drama perilously distract hard-working Americans away from any possible solidarity that might come if they realize many Americans are as frustrated as they are. It detracts Americans away from the power of shared experiences or any consensus on solutions. Polling data suggest Americans, by and large, recognize the existential problems we face now and in the future and that our concerns are being largely ignored. The data also suggests ways to fix these problems with the consensus that we already have. We live in a new political information system that inadvertently—and at times explicitly—keeps ordinary Americans from recognizing and confirming our commonalities. The aspiration in this book is that enumerating our shared concerns might inspire a rational majority in the US to reassert itself to energize a more deliberative form of democracy than the one we have been relegated to.

My motivations for writing this book also run deeper, from my own experiences growing up and later from research conducted primarily in Mexico and in the United States. I grew up in two worlds: ethnically, financially, and politically. As a half-Hispanic and half-White American, like many so-called "halfies," I always felt at home in two different cultures in the United States, but also very much apart as well. I have always felt welcomed by Mexican-American families, even though my Mexican ancestry derives from a well-off family whose properties were confiscated during the Mexican Revolution—not a stereotypical story of cross-border immigration. Nonetheless, like any multigenerational immigrant story, it is a narrative about starting over with little in possession. My mother's family is of Anglo-Celtic origin and was part of the internal immigration of Dust Bowl farmers forced to relocate to Northern Arizona, where water was plentiful—they started over with even less.

My early childhood, however, is remembered fondly, living in a small creekside house in prosperous Marin County, California probably most known now as the home of Lucasfilm's Skywalker Ranch. Naturalized to the privilege around me, my father died when I was only seven years old, and my own immediate family also had to start over: a single mother and three children moving to Southeast El Paso, Texas, very close to the Southern border with Mexico. I began to know something about the other side of America, those struggling on the economic margins. In that geography, my curiosity about "the other side" began to be cultivated. What stands out in my early childhood memories are acts of generosity: from wealthy parents of other kids in Marin County who welcomed a different-looking kid and from those dirt-poor classmates in El Paso who had little but shared all they had.

My experience from the other side in El Paso, Texas, was fairly brief. A new stepfather helped bring my family back to California. He took it upon himself to teach me the value of a hard day's work, taking me along as a teenager on his construction jobs, he was a crane operator. I suffered through the pre-dawn work trips and his conservative rants in the cab of his truck, railing against taxes and "those people" working the system of social welfare. As I grew older, I learned more about my stepfather's experiences in World War II, and I came to believe he had fought life and limb for the right to speak his mind and be heard. I would never begrudge his views again, no matter how much I disagreed with his outlook. Like many Americans, my family was composed of white-collar and blue-collar members of diverse political ideologies. As I became a working adult, trying to make a living in a new American economy of gig workers, I worked a variety of jobs talking to people of all stripes in "the back of the house," in industries like restaurants, television, mortgage lending, and higher education; listening to the common aspirations of those working day to day and observing the challenges they overcame in pursuit of their goals.

I took these experiences with me when I began doctoral research in 2004, researching the Maya quest for democracy and autonomy in Chiapas, Mexico. On January 1, 1994, the Zapatistas, a politicized group of mostly indigenous Maya rural laborers arose rebelling against trade liberalism with the onset of the North American Free Trade Agreement (NAFTA) scheduled to take effect that day, which meant the wholesale corn prices of small-scale Maya farmers would be slashed. Maya families who made a small living from growing corn would have to sell their labor down the mountain to larger agricultural companies, and their autonomy and sense of self-worth would be diminished. Since 1994, the wage gap between the poorest and the richest workers in Mexico, the US, and many other parts of the world has noticeably increased. However, the Maya citizens weren't helpless: over 100 municipalities in Chiapas, Mexico, threw out their coopted town leadership soon after NAFTA took effect. However, the economic fate of Maya workers remained closely tied to national Mexican policies that have only recently evolved.

The lesson learned from research in Latin America and in communities in the United States is that democracy has to begin from below. Societal change and transformation begin when people recognize and act on their collective strength and unity together. Fomenting division and polarization are strategies used by factional minorities to grasp power, but these strategies are based on insecurity and subterfuge. Certainly, the American people have grown more divided in a social mediascape that rewards notoriety and wealth. Still, many more Americans in the last few years have become more conscious of national politics and the failure of our leadership to acknowledge what the polls are telling us—too many of our politicians take their marching orders from a powerful few.

When one travels the world, a new appreciation for our home country can take hold of you. The United States pioneered a new form of democratic-republican government when monarchs and despots ruled the world, and free public education empowered our nation into the 20th Century. The United States—like the United Kingdom—endured a civil war that would eventually forge a new and more inclusive nation that prioritized the growth and sustenance of a thriving merchant class. Blessed with abundant natural resources, the United States was the first nation to preserve wild lands and natural wonders for the benefit of all. Now, leadership in the US House of Representatives seems to be mired in petty squabbles, obstruction, and fundraising from division and polarization. If change and growth in our nation will not come from strong and bipartisan consensus from our leadership, then it may have to come from below. The first step is to quantify our accord, to enumerate where we agree, where we have strength by numbers to galvanize our national leadership toward making our democracy healthier, our citizens wealthier, and our ecology and resource industries sustainable now and for future generations.

Though my family is composed of members with diverse Left and Right perspectives, I know our differences will never divide us—our shared experiences have bound us together with far more power and cohesion. It is my aspiration that this book might offer a similar experience, reminders of our shared national experience and outlooks, and that it might help us to talk to one another again in civil discourse acknowledging all deserve to be heard.

A Note On Sources In This Book

Accurately representing the number of attitudes, beliefs, and solutions for the nation's most urgent problems would entail consulting with every American. The conclusions follow from non-partisan polling data, which can only capture a general attitude in the United States. Still, the data also compel me to understand the issues from both sides, as much as I can, to seek the middle ground majoritarian view. Much of this research is also guided by ethnographic research undertaken in the US and Mexico.

One of the goals of this book was to try to allay some of the fear, division, and animosity that has been thrust onto the American public sphere with an embedded strategy to keep us divided and to instill mistrust in all our American institutions, the reasons for which I will detail later. Following this goal, I purposefully chose sources for this book that are verifiable, non-partisan, multi-genre, and available on the internet or contained within accessible published books. I sought to use sources that did not require special academic access, preferably nonpartisan and multi-genre, to demonstrate that it is still possible to get a view above the political forest even as we clamber through the thickets and thorns of polarized speech. I also wanted to be as transparent with my information as possible and to reference more complete discussions of the whole book and article sources. I hope by using widely available sources I am sending a message that truthful, factual, and non-partisan information can still be obtained online in the public sphere.

Why Consensus Matters

When hyperreality came to the White House

On 22 January 2017, newly elected United States President Donald J. Trump's campaign manager, Kellyanne Conway, spoke with NBC journalist Chuck Todd on *Meet the Press* to try and explain White House press secretary Sean Spicer's false and "easily disprovable claims about the size of Trump's inauguration crowd."[2] Spicer's original comments were meant to defend Trump's statements that the size of his 2017 inauguration crowd was larger than that of President Barack Obama's first inauguration in 2009. Photographic evidence proved it was not. "Don't be so overly dramatic about it, Chuck," Conway told Todd when he noted that Trump's presidency began with this fallacy. "You're saying it's a falsehood...our press secretary, Sean Spicer, gave alternative facts to that."[3] At this point in the conversation, "alternative facts" became part of the lexicon of the US public sphere. In a few short years, an increasing number of Americans became mystified by television news coverage of the national political landscape.

Just before the 2020 US Presidential election, Pew Research polling revealed majorities in both parties believed that "made-up information causes a great deal of confusion, with around seven-in-ten Trump supporters and 60 percent of Biden supporters saying this.[4] We hear so much about our polarization in America, in the news media, and from politicians who stress our differences. But we don't have a very accurate idea of how the issues divide us as a nation, and almost no idea if we have some reasonable consensus on our most concerning issues.

Increased inflation, initiated by supply-chain interruptions during COVID and Russia's invasion of Ukraine, has many Americans paying for the cost-of-living increase with credit cards, unable to keep their wages rising with inflation—exacerbating the political disjuncture between positive economic facts and figures quoted by the Administration of President Joe Biden and the economic pain felt by most Americans. Political disconnection from the Left and post-truth on the Right have left many Americans wondering if unresolvable political division and reality TV have taken control of the wealthiest most powerful democratic nation in the world. Polls indicate the American people *en masse* have lost trust in their institutions, politicians, and even other citizens, leaving open an important question that has filtered into the minds of many Americans: Will Republicans and Democrats ever be able to find accord, some reasonable bipartisan compromise in a world facing immensely consequential challenges?

With a cursory examination of partisan television news sources, and statements of politicians from the fringes of the political spectrum, it is not difficult to imagine the US electorate is deeply and hopelessly divided on critical issues in economics, the environment, diversity, gun rights, and even truth itself. We live in an attention economy, where media, advertisers, pundits, and politicians compete ferociously for our attention. It is a mediascape drawn to the most divisive politicians and the most outrageous statements that drown out voices from the middle ground, and the loudness of the polarization has sometimes been deafening. Americans have grown weary of politics as performance and the false choice that there is only a Right way of thinking or a Left way of being.

However, looking closer at polling data, what we perceive of one another and of the opposite political party don't always correlate with our presuppositions of what we imagine those differences are. Among the academics who have tried to bridge the gulf in our political misperception is University of California sociologist Arlie Hochschild. In July 2019, she published an article in the British daily newspaper *The Guardian* titled "Think Republicans are Disconnected from Reality? It's Even Worse Among Liberals" that used polling information by the think tank *More in Common* to argue a case for misperception. One of the *More in Common* findings Hochschild emphasized was that:

> The wilder a person's guess as to what the other party is thinking, the more likely they were to also personally disparage members of the opposite party as mean, selfish or bad. Not only do the two parties diverge on a great many issues, they also disagree on what they disagree on.[5]

While we don't have a clear sense of what the other side in America believes, we do have consensus, even unanimity on some issues. To start, Republican-leaning Americans and Democrat--leaning Americans are equally concerned about not being able to communicate with each other. Sixty-two percent of those polled in both parties believe that the inability of Republicans and Democrats to work together is a "very big problem," with both sides mirroring the scale of the problem in near-perfect alignment.[6] If the electorates in both parties want our politicians to work together, why aren't we hearing that message loud and clear from the voters themselves? I believe the answer goes back to Arlie Hochschild's observation: through all the political tribalism, shifting ideologies, and divisive rhetoric, members of the two parties aren't exactly sure what they disagree on, and therefore, a powerful collective voice for majoritarian democracy has been reduced to a confused muffle.

Certainly, Americans of each party affiliation have different policy priorities they'd like to see enacted in Congress, and differences now divide people within the same parties along a continuum of ideologies from more liberal to more conservative; we also differ by group identification, ethnicity, and age cohorts. Let me make clear from the outset: Americans are individuals, first and foremost, not simply affiliations or generalizations. In fact, over-generalization is one of the curses of polarization and division. However, if one looks at the big data of national polls across multiple issues, what emerges is a clear majority of Americans in support of legislative action on urgent issues where none is being undertaken. The purchasing power of Americans has declined overall, with inflation forcing many Americans from middle to lower income brackets; tens of thousands of immigrants have flowed over the borders of the Western nations, including the US; pregnant women are facing the realization that obstetricians are leaving their communities; and gyres of plastic hundreds of square miles circle within our world's oceans—indecision, obstruction, and lack of legislative action have real consequences in the world we live in. And the US Congress cannot even get started on problems that may take decades to fix.

The purpose of this book is to shine a light on the surprising amount of consensus in the United States that exists right now on critical issues, to try and demystify the issues at hand, to get past the sound bites and distracting jingoism and get to the root cause of Americans' very rational frustrations. In documenting consensus, it is important to try to take us all back to the basis of urgent problems, to try and ground our national discussions registered through polls in history and comparative policies to point out the ways—even in a seemingly polarized nation—people and institutions around the world are working to alleviate some of the world's most urgent problems right now, undeterred by political primary talking points or the enrichment of campaign funding coiffures.

Is "consensus" itself a contentious term?

Consensus in this book refers to national consensus registered through small, diverse polling samples of majority/minority views in the US population. Certainly, within states and even counties, consensus matters as well, and congressional delegates to the US House of Representatives must consider the majority attitudes of their constituents to be elected to Congress. But it is worthwhile to point out that despite our regional, demographic, and partisan differences, our national consensus suggests a glowering disjuncture between the political will of the majority of US citizens and the legislative priorities of the US House of Representatives. In Chapter 5 of this book, I will cover reasons why this disjuncture persists. The first job at hand is to try to clarify how we perceive the major political issues by party, where consensus may be found, and to discuss what consensual solutions may avail themselves moving forward.

Implied in all of my arguments in this book is that majoritarian democracy is the strongest and most sustainable form of government over the long term because it allows for direct political ownership, an individual stake in the destiny of the nation-state for individual citizens—when it works properly. It is flexible enough to evolve with the pulse of the nation, and it prioritizes crowdsource knowledge, which is ideally a multiplicity of perspectives. Whether majoritarian democracy is the most resilient form of government is debatable, however. It relies on successful deliberative communication and constant political recalibration in an ever-changing world. It is also subject to constant threats by powerful minority factions and mon-eyed interests or want-to-be dictators who make straw man arguments and deliver their points home with captivating performances of conviction.

It is also understood in this book that majorities themselves can be driven by innate prejudices and incomplete knowledge, as the philosopher John Stuart Mills pointed out. Resilience in major-itarian democracy is also subject to the rules of political inclusion in a given society (who is granted citizenship), the quality of the information given to the political public, and a healthy public sphere that allows for civil, mediated discourse. Majoritarian democracy is also sustained by tolerance for minority views and further cultivated by receptivity for new and collaborative solutions.

Does finding and acting on consensus in the US matter?

The United States has many founding stories, origin myths, and origin realities that have come to inform who we are as a people and what unifies us. Consensus and deliberative action figure prominently in the story of America, in events we celebrate, and in ways that are far less conspicuous but no less significant for what they teach us about ourselves. Foremost of our origin stories revolve around the consensus reached in the signing of the Declaration of Independence on July 4, 1776. It is a noteworthy event for the politics of today because the consequences of that consensus were perhaps the greatest of political gambles.

Before that momentous decision, King George III had declared the colonies in a state of rebellion, blood had been spilled at Lexington and Concord, Massachusetts, and American militias had assembled into an army to defend Breed and Bunker Hills in Boston. Signing a document was only the affirmation of a revolution in progress. Nonetheless, the amount of accord and the risk to those assembled in the Continental Congress when the Declaration was signed was very real. In an 1811 letter to John Adams, Benjamin Rush described the signing ceremony on July 4 as a scene of "pensive and awful silence." Rush said he and the other delegates were called up, one after another, and then filed forward somberly to subscribe to what each thought was their ensuing death warrant.[7]

It is difficult to read into all the risks and rewards the signers contemplated or the social pressures they must have been feeling. One delegate dissenter, Thomas Willing, declined to sign the Declaration but subsequently led a 1778 military expedition to raid the holdings of British loyalists in Natchez, Mississippi, and donated money to the revolutionary cause. He later became the wealthiest man in America for a time. His dissent did not deter his patriotic gambles or social prospects, as it did with many British loyalists after the Revolution. Another dissenter, Charles Humphreys, believed the Declaration would escalate the conflict into full-blown war, which he could not support as a Quaker; he, too, prospered. Both dissenters, however, profited in their professions by slavery, signifying the unre-solved contradictions in the most famous preamble ever written: "We hold these truths to be self-evidence, that all men are created equal…" In a very significant way, consensus in America would be determined by which men (and women) would be included in this preamble, how Americans imagined their citizenry, and how our notions of national identity evolved.

Wendy Wall, a professor of history and Queen's University, in her book *Inventing the "American Way," The Politics of Consensus from the New Deal to the Civil Rights Movement* suggests that US national political census has been significantly shaped by the priorities of each era. For Wall, between the mid-1930s and the end of WWII, the focus of American politics and consensus "moved from class-based concerns to a preoccupation with pluralism and individual rights… many liberals who had previously worried about the dangers posed to the nation by economic inequality and an oppressive business elite became increasingly concerned that divisions of any sort might tear democracy apart."[8] During that era, consensus in America was significantly shaped by the rise of fascism and war, which eventually became all-consuming.

Collective visions for an "American Way" in the US have included historical revisionism, at times flipping the roles of victims and perpetrators. In the *Lost Cause* narratives of the Civil War, for example, slavery became deemphasized as a cause for the war, and the rise of the Ku Klux Klan was rationalized in a reimagined Recon-struction South where lawlessness and violence by "uppity" Blacks needed to be quashed. So often in the United States, populist sen-timent can be distracted from underlying and undisclosed causes of discontent: the disempowerment of a once powerful minority or the loss of identity tied to status, for example. Frustration and discontent by emergent populism have all too often been directed toward easy scapegoats like women, Jews, or immigrants in the US. So often, the underlying discontent in the US is also lodged in structural/perceptual frustration of the citizenry, unable to even recognize or much less navigate the structures that hinder one's path toward their American dream.

Organized labor became popular during the Great Depression. It was an important part of the American workforce identity up until the years of President Ronald Reagan when it became associated with corruption, unfair dues, and inflexibility in a free market world—some of which was deserved in the Jimmy Hoffa era. Defining consensus in America is a loaded discussion because so many groups with a vested interest in their version of America have weighed in and prioritized their conception of the term. At one time, consensus in America proved simply impossible. The South's unacceptance of President Lincoln's overwhelming electoral victory in the 1860 presidential election is the shortest answer for the cause of the American Civil War. This momentous election also previewed warning signs of the disjuncture between consensus in the Electoral College and (lack of) consensus in the popular vote. Finding consensus in America outlines a history fraught with contention and deep prejudice—the unwillingness of those who represent the enfranchised majority to incorporate the disenfranchised minority into the voting roles. The story of consensus is also a tale of sacrifice and triumph, of young men and women of diverse backgrounds who have spilled blood so that we may all benefit from a more inclusive nation.

Political intractability, polled as the third greatest concern in the nation by Pew Research in 2023, only emphasizes how important it is to take the pulse of national accord and why non-partisan polling organizations are vital for the health public sphere.

Locating, yes, but ultimately acting on consensus—this is the basis for democratic rule, and it has been so from the dawn of humanity. Consensus was registered in the ancient Greek *ecclesia* (assembly), and it was an important factor in American Indian society before and after the European wave of immigration to North America. To *caucus* in America is to meet with other members of a political party to nominate candidates. The term most likely derives from a Native American Algonquian word for "counsel," *cau´-cau-as´u*. Benjamin Franklin is among the founding fathers who spoke about the Iroquois Confederation as a novel and useful form of representative federalism.[9] Ruling by consensus is also deeply woven into the fabric of Anglo-Saxon governance. It was one of the reasons the English House of Commons evolved from being the King's assembly to help procure money for war to being an assembly that rules over the nation and keeps a Monarch at bay. While democracy is a borrowed inheritance, to caucus is a truly American practice.

Key to the framework of majoritarian rule is trust in the political process through transparent and public voting processes and communication. Also key to trust in the US political process is maintaining trust in other Americans and having a healthy public sphere with which to communicate. However, as the political philosopher Niccolò Machiavelli pointed out, those who hold office and prestige have often resorted to covert machinations and subterfuge to retain power. Politics, as it has been practiced in Western societies, is full of strategy, employed in coalition-building, for one, and in the shaping of political performance, for another—playing to a given audience. However, in the politics of this moment in the United States, many national politicians are occupied with planting false flags (no actual-win victories), creating false urgencies, distracting from issues where they have no answers, and deflecting from speaking to concrete policies. Why? What is the strategy? Politicians may avoid policy questions, knowing they may have to change their views from the fringe for a primary election to the center for a general election. They may also realize their views are highly unpopular to the majority of Americans, so providing a concrete vision for America is far less politically effectual than simply calling out the other side in an endless diatribe. They may simply not have any realistic policies couched behind their platitudes. Or they have realized their policies are ineffectual, "done and been there" old recipes for disaster in America when referenced with quick historical policy fact-checking.

A good deal of political fundraising is based on grievance politics, so structurally the political party system ensures political accord is seldom reached, never acknowledged, and is most often represented in the politician's misperception of the majority view. A politician who casts their views as a representative of a district, state, or nation is often fueled by strategic conviction that flies in the face of polling data or election results. Certainly, the surprising unpopularity of abortion restriction measured in "red states," where voters vote predominantly for the Republican Party, has proven how limited a few politicians' view of the popularity of legislative initiatives can be, perceiving only the views of a subset of their electorate. Politicians also recognize that polling information is also limited in its scope, limited by the framing of the poll questions asked, and by the fact the polls only track the attitudes of Americans at the moment. A candidate's popularity in polls that ask the question "Who or what would you vote for?" from policy and candidates more accurately represents a general and tepid wish list. Political polling doesn't account for that day when the voter enters the polling booth, and the question for them then becomes, "Which choice can I live with?" In a more deliberative democracy, where the populace demands more from their candidates and political system, where we have listened to the concerns voiced by the other side, the question that should be answered for us on election day should be "Which candidate and what policies will demonstrably change our lives for the better?"

Finding consensus is now harder than ever because our attention economy privileges discord, notoriety, and celebrity over the candidate's fitness to govern with a clear vision of the future. But it is our fault as much as it is mainstream media. Which of us can say we spent a few hours watching C-Span today? Most of us do not have extra time to stay up with all the legislation proposed by the US House of Representatives or in our state legislatures. Televised town halls and debates that specifically address the abiding concerns of Americans are a good start for debating policy differences. However, the real work of consensus for a politician is far from dramatic. It is the hard, tedious, and mundane work we pay national politicians to do, hashing out the details of agreements and working to improve the lives of the American public.

Political news reporting fills in news content with what is available, but it is constrained to report what they see and hear in a dysfunctional political system. But once upon a time in America, television political reporters on just three major TV channels endeavored to explain both sides of any one political issue. They were duty-bound—and subsidized by their stations—to report on the boring work of consensus as well. Now, many ordinary Americans, with the addition of politized media, view national politics as an eternal soap opera in an unfortunate and circular gyre of partisan distraction. Political policy discussion and consensus in America are also constrained by new hyper-condensed and repetitive news formats, which have distracted audiences taking in information-in-milliseconds and trying to make sense of complex policy choices in tweets and soundbites.

Why is it hard for us to discern how we are alike and what we agree on?

As human beings evolved into diverse and disparate societies all over the world, small-scale societies developed distinct cultures and languages. When bands of human beings encountered one another during periods of migration or gatherings for trade or conviviality, cross-cultural communication became reliant on translators or on non-verbal communication that could be interpreted by a receptive "listener." As tribes and bands spread apart in space and time, so too did culture become far more differentiated among human beings, which engendered forms of ethnocentrism: the belief that one's cultural ways, with customs and beliefs that were logical, grounded, and well-understood, were better than others one encountered whose ways seemed foreign, illogical, or less humane.

In Native America, ethnocentrism is exemplified in the names tribes and bands gave themselves. For the small bands of people living in the Western Amazon that call themselves the *Ayoreode*, their name means "human beings" in their language, for example.[10] The tribal names of many Native American groups are similar to "human beings" in their language. This makes sense if an outsider were to ask them, "Who are you?" they would answer, "We are human beings?" then respond, "And who are you?" (who look and behave so differently). The implication is that outsiders are not quite human, meaning others have ways that don't make sense and or seem alien to the *right* way of living. The fact that ethnocentrism is common across cultures is relevant to modern society in two ways:

- Human beings have always been closer and more invested in people they know or understand.
- Seeing differences in others is the easiest way to define yourself by determining what you are not.

Cognitive anthropologist Gregory Bateson was the first modern researcher to delve deep into the process of defining oneself through others. In his ethnography *Naven: A Survey of the Problems Suggested by a Composite Picture of the Culture of a New Guinea Tribe drawn from Three Points of View*, he described this process in scholarly terms as the "differentiation in the norms of individual behavior resulting from cumulative interaction between individuals."[11] He gave the process a name, *schismogenesis*, translated from Greek as the "creation of division" between people. As a neurological shortcut to our interpretive centers, human cognition is far more adapted to seeing differences in others than recognizing "sameness" in each other. However, human beings are genetically very uniform—more alike genetically than any given troop of chimpanzees or single group of penguins, for example. Minute changes in our immense genome have created different eye, skin, and hair colors, to name a few of the physical features that differentiate us.

It is also much easier to register differences between each other at first sight but far harder to do the work of talking and listening to each other's views and learning how we are experientially similar or different—this takes time. In this way, staying with assumed differences of another and never seeking to know another beyond first impressions leads to prejudice. It is a default cognitive mechanism that can lead to polarization because:

- In the modern world, we are inundated with human beings we will never know, so it is easier to view human beings in preconceived generalities and associations rather than trying to individualize the thousands of faces we encounter through media.
- It is easier to keep our generalities of people in place than enter into a space of cognitive uncertainty required to change our outlook or correct our initial assumptions.

Though we are the same species, *Homo sapiens*, "the knowing human," with very little genetic differentiation, we are far more in tune to notice differences in one another than sameness and far more prone to understand that which is familiar to us than that which is different. However, a better descriptor of our modern species might be *Homo communicatus*, a human species defined by our ability to communicate exceptionally well. It is my aspiration, in any case, that through communication we can better understand our common humanity, our sameness, and look beyond our more obvious differences.

Why is losing trust in our institutions and each other harmful to democracy?

In 1991, even before the full societal changes brought on by the Information Age, British sociologist Anthony Giddens suggested modernity itself could be partially defined by the reliance upon trust in people and institutions in an ever more abstract world.[12] In pre-modern societies, elders possessed the knowledge to carry generations forward, and the truth of someone's vision or views could be confronted face-to-face and in direct consultation. Members of society, connected by relationships of extended families, generally had each other's best interests in mind. Deception in small-scale societies was acknowledged as a vice underscored in folk parables. In modernity, human beings are increasingly reliant upon experts and mediators of knowledge like researchers and professional journalists for truth and reality. This reliance upon the trust of others in modernity leaves us vulnerable to systems and institutions, increasing overall caution in society and elevating fear, frustration, and even paranoia in some who see the system as rigged against them but are unable to determine how or why.

Anthropologically speaking, human beings evolved neurologically to prioritize visual and aural inputs of other human beings' faces and eyes particularly. Our pre-human ancestors depended upon minute perceptual clues in each other's expression in an African world dominated by social predators. Our species prioritized the ability to communicate with each other and with our surroundings as the primary means of survival. We became a species reliant upon our ability to meta-communicate: to read the signs of animals in nature, to interpret each other's intentions through communication, and to think about what each other was thinking. As we began to learn and speak languages, we prioritized effective ways of communicating; we learned to listen more intently to those who spoke with conviction and purpose.

In the twentieth century, during the cinema and television age, we transferred those skills to our media, looking "into the eyes" of people on our flat screens for intentions and motivations. As sentient animals sensitive to the passion and emotional appeal of others, we responded to suffering and testimonials where authentic emotions held our attention, and we still conflate the conviction of the character on the flat screen as someone's inner truth. But conviction is a double-edged sword that also measures the depth of a singular vision, so it was always tempered by deliberation and shared knowledge in the quest for a weighted consensus. It was one of the elements that the framers of the US Constitution considered when they weighed the checks and balances of good governance in having a Senate, a House of Representatives, and a chief *presider* of the federal government, the president. They wanted no one voice or faction full of conviction to have more power over the balance and rationale of the many.

Our world is so complex a great extent of childhood is occupied with learning to negotiate the volume of information that we find in it. However, we're still constrained by our evolutionary cognitive shortcuts that attempt to synthesize overabundant data with some meaning. We live in a world of artificial intelligence, and we're easily diverted from the things that should be important to us and give us purpose and meaning. In a world where false urgency is the norm, where *the boy who cried wolf* cries out a thousand times a day, day after day, we are distracted to numbness—distracted from the very real urgencies posed in the world we live in. But many Americans are nostalgic once again for a time before Zoom, and COVID-19 made us into video-cam zombies: we want to know what others think, we want to know why they think what they do, and we want to move forward together. Without civil conversations with the people working within institutions, we may be left with a vague and abstract suspicion of what motivates an individual or institution's belief system, mission statement, or policies. Nonetheless, modern societies are dependent on the cultivation and maintenance of societal trust to function successfully.

Does postmodernity add to our polarization?

In a distracted world where consensus is hard to measure or even to imagine, it doesn't help that the universe, as physicists have come to know it, has proven much more unimaginable to the senses in the twentieth century than it was envisioned by Einstein and earlier scientists; or in the last century, social scientists embraced ideas that focused on a critique of institutions and a critique of progress as we knew it. In the late 1970s, social scientists began to question how knowledge itself was produced, filtered through biased lenses, and driven by questions from a narrow subset of the population—elite white male perspectives, for example. The net effect of this post-modern and poststructural research questioned even how truth was constructed in the social universe. Postmodernist research began to look past the easy master narratives of experts to the more difficult and transparent first-person stories of the individuals, opening up field notes to examination, looking at *process* in research more than grand syntheses of concrete conclusions. In postmodernity, truth becomes a quest for relative truth, filtered through an individual's situated perspective, their experience, and even their status or privilege in their role in society. In poststructural research, the basis and method by which empirical knowledge had been constructed were questioned. The scientific logic of the modern penal system came under scrutiny, for example, as a state apparatus designed to anonymize, pathologize, and ultimately warehouse undesirables in society, so-called progress justified by scientific rationalization.

Sound familiar? It should. Some of the ideas and methods from this research have bubbled up into popular modern consciousness. Beginning during the Obama Administration, institutions like the justice and carceral systems began to be questioned for fairness— and rightfully so in a nation that imprisons more people per capita than any other nation and a disproportionate number of black and brown Americans. Institutions that seemed trustworthy for many years, like our banking system, came under scrutiny with the world economic collapse even before Obama entered office in early 2009. Questioning the origin, purposes, and development of institutions that seemed fallible or even broken was a natural consequence of the reflexivity embedded in this new postmodern condition where solutions to real-world problems might become buried in the subtleties of argument or insatiable critique.

However, I would also suggest that the questions posed by postmodern and poststructural research have been valuable and necessary in a world moving at light speed into a future of unknown consequences. By 1962, for example, modernity had brought with it atomic energy and pesticides like DDT that turned thriving entire ecosystems into desolate wastelands, as Rachel Carson documented in her 1962 book *Silent Spring*. Modernity's emphasis on ease and convenience, unchecked growth, and fierce competition seldom questioned basic and contradictory data on whether our fundamental institutions had become too big to fail or that the endless manufacture of plastic would find its way into one-thousand-square-mile gyres of trash circulating in our oceans. The language of postmodernism and poststructural theory are embedded in concepts like *structural racism* or *geographies of violence*. Consider that the construct of race has been outmoded for 100 years; there is no such thing as the "races" of people as we once knew them, and yet racism, antisemitism, and Islamophobia are alive and well. We still need to interrogate why systems of prejudice exist in the world and, more importantly, why race is still used to objectify and discriminate against other people. We can't move forward unless we excavate a bit into the structures that hold us back.

Postmodern and poststructural theory and research have been key to questioning our earlier and easier conceptions of progress coming into the atomic age. Still, this research also had an Achilles heel. By asserting that institutions themselves are always a part of power and privilege or conceiving that institutions themselves are all nefarious—like the US government—then, in a real sense, all progress up to now is broken. Postmodernism and poststructuralism, as critiques that question the frameworks by which knowledge is created, can be taken to a nihilistic extreme where truth itself in society becomes all but contextually relative—a problematic framing the presidents of three major higher education institutions faced when they became entrapped by their semantics in front of US House of Representatives lawmakers on 5 December 2023. They could not explain their institutional policies on antisemitism with clarity and conviction without considering nuance and contextualization in a very loaded and oppositional line of questioning.[13]

Circling back to the first days of Trump's presidency, when Kellyanne Conway stated Sean Spicer was using "alternative facts," I understood Conway's admission in two ways. On one level, I knew what she was referencing—the size of Trump's inauguration crowd—was relative to one's perception idea of what a large crowd looks like. But Sean Spicer was trying to defend something factually indefensible Trump himself had said, that his inauguration audience had been larger than Obama's. This simply wasn't true. Conway's admission was also a warning sign that perhaps the nihilism embedded in postmodernism had reached the arena of politics and policy. Had we entered a *post-truth* era from the debris field of postmodernism framing?

Lee McIntyre wondered the same thing in his 2018 book *Post-Truth*.[14] McIntyre went further, attempting to trace how the critique of knowledge, a common quest in the social sciences from the 1990s on, could have been transfigured and coopted by the Right to mystify basic facts and prevailing knowledge. Certainly, the reasoning and intent have changed from social critique to purposeful misdirection. Still, the end outcome of Leftist pure critique and relativist truth in Right-wing declarations is similar. At their worst, both instill a sense of nihilism from arguments that don't produce any new solutions or suggest institutional reform. In the US public sphere, we are increasingly subject to circular arguments by political operatives who work to mystify truth rather than clarify; to invalidate social, economic, medical, and political progress in the United States and turn it all into simplistic and easy "anti" slogans. Making health care affordable, reducing pricey prescription drug expenses, lowering the cost of higher education, taxing and redistributing the wealth of billionaires, and transitioning to green technologies are all popular policies measured in national polls. If these policies are "socialist" as judged by the far Right-wing minority, then the majority of Americans are either socialists or jingoism has its limits.

What I would suggest in this book is that an old/new political strategy has reemerged in the US born from the plausible deniability strategy of big tobacco's research of the 1990s. It is a communication strategy implicitly used by the far Left and explicitly used by the far Right that coopts some of the worst nihilistic tendencies of postmodernism. In this new political domain, policy arguments are undertaken with little or no foundation of truth or valid research, and the reasoning or logic is circular and self-affirming. It is a political strategy of mystification used by the tobacco industry for decades to suggest alternative science for the health of smoking exists in the face of overwhelming data that concluded people do indeed die from their smoking habit—as my mother did. If your political position in the country is unpopular or your policies outdated or dysfunctional, it is best not to argue your case on its merits. It is best to mystify and confuse the American public and suggest alternatives without specifics, particulars, or referents so Americans don't know what to think, what to support, or even what the truth is.

How can we start getting back to the facts and to common ground?

As postmodernism and poststructuralism asserted their allure on the social science academies in the 1980s, an interdisciplinary scholar emerged whose work has become particularly relevant for our time. His research but also his early life, and his transformation are relevant today.

Jürgen Habermas was born in Düsseldorf, Germany, with a cleft palate that hindered clear speech, and he underwent two surgeries in childhood to fix this condition. He has written that his speech disability may have made him feel differently about human "dependence and vulnerability, and a sense of the relevance of our interactions with others."[15] Born in 1929, he came of age during the Nazi era and turned 11 years old in 1940 when he became a Hitler youth. Habermas' early life ensconced in Nazi Germany, and a son of a Nazi sympathizer strongly influenced his work. The indoctrination campaign of Nazis and the ascendancy of totalitarian fascist rule in a country with a proud history of enlightened scholarship informed his lifelong scholarly output. His work, influenced by American pragmatist scholar Thomas Dewey and academics of the Frankfurt School, became dedicated to strengthening democratic processes in modern nations. Like other philosophers before him going back to Aristotle, and with resurgences by scholars like Hannah Arendt, Habermas believed the fate of democracy was dependent on the active engagement of the citizens of democracies. In the democracy of communication itself—all citizens have the same "capacities of discourse, social equality [when] their words are not confused by ideology or by other errors."[16]

Habermas' optimism for the transformative potential in the public sphere has been panned as wishful thinking by some. Indeed, he turned away from the political skepticism and disdain for modern material culture of his mentors, Max Horkheimer, and Theodor Adorno, and he has criticized the circular reasoning of postmodern critiques.[17] Rather, he aspired for a future where representative democracies evolve into deliberative, discussion-oriented, and engaged nation-states that valorize equal rights, open communications, and renewed interest in civic responsibility. Having grown up in a totalitarian fascist government, it was clear to Habermas how corrosive propaganda could be to a national population and deadly for those scapegoated for a country's financial woes. He witnessed first-hand how charismatic leaders could take control of the conscience of a nation. Significantly for Habermas, policies in public debate are not enough; they must be followed by political action—and many public servants in the United States still work with these goals in mind.

For all the dysfunction in the Republican-led House of Representatives, where the spotlight became focused on the most extreme views in the most unproductive year the House has ever recorded (2023), there are House members poised to work every day to pass bipartisan legislation. Take, for example, The Problem Solvers Caucus, a group in the House of Representatives created in January 2017 as an outgrowth of meetings held by the political organization No Labels. The Problem Solvers Caucus includes members equally divided between Democrats and Republicans, and they are posed to help the House find accord through the most difficult issues—given the opportunity. There are former politicians and current politicians who were and are laudable for their work across the aisle, like George Romney, Senator and former presidential candidate Mitt Romney's father (1907-1995), who supported the Civil Rights Act of 1964, and believed polarized ideologies were destructive for the nation; or Charlie Baker, the former Republican governor of the deep "blue state," of Massachusetts (served from 2015 to 2023). Baker left office with a 75 percent approval rating by finding bipartisan consensus wherever he could, and Maryland's current senator, Chris Van Hollen, has doggedly fought for campaign finance reform, seeking to limit the corrupting influence of big money in US politics with the bills he has helped sponsor. We don't praise the people working across the aisle or our politicians working for the American people on bills that would limit their political coffers. Too much of our attention is focused on the drama of polarization, where it is found or where it is manufactured.

I have addressed what this book is about, but I also want to state what I hope to prove. I hope to demonstrate that the majority of Americans are rational and highly motivated to move beyond the politics of polarization, that we should try to understand our differences, trust one another and our common purposes, that bipartisanship should be prioritized once again by all members of Congress to focus on the most urgent concerns of Americans; that they should find consensus, and pass bipartisan legislation, even if it puts their political incumbency at risk—remembering others have sacrificed more for American freedom and liberty. We can embrace forward-thinking once again, this is what made America great. Let me now cover our prevailing concerns and synthesize what consensus looks like in the United States today, searching for a path forward.

Chapter 1

The Cost Of Living, Economic Equality

Introduction – A Fundamental Flaw?

A spotlight shown on our political differences in economic policies and the causes of economic inequality on October 23, 2008, in the US House of Representatives. Alan Greenspan (b. 1926), who headed the Federal Reserve for 18 years until early 2006, appeared at a hearing examining the role of federal regulators in the mortgage-backed securities crisis that turned into the Great Recession of 2008.[18] As head of the Federal Reserve in the United States, Greenspan was head of the central bank that uses the nation's money reserves to control and maximize national employment, stabilize prices, supervise and regulate banks, and moderate long-term interest rates that affect interest on mortgages and car loans. One of the presiding members of Congress, Democrat Henry Waxman, read from several statements of Greenspan:

"'I do have an ideology. I judge that free, competitive markets are by far the unrivaled way to organize economies. We've tried regulation. None meaningfully worked." That's what you said.

Then he asked Greenspan point blank:

And my question for you is simple. Were you wrong? Greenspan replied:

I made a mistake in presuming that the self-interests of organizations, specifically banks, and others, were such that they were best capable of protecting their own shareholders and their equity in the firms.

Waxman pressed him:

You found that your view of the world, your ideology, was not right. It was not working?

And Greenspan replied:

That's precisely the reason I was shocked because I'd been going for 40 years or so with considerable evidence that it was working exceptionally well.

Surprisingly transparent and scholarly, Greenspan admitted he had not anticipated a "flaw in his model," believing bankers would supervise themselves enough not to warrant much regulation of their industry.

In fact, banking deregulation had produced credit default swaps (CDS) that began to emerge in the 1990s and increased in use in the early 2000s. By the end of 2007, the outstanding CDS amount was $62.2 trillion in the US, almost twice our current national debt. These CDSs were highly leveraged financial instruments created after banking deregulation during the late 1980s. They presented a major risk to major banking institutions if US home foreclosures ever increased on a large scale. In 2008, this possibility became a reality in the US, and the overall wealth of many middle-income Americans collapsed in the Great Recession.

In the years following, Americans recovered financially. But by the end of 2023, after three years of rising prices in rent, mortgage loan rates, health, and groceries, an increasing share of middle--income Americans began to ask existential and inter-generational questions about the state of their finances and the decline of their purchasing power: Will I still be able to afford my monthly bills? Can I work even harder to rise above my expenses? Can I find more affordable food somewhere? A national poll taken every year for four years asked, "How would you assess the financial situation in your home?" In June 2019, 32 percent rated their financial situation as "leaning toward poor," by March 2023, after the effects of inflation became more widely felt, 47 percent of Americans stated their financial situation was "leaning toward poor," almost half of Americans.[19] Credit card debt in the US in 2023 surpassed $1 trillion by mid-2023, and by the end of 2023, rising delinquency payment rates with credit cards used more frequently to pay for expenses like gasoline indicated that many Americans were struggling to maintain costs of living.

In June 2023, a Pew Research poll indicated that 52 percent of Democrats and 77 percent of Republicans believed inflation was a very big concern; 73 percent of Democrats and 54 percent of Republicans believed the affordability of health care was the nation's second top concern (see figure 1).[20] Taken together, and for the few years leading up to 2023, Americans believed the cost of living overall was the biggest problem in the nation. Competing visions for what improves the American economy have divided the United States since its beginning. Going by entrenched economic policy polarization in the US House of Representatives in 2023, it would seem that Americans are hopelessly divided on solutions to our economic woes. However, it is not so. The fundamental mantra underlying Democratic and Republican economic policies, that all Americans should be lifted in the US economy, has been the same for decades. Differences arise when we get into the specifics of the question, "How do we get there?"

This chapter questions our perceived divisions on economic issues in the US: What are some of the root causes of the rise of cost-of-living expenses and the decline of purchasing power in the US? Why did economic inequality in the US grow in the last forty years and decline in the sixty years before then? America is a rich nation by any standard, producing enormous wealth and tax revenue. However, the US Government has also borrowed beyond tax revenue to meet national expenditures for many years, and this has increased our national debt substantially. Why has our national debt increased so much? Is there any consensus on how to prioritize our national tax dollar spending, where to cut back or get more tax income, or where the middle ground is on a fair national income redistribution? To begin, let's look at our perception of the national economy and inflation concerns and how Americans differ on economic solutions from partisan perspectives.

Where do we believe we differ on economic issues and problems?

For a few years up to the end of 2023, the top concern for a majority of Americans was inflation. Inflation is the rising cost of goods and services and may entail the loss of revenue for small businesses—should inflation turn into recession as Americans hold back spending to afford the extra costs of living. But most significantly, inflation decreases purchasing power, the amount of goods and services that can be purchased with a dollar. In a July 2022 Pew Research poll, when voters were asked what is contributing to the rising prices in the US, 71 percent of Republicans and 90 percent of Democrats believed businesses "taking advantage of economic conditions to increase profits" contributed to inflation "some" or "a lot," along with the impact of COVID-19 on manufacturing and shipping (79 percent and 89 percent, respectively).[21] Democrats tended to believe Russia's invasion of Ukraine had more to do with the price hikes than Republicans, and Republicans believed government aid to deal with the impact of COVID-19 had more to do with the rise in costs; a majority of both parties believed that the low-interest rates that banks offered coming into supply-chain shortages were also contributing factors.[22]

Nearly every year, the US government spends more than it collects in taxes and other revenue, resulting in a deficit.[23] The national debt reached a historic high at the end of 2023, but it is a deficit that has been built up over time—building considerably in the 1980s, and escalating in the 2000s. Tax cuts, particularly on the wealthiest Americans since 1981, combined with unpaid for wars in Iraq and Afghanistan, the 2008 financial crises, and the cost of paying for the first coronavirus relief package or CARES Act, increased our national debt passed $34 trillion by the end of 2023.[24] Seventy-two percent of Republicans in a June 2023 poll believed the federal budget deficit was "a very big problem," along with 39 percent of Democrats, for an overall majority of 56 percent of Americans. In just a few years, from 2021 to 2023, concerns about the national debt increased from 42 percent of Americans who believed tackling it should be a top priority to 57 percent who believed the same in 2023, with some partisan differences.[25]

A critical and increasing expense for Americans has been the rising cost of health care. Some of those specific concerns registered in a poll published by the Kaiser Family Foundation in March 2022 indicated that 61 percent of Americans don't want the cost of prescription drugs to surpass inflation, understandable for seniors dependent on the small cost of living increases in social security payments. Fifty-three percent of the respondents wanted the costs of insulin capped at $35 a month, and placing a limit on out-of-pocket expenses for seniors should be a top concern for Congress to take action on. Both the cost of nursing homes and the inadequate level of care were also concerns embedded in the overall rising cost of health care, a concern of a majority of Americans.[26]

The rising cost of health care and overall price increases of inflation do not affect all income classes equally in the US, it hits the broad middle and lower-income populations much harder than high-income Americans. One of the top abiding economic concerns in the US, of greater concern just before and during the lockdown of COVID-19, is the amount of income inequality in the United States. In a Pew Research comprehensive poll taken in September of 2019, a majority of Americans, 61 percent, believed there was too much income inequality in the US. Significantly, a large majority of Democrats (78 percent) represented by all income levels believed there was too much income inequality in the United States. Republicans were divided on their perceptions of income inequality: 41 percent believed there was too much income inequality, and 43 percent believed there was the right amount.[27]

Americans are mostly in accord with economic concerns gripping the nation but not on the causes or fixes for economic inequality. Though there are stark differences in the causes of economic inequality, both parties view "problems in the education system" as part of the overall cause to a small degree. Republicans mostly attribute economic inequality in the US to "the different life choices people make" (60 percent), or that "some people work harder than other people" (48 percent), or to "illegal immigrants" (32 percent).[28] Democrats tend to believe the causes of economic inequality center around lax "regulation of corporations" (54 percent), an "unfair tax system" (56 percent), "discrimination" (50 percent), and "starting life with less opportunity than others" (52 percent). As one of my politically independent Gen-Z college students responded when asked what goes into continuing wealth disparities in the US: "The luck that goes into being born, based on race, wealth, social status." Of the 41 percent of Republicans who believed there was too much income inequality, lower-income Republicans in that group by a wide margin (77 percent) believed fixing income inequality in the United States required either "major changes or needed to be completely rebuilt," an indicator that disparities on economic policies are class-driven within the Republican Party, much less a factor in the Democratic Party.[29]

Significantly, lower purchasing power for some in the middle class coupled with a more noticeable divide between the haves and the have-nots has many Americans questioning if social mobility in America is as strong as it once was. Fully 78 percent of those queried in a June 2023 *Wall Street Journal*/University of Chicago poll indicated they "do not feel confident" that their children will be better off.[30] Drawing from this last poll, it is worthwhile to briefly revisit the economic history of the United States to try and answer why Americans feel so dour about the economic prospects for their children and the promise of social mobility today.

How did industrialism set the stage for the US economic concerns of today?

In an argument driven by economic data of the last few centuries, French economist Thomas Piketty looks at the Western history of social and economic inequality in his book *A Brief History of Equality*. In his book, Piketty flips the script on the dour notion that economic history in the Western world has been an inevitable march toward uneven development and inequality, suggesting when democratic values and input shape capitalism, economic systems have actually produced more equality in the past:

> Let's start at the heart of the matter: Human progress exists: the human movement toward equality is a battle that can be won, but it is a battle whose outcome is uncertain, a fragile social and political process that is always ongoing and in question.[31]

Looking back through one thousand years of Western socio-economic history, it is not difficult to come to the same conclusion. In the European Middle Ages, wealth and status were concentrated in the hands of the aristocracy and clergy. Peasants, numbering close to 90 percent of the population, held little power over their destiny. One was born into a social caste and remained in that caste their entire lifetime. Social mobility was almost non-existent. Housing for peasants consisted of hand-built small dwellings of mud brick with dirt floors. Sewage ran down the streets, and in bad weather, livestock were often pulled into the living quarters of commoners. Slowly, with eras punctuated with economic progress in trade and mercantilism, European wealth increased and a merchant class emerged in greater numbers in Late Medieval Europe. One's station in life began to be less constrained by social status at birth.

By the time of the English Renaissance in the 1500s, those born into the *yeoman class*, what we might think of today as someone born into the house-owning, middle-class, were producing ambitious men like Thomas Cromwell who rose to aristocracy as Chief Minister of King Henry VIII, or William Shakespeare who was able to apply a solid grammar school education of the classics to become the best-known dramatist of all time and co-founder of an acting company patronized by King James I of England. The economy of England that Shakespeare was born to was prone to hyperinflation, food and labor shortages caused by under-developed agricultural technologies, and periodic waves of epidemics of "sweating sickness" and bubonic plague. Gifting economic monopolies to court favorite aristocrats and companies was the order of the day, ensuring wealth was confined to the few and connected. On the very last day of 1600, Queen Elizabeth I granted a charter to a group of London merchants for exclusive overseas trading rights with the East Indies, "a massive swath of the globe extending from Africa's Cape of Good Hope eastward to Cape Horn in South America. The new English East India Company was a monopoly in the sense that no other British subjects could legally trade in that territory." However, England at the time was competing vigorously with other nation-states like Portugal and Spain to establish trade dominance around the globe.[32]

By 1776, the efficacy of trade monopolization and importation tariffs as economic policy began to be questioned by leading intellectuals in England and Scotland. In his book *An Inquiry into the Nature and Causes of the Wealth of Nations*, Scottish moral philosopher Adam Smith envisioned a world where free trade would prosper and grow guided by self-motivated producers in an economic system that worked through an *invisible hand* to improve economic equality for all.[33] Smith vigorously attacked the remnants of aristocratic economic policies that hindered mercantile expansion, like tariffs, arguing that imposed trade restrictions and manipulations in the free exchange of trade create inefficiency and a higher cost of goods for everyone. In Smith's theory, countries should cultivate home economies that best use their land and climate. In the United States, where agricultural land was plentiful, citizens could prosper by producing raw goods of cotton, tobacco, and furs, trading for finished goods in the early manufacturing sector in Great Britain. For Smith, the role of an efficient and fair national government called for subsidizing a government including the military, but not the coiffures of the aristocracy.

Smith believed fair market prices in an interconnected economy could only be achieved without the price manipulation inherent in monopolization. In his time, the immense import/export of the Dutch version of the East India Company chartered and based in Amsterdam possessed quasi-governmental powers, including the ability to wage war, imprison and execute convicts, negotiate treaties, strike coins, and establish colonies.[34] Today Adam Smith is considered the patron saint of *corporate libertarianism*, or a world in which capitalism and multi-national corporations function in a world without regulation. But Adam Smith's construct of the world economic system was one in which small merchants bought and sold from one another, an economy that would—by the invisible hand—create a greater economic distribution of resources.

Smith acknowledged that economic inequality would continue to exist, but his underlying philosophy was that human self-interest would translate into initiative and increased efficiency. Smith was a moral philosopher, first and foremost. He saw economic trade positively, tied to trust and the rule of law—as did other philosophers of his day. His brand of free trade was dependent on economic fair play with transparent exchange and a well-regulated banking sector. Concerned for the most vulnerable in society, Smith willed his estate to the impoverished of his home city of Edinburgh. He also foresaw some of the problems that would come from a free trade economy where the division of labor classes could indenture many to repetitive work. Smith could not have imagined the scale of his forecast made possible by rapid industrialization in the United Kingdom in the 1840s. In the grand sweep of economic progress in the US and Europe, a new business class, the bourgeoisie, emerged. It was not a world that created prosperity for all.

In 1842, an army veteran and son of a wealthy family from Prussia sent their 22-year-old son Friedrich Engels to work in one of the cotton textile mills they owned in Manchester, England. There, young Engels met a fierce Irish mill worker, Mary Burns, who held strong views about social justice. Burns guided Engels through Manchester, showing him the impoverished neighborhoods of the inner city. In 1845 Engels published *The Condition of the Working Class in England*, based on personal observations and research in Manchester and Liverpool.[35] During the same time, Charles Dickens published his novel *Oliver Twist*. Both authors used narratives that were grimly realistic to expose the decrepit living conditions of the urban poor of nascent industrialism. In *Oliver Twist*, Dickens unmasked the cruel treatment of orphans who were placed in workhouses in mid-19th century London—part of Dickens' own experience as a child. For Engels, living conditions of the Irish immigrant worker tenements were callously ignored by the emerging bourgeoisie class of the UK's industrial cities, which drove him to document what he saw in graphic detail:

Several tanneries…fill the whole neighborhood with the stench of animal putrefaction. Below Ducie Bridge, the only entrance to most of the houses is by means of narrow, dirty stairs and over heaps of refuse and filth.[36]

Rapid industrialization greatly worsened the health and living conditions of the pool of laborers that flocked to the cities from the countryside of the United Kingdom and across the shore from Ireland. Years later, Engels reflected upon his observations in the slums of the big cities of Great Britain and concluded that the British Isles had outgrown their juvenile state of industrialism. Public pressure forced municipal authorities to improve infrastructure, including sewage and drinking water systems. But Engels saw similar squalid conditions emerging in the US in the late 19th Century, in the slums of New York.

As industrialization began to spread worldwide, the housing and work conditions required to supply the great machine of capitalism would also spread with it. By 1890, social and economic inequality could be visually mapped in a stroll through New York City, where the mansions of the industry-owning elites lined 5th Avenue next to Central Park. Across town, the industrial workers resided in the tenement housing on the Lower East Side near the East River. The lives and living conditions of the tenement dwellers there were documented by police photographer and Danish-American immigrant Jacob Riis and published in his book of photographs titled *How the Other Half Lives* (1890).[37] The eye-opening images in the book, of grime-covered children sleeping in the streets and crime-riddled alleys and slums, caught the attention of the police commissioner of New York City, Theodore Roosevelt. Riis' work would inspire Roosevelt and others to work to improve the living conditions of poor immigrant neighborhoods and, eventually, to instigate reform policies to mitigate the worst effects of turn-of-the-century capitalism.

Roosevelt initiated a domestic policy as New York's governor—later as the US president—of the "Square Deal," borrowing from the populist parlance of his day. The economic policies of his Square Deal worked to enforce anti-trust legislation—breaking up corporate monopolies—and to enact consumer protection laws to keep food safe and free of poison. Teddy Roosevelt helped to break up big monopolies like John D. Rockefeller's Standard Oil, which, in the year 1904, controlled 91 percent of oil refinement and 85 percent of petroleum sales in the United States.[38] As a Republican, Roosevelt wasn't pro-labor, per se. Still, his Square Deal was the first turn toward progressive presidential policies and government legislation that was to culminate with Franklin Delano Roosevelt's New Deal measures during The Great Depression. Progressive reform-minded presidents like Teddy Roosevelt, Woodrow Wilson, and Franklin Delano Roosevelt aimed to regulate capitalism, create buffers of social security for job loss and old age, and ensure job injury compensation—measures that softened the worst blows of economic insecurity in the middle and lower classes.

Teddy Roosevelt's progressive reforms were popular in their day, particularly regulations imposed upon industry following events and publications that exposed the excesses of unchecked industry and capitalism. The publication of Upton Sinclair's book *The Jungle* in 1906 raised public health concerns in the description of passages exposing the unsanitary conditions of the meat packing industry in an urban public already susceptible to communicable diseases like polio, tuberculosis, and diphtheria.[39] The Triangle Shirtwaist Factory fire in Greenwich Village, New York City, 1911, was one of the deadliest industrial disasters in US history and brought building codes that ensured safer working environments and work safety reforms. In 1934, the US Division of Labor Standards—which later became the Occupational Safety and Health Administration (OSHA)—was created to oversee labor safety. The net effect of added regulation and reforms countered the effects of industry and landlords driven by profit over safety. The slow accumulation of reforms amounted to social and economic progress through safety. These reforms created a common set of rules in a national economy of increased technology and labor hazards that came with expansive productivity.

Institutionalized redistribution

Redistribution is a way of redistributing resources, like food or capital, like money, to people in need in society. In small tribal societies, redistribution was a mostly unspoken, organic strategy to feed one's elders and children as a laboring adult. At the beginning of the 20th Century, redistribution and economic policy became more institutionalized within the governance of the United States as progressive forms of taxation. Many of Thomas Piketty's most illuminating points in *A Brief History of Equality* are centered around the years 1914-1980, an era he coins "The Great Redistribution."[40] According to Piketty, several factors contributed to wealth and income equality increasing markedly during this sixty-six-year period ending in 1980. One very important factor, beginning in the late 1800s, was the introduction of free public education in America, which gradually rolled out in the Northeast culminating in the segregated South. The United States helped pioneer a free public education system for the rest of the world, and this educated labor pool was better able to participate in the technical demands of late industrial capitalism.[41]

At the close of the 19th Century, the political Populist Party in the US with roots in the Farmer's Alliance and agrarian movements organized. One of its goals was to alter how the US government raised revenue: away from tariffs on goods entering the US and excise (sales) taxes on commodities like gasoline and imported farm equipment that unfairly taxed the poor and agricultural communities. Though income taxes had been levied upon Americans off and on since the beginning of the Republic, income taxes were ruled unconstitutional by the US Supreme Court in 1895. Rural populists and progressive Republicans and Democrats alike favored creating a national income tax to shift the revenue burden onto wealthier US individuals.

A Republican senator, Norris Brown of Nebraska, proposed the 16th Amendment (income tax) to the US Constitution, and it passed with a strong bipartisan consensus on July 12, 1909. Midwestern and Southern states were most supportive of the amendment because income taxes proportionately targeted wealthier Americans in urban centers. In 1913, with the support of the rural populist coalition, the 16th Amendment was ratified, creating modern income taxes in America.

Ironically, in early 2023, a Republican-led Libertarian faction in the House of Representatives tried to abolish the income taxes in the US. They proposed The Fair Tax Act of 2023, a bill that proposed a national sales tax on the use or consumption of taxable property or services.[42] The bill would have created a 23 percent national sales tax administered by the states and would have replaced current income taxes, payroll taxes, and estate or gift taxes. This regressive tax policy would have shifted the burden of taxation once again to middle and lower-income families, increased the cost of groceries and commodities, and reversed a revenue-generated tax system galvanized from below by a rural tax movement more than a hundred years before.

As the US entered World War I in 1917, the nominal tax rate

jumped from 7 percent in the first year of income tax in 1913 to 77 percent for those making more than one million dollars in annual income, the top 1 percent of the population. *Progressive taxation*, meaning a system whereby tax rates increase with income, would become the institutional norm in the US and commonly used worldwide. The highest nominal tax rate went up to 94 percent by the end of World War II, then settled at 91 percent during the Republican Eisenhauer administration for those making more than $3 million a year in today's salary. John F. Kennedy cut the highest nominal tax rates on the wealthiest down to 70 percent of income with the Revenue Act of 1964, signed into law by his successor, Lyndon Johnson. This highest nominal percentage rate remained in place up to 1982.

Average working hours per week were reduced substantially during "The Great Redistribution" era as well. In 1870, the hours worked for full-time production workers in the US hovered around 3,100 hours a year, or around 60-hour weeks.[43] The number of hours in the average production work week had only slipped down to 57 hours by 1913 despite greater public and political acknowledgment of exploitive US labor conditions.[44] By 1980, with high labor organization participation and working conditions reform, the average work week was reduced to 36 hours—when average weekly work hours leveled out to the present time. Child labor, common in the US and Europe until 1900, was also eliminated—though not in the rest of the world. One of the important differences between the way people worked in the year 1900 and the way we work today is that far fewer Americans engage in hard and repetitive manual labor. Our economy has shifted over time toward a burgeoning service sector, and with better technology, there is far less hands-on heavy work today. Hard labor in America has been reduced in terms of worker numbers, average hours worked, and the degree of physical demands.

Americans are not working their bodies to early death and injury as we once were—there has been progress.

Piketty points out that during the "Great Redistribution" era in the United States, huge infrastructural projects were undertaken, including the interstate highway systems, the electric grid, and electricity-producing projects, including nuclear power plants. Free public education in the US and free higher education for GIs after WWII produced the most highly-educated workforce in the world, laying the structural foundations for income increases along all social and economic strata in America, including the very wealthiest.

What happened to middle-class wealth and progress on economic equality?

Real wages overall in 2018 in the US—wages adjusted for inflation— were about the same as they were in 1978 for a great majority of Americans.[45] When you consider that most of the growth in yearly income came for the highest 10 percent of earners in America and that some costs like health care, housing, and—for the last twenty years—higher education have surpassed the rise in inflation costs, purchasing power for the majority of Americans overall went in reverse in sectors we normally associate with social mobility: higher education, home ownership, and good health care. While the median wages for women rose 29 percent from 1979 to 2019, representing significant gains by women in higher paid positions, the median real wage for men went down 3 percent, and in the bottom 10 percent of men's salaries, down by 7.7 percent, according to the Congressional Research Service.[46]

By 2018, however, the total annual income generated by the top 20 percent of earners in the US had increased to 48 percent of all wages in the US (up from 29 percent in 1970), while the middle-income share of total income lowered to 43 percent from 62 percent of all income in the US during the same time.[47] This downslide in the share of earned income erased much of the progress in salary equalization for sixty-five years in the US from 1915 to 1980. Coincidentally, business executives and upper-tier management in administrations, legislators, and those in authority to increase the wages of others—the upper 10-20 percent of earners in America— are the only income group whose purchasing power has kept pace or surpassed overall inflationary costs. And it is only among Americans in the upper five percent of earnings where salaries have kept pace or surpassed the geometrically rising costs of health care, higher education, and homes.

Certainly, the choice of our occupation, and personal effort and determination play into higher salaries earned. According to policy analyst Michael D. Tanner with the libertarian think tank Cato Institute, the highest proportion of the top 1 percent of highest earners in the US come from occupations representative of "executives, managers, and supervisors" (30 percent), the medical field (14 percent), financial professionals (13 percent), and attorneys (8 percent). In these occupations, long hours are often logged, and as Tanner points out: higher income tends to come with longer working hours.[48] Republicans, by and large (and some Democrats) favor explanations for these causes of income inequality in the US, due to one's choice of occupation and hours put into work.

However, it is important to consider that occupations that garner higher salaries generally require a university degree and more often a post-bachelorette education. It is also important to consider the physical demands that differentiate blue-collar and white-collar jobs. High-paying white-collar positions at the executive level are not without pressures to perform, but work duties are variable, stimulating, and self-directed. Work duties may include activities that blend into communicating needs with others, meetings, and organizational duties that can be mentally but not physically taxing. Work in blue-collar jobs is often physically taxing, to the point where working more than an eight-hour day can be dangerously repetitive and physically unsustainable. A former area manager for Amazon told me that the business model at Amazon fulfillment centers necessitates constant hiring of new floor workers (associates)—who do "mind-numbing" repetitive package-assembly work all day—due to the high turnover rate in associate positions. The ten-hour shifts are physically taxing and unsustainable for the many.

The expectation that blue-collar workers in the United States can take on more hours to afford the rise in the cost of living is unrealistic. A waiter, farm worker, construction laborer, or retail cashier cannot work more than eight hours without physical recovery; they cannot work more to get ahead. Those Americans whose wages await executive decisions to provide cost of living increases have been most affected by inflation. At the same time, the rise in the cost of living has not affected those upper-income earning Americans whose salaries have risen correspondingly with inflation costs. So, how did US economic policies contribute to lowering the earning potential of middle and lower-income Americans?

How the US become an unequal society

For economist Joseph Stiglitz in his book *The Great Divide: Unequal Societies and What We Can Do About Them,* the growth of economic inequality—or the "flaw" in the neoliberal model in the US—began when national economic policies shifted in the early 1980s, the financial sector underwent dramatic deregulation and tax rates on the wealthiest Americans were significantly lowered. [49] Coming to office, President Ronald Reagan recalled how, as an actor, he made $400,000 per picture during the heyday of Hollywood studios in the early 1950s, but with the top federal tax rate at over 90 percent of earnings at the time, he took home little of his salary.

Reagan told his White House chief of staff, Donald Regan, that as a studio actor, he always chose to loaf around rather than make more than two pictures a year: "Why should I have done a third picture, even if it was *Gone with the Wind*?" Regan remembers Reagan asking. "What good would it have done me?"[50] As a top 1 percent earner, Reagan's views were forged as an anti-communist in the 1950s, working for General Electric's advertising agency, BBDO, as a television show host and company spokesperson. Reagan believed, along with Milton Friedman and former Federal Reserve chairman Alan Greenspan, that an excess of profits to the wealthiest individuals and corporations in the US would initiate innovation and new enterprise that wealth would filter down to the middle classes.

In reality, deregulating banks and savings and loans created new financialization markets that made it possible for banks to turn from making 80 percent of their profits from small loans and businesses to making 80 percent of their profits on financial instruments, essentially reinvesting money back into their own Wallstreet financial sector. Wealthy businesses and people tended to conserve their resources rather than invest in the new and potentially risky enterprises of others. New enterprise is more often generated by people driven toward success who are not risk-averse, who learn from failure; who are undeterred by challenges, and who are fueled by a determination to fulfill their vision. Big multinational corporations use their profits to help buy up other competing businesses, to minimize risk challenges and competition by monopolizing as much of the market as possible. In economic terminology, the profits of trickle-down economics went into increasing "rents," the conservation and monopolization of wealth assets rather than investment in new industries that fueled job creation, new positions, and social mobility through mid-level management job creation.

After the first two years of his new economic policies, Reagan himself was surprised to learn that lowering taxes did not bolster the economy very much. The National Debt spiraled up, and by Reagan's second term, he was forced to increase taxes, mostly on middle-income Americans, to compensate for the lack of tax receipts his administration believed would follow. The neoliberal mantra for years was to stay the course; after some time, all Americans would be financially enriched. This was never the case for the real purchasing power of 80 percent of Americans. Labor union membership dropped, and pay increases for the lower and middle classes never caught up to the rise in inflationary costs. By 2008, the share of total wealth in the US had more than tripled for the top 1 percent, rising from 7 percent (1980) to 20 percent of the total wealth of the US.

With exceptions in the cost of clothes, recreation, and transportation, in the last forty years that the US has floated neoliberal economic policies through every administration, the dollars earned by 80 percent of Americans today afford cheaper televisions, clothes, and toys, but far less in housing, healthcare, and higher education than they did in 1980—the expenses that take the most out of one's paycheck.[51] Even after the financial losses and foreclosures that many middle-class Americans suffered after the 2008 financial crises, corporate mergers, buying up stocks and bonds at a reduced value, and corporate conglomeration only increased the financial windfalls of the very wealthiest Americans. *Forbes Magazine* titled one of its articles "2010-2020: A Decade of Billionaires."[52] *Barrons Magazine* noted that the world added 412 billionaires in 2020, at the height of the COVID epidemic, and one million millionaires, many of whom made their fortunes on cryptocurrency and financial speculation.[53]

Even though the nominal tax rate for the wealthiest upper tenth of 1 percent in the US is 37 percent and has declined from 70 percent in 1964, most billionaires don't pay close to this tax rate in actual taxes. Most of us learned this fact publicly when Trump's tax records were unsealed from 2015 to 2020. Trump paid $750 a year in federal taxes in 2016 and 2017 and paid no income tax at all in 2020. The "effective tax" percentage on the wealthiest in the US is far smaller than 37 percent, estimated to be 23 percent overall.[54] The wealthiest Americans do pay substantial income tax amounts annually. As a percentage of the population, they pay the most taxes. However, in 2018, the top 1 percent also earned 21 percent of the total income in the US. It is worth considering how much of the US national debt could be paid down if the effective tax rates on the wealthiest Americans were closer to the nominal tax rate set by the US Congress. Close to $160 billion has been estimated to be lost each year in evaded tax revenue by the top 1 percent.[55]

Joseph Stiglitz's most illuminating points in *The Great Divide* dispel the persistent myth that vibrant economies naturally create wealth inequality. He argues that the increased wealth and income inequality in the US has actually hurt the overall economy of the US, citing research from sources as conservative as the International Monetary Exchange. He reminds us that income inequality is a policy choice, not the inevitable consequence of economic growth and prosperity.

Why have costs escalated in housing, health care, higher education, and groceries?

The second most concerning issue for Americans in 2023, the cost of healthcare in America, totaled $74.1 billion in 1970. By 2000, health expenditures had reached about $1.4 trillion; in 2021, the amount spent on health tripled to $4.3 trillion.[56] From 1970 to 2000, inflation rose 344 percent in the US. Still, healthcare expenditures increased in the US during that time by 1,890 percent. Though the cumulative inflation rate from 2000 to 2021 was just 57 percent, from 2000 to 2021, healthcare expenditures in the US grew by 307 percent, representing over $12,000 per person in the US and 18.3 percent of the total US Gross Domestic Product (GDP). The Hamilton Project, sponsored by the Brookings Institute, has summarized the many negative and positive variables that outline the enormous cost in healthcare costs in the last 50 years.[57] Right now, the United States spends much more on health care as a share of the economy (17.1 percent of GDP in 2017) than any other large advanced economies like Germany (11.2 percent) and the United Kingdom (9.6 percent).[58] Public health insurance in the United States "covers only 34 percent of the population, much less than the universal coverage in countries like Canada and the United Kingdom, indicating that it costs far more to provide coverage in the US system than around the world."[59]

The aging bubble of baby boomers in the US populace has contributed to a severe labor shortage in US healthcare providers, with not enough healthcare labor to suit demand. The severe labor shortage has also been driven by other untimely and structural factors in the US health system as well. College nursing programs are heavily impacted and turn away students with high GPAs because they don't have enough faculty to teach. The US physician labor supply has not kept up with demands because residency or "training" programs for doctors have been constricted by the costs of such programs, even though applications have risen rapidly. Also, many healthcare providers simply burned out during and immediately after the COVID crisis. One study in the article "A Dozen Facts about the Economics of the US Health-Care System" from The Brooking Institute states that labor compensation accounted for 49.8 percent of 2012 healthcare revenues.[60]

Healthcare labor is driven by supply and demand; where demand is extreme—due to a systemic shortage of medical personnel—salaries have increased substantially. Administrative healthcare costs are also higher as a share of the Gross Domestic Product in the United States than in other countries. The US, far and away, has the highest health administrative (i.e., nonclinical) costs, which take several forms, including claims processing and payment, prior authorization and eligibility determinations, and quality measurement. Also, in the US, the cost of drugs is far higher than in other countries. And, "While a certain amount of this administrative expense is inevitable and necessary for a well-functioning system, public or private, the excess of US costs over those of other advanced economies is part of the explanation for high US healthcare costs overall."[61]

Higher education

Several factors have been at play in higher education that have increased the cost of college. In order of significance to the bottom line, they are: (1) reduced funding from state governments, (2) increased investment and costs of student support services, (3) inflationary costs of health care and operations, (4) and in "Tier 1" universities, those schools that have over $100 million in research revenue and are in great demand with low admission rates, these schools can sustain higher priced tuition costs because demand remains high—though enrollment nationally in higher education is 10 percent lower in just five years, and will continue to decrease with less college-age students coming of age in the US[62] Decreasing state funding has markedly affected the overall structural costs of managing state budgets. More of the pie of the state from declining revenues after the global recession of 2008 had to be allocated to other state expenditures, including the rising costs of health care for state employees and other costs in the state expenditure pie, including law enforcement, K-12 education, and state pension funds. Public universities have had to increase tuition costs to match the decrease in state funds, which have gone down as a percentage of state funding for many years.

Student service programs initiated by students, faculty, and administrators over the years require staffing: programs like Title 9, counseling, health care, and student center staff. Administrative bloat can be attributable to ideas for programs that foster the well-being of students but also require staff. Still, administration salaries in top-level jobs have also been increasing over national inflation costs. One of the harmful consequences of administrative bloat has been the additional precarity added to non-tenure faculty, those who teach the largest classes generally and whose employment is subject to financial shortfalls in the system. We have created a higher education system that mirrors the global economy where an administrative class has seen substantial pay raises, a tenure track faculty that has received modest salary increases, and a burgeoning "temporary" non-tenure college instructor class whose workload has increased, whose salaries have remained mostly stagnant, and whose jobs remain subject to the vagaries of enrollment and state budgets. Inflationary costs of energy, rents, housing for students and providing matching retirement and health funding for permanent faculty and administrative personnel have also meant the extended costs of higher education have risen dramatically.

Perhaps the most substantive issue brought about by the high cost of higher education in the US is the deferred cost to US society—we aren't incentivizing the education of a highly trained, technologically advanced, and intellectually empowered population that we once were. According to the Organisation for Economic Co-operation and Development, higher-income students spend about twice the amount of money to attend an American university than they do in universities of other developed nations.[63] In Demark, for example, graduate school has no tuition costs for students. The state pays them to study toward a terminal degree while they help to help teach undergraduates. Training and education for the fields that promise high-paying jobs are impacted, and the US government is no longer in the business of supporting big-scale visionary projects like NASA that galvanized middle-income college students toward meaningful work and new fields of entrepreneurialism.

Housing

The onset of inflation contributed to the cost of rent and home-ownership becoming more of a burden on US citizens. Nearly half (49 percent) of Americans polled in October 2021 stated that the availability of affordable housing in their local community was a major problem, with another 36 percent stating that it was a minor problem (85 percent total).[64] Only 10 percent of young adults 18-29 believed affordable housing was not a problem. Residents in the West have seen rents and housing prices rise most significantly, with more houses bought with cash (about 30 percent) than ever before and houses bought over market prices. High home prices have grown overall household wealth for many older homeowners, for some, substantially. Home prices rose more than 20 percent on average in the US in just one year, Q1 2021 – Q2 2022.

Those who have built equity through homeownership after the housing price meltdown of 2008 have been fortunate. A new wave of institutional investment has Wallstreet getting involved in buying single-family homes across the nation, with some estimates that institutional investors may control 40 percent of US single-family rental homes by 2030, according to MetLife Investment Management. [65] Institutional investors purchased 29 percent of homes in California and Texas and a greater percentage in other Sunbelt States like Arizona in 2021.[66] Corporate investment in single-family homes may invite price instability in the near future, bringing financial speculation further into the industry. It is already inflating home prices and rental costs.

Housing demand is sky-high, and unfortunately, the bureaucratic limitations for new construction and pressures created by years of structural NIMBY (non-in-my-backyard) policies have only exacerbated a now severe housing shortage in some communities in our nation. It doesn't help, either, that the housing industry is one of the few industries in America that has become less efficient and not as productive over the years. The substantial rise in construction costs, including raw materials and labor, is partly to blame. Much of the rise in costs is attributable to the geometric rise in land value in some areas of our country where available land to build upon is a diminishing resource.

With 70 percent of the overall assets in the US owned by just 20 percent of the US population, an ever-more distinct line has been drawn after 2020 between homeowners and renters unable to afford homeownership.[67] High home prices, especially in coastal cities in the US, are just one symptom of overall economic inequality in the US. It has led to an increased perceptual gulf between the haves and the have-nots and the erosion of our once-hallowed optimism for upward mobility in America.

Where is consensus on economic policy and equality?

In an article published in 2011, "Building a Better America—One Wealth Quintile at a Time," a Harvard economist and a psychologist from Duke University conducted an online survey of 5,522 people whose combined household income was close to the national medium, in a voting distribution that was bipartisan.[68] They asked respondents to examine three pie charts representing hypothetical wealth distributions in three nations. The first unnamed pie chart represented an equal distribution of wealth across five income groups by percentage represented in the US from the top 20 percent quintile to the lowest 20 percent quintile. Forty-three percent of the US respondents favored this equal distribution of wealth across classes, a "utopian" equal share of wealth as the fairest distribution. Forty-seven percent of respondents chose a second pie chart that represented an unequal income distribution, with by far the largest share of wealth concentrated in the hands of the top two upper-fifths of income groups. Only 10 percent of respondents chose a third pie chart representing the true enormous national wealth gap in the US. Norton and Ariely, the authors of the report, concluded:

> All groups—even the wealthiest respondents—desired a more equal distribution of wealth than what they estimated the current United States level to be, and all groups also desired some inequality—even the poorest respondents. In addition, all groups

agreed that such redistribution should take the form of moving wealth from the top quintile to the bottom three quintiles. In short, although Americans tend to be relatively favorable toward economic inequality than members of other countries (Osberg & Smeeding, 2006), Americans' consensus about the ideal distribution of wealth within the United States appears to dwarf their disagreements across gender, political orientation, and income.[69]

What was more startling about Norton and Ariely's survey was how inaccurately respondents estimated wealth distribution in the United States. Respondents estimated the top 20 percent of earners in the US owned about 58 percent of all the wealth (it was closer to 84 percent), and they estimated that the 40 percent of Americans of lowest wealth possessed about 10 percent of the nation's wealth (the true number is about 0.3 percent). In short, this survey indicated that Americans were comfortable with either true economic equality in the US or having some economic inequality, but 90 percent of those surveyed desire more wealth equality than the enormous wealth differential that exists in the United States. Americans, by and large, do not fully comprehend the extent and scale of economic inequality in America. Moreover, the second "unnamed" pie chart chosen by 47 percent of respondents comfortable with moderate-to-large economic inequality had unknowingly chosen the actual wealth distribution of Sweden in 2010.

One of the perennial issues confronting political leadership in the US has been the scale of our national debt. The US national debt ballooned up to 31.4 trillion dollars by 2022, and Americans, particularly Republicans, are concerned about this enormous deficit. The United States, however, has always carried some national debt. We have, in fact, never fully paid for the American Civil War, which represented the first time our national debt ballooned to 33 percent of our annual Gross National Product.[70] Historically, our national debt increased substantially during times of war, including the Civil War, World I, and the Vietnam War, and during times of national emergency. In the 1980s, the budget deficit tripled for the first time without any immanent national crises due largely to tax rate reductions that decreased revenue. The Clinton Administration was far more conservative on the national debt, balancing the budget and reducing national debt for eight years. The second war in Iraq increased the budget deficit once again, as did the conflict in Afghanistan. No added tax levy was imposed to pay for the war (unlike the US Civil War and World Wars I and II), adding substantially to the debt. The financial crises of 2007-2008 also added substantial debt. One-quarter of our total national debt, or $8.18 trillion, is due to tax cuts and the initial economic hit by COVID-19 incurred during the Trump Administration. Unpaid wars and economic crises have pushed the debt to enormous proportions.

The two alternatives for cutting the national debt have always been to (1) reduce spending—usher in economic austerity by cutting social program costs and/or military spending—or (2) increase tax revenue. Forty years of economic data demonstrate that austerity measures would hurt the US economy overall—any cuts to income or adding to the expenditures of the bottom 80 percent generally do. Those who spend the most on goods and services are the most populous in our society, the middle class. It is also very unpopular to increase taxes in the United States. However, attitudes about paying income taxes differ most when combining higher-income and political party affiliation: far more (71 percent) upper-income Republicans believe they pay more than their fair share of taxes than upper-income Democrats (37 percent), for example. Lower-income

Americans have more consensus on taxes; only 37 percent of Democrats and 41 percent of Republicans in lower-income groups state they pay more than their fair share of taxes.[71]

A Pew Research survey of US adults in April 2023 found that what bothers Americans most about the federal tax system is not that lower-income people don't pay their fair share of tax, with 34 percent of US citizens bothered "a lot" or "some." What bothers Americans most, "a lot or some," about the federal tax system is that "some corporations" (83 percent) and "some wealthy" people (82 percent) don't pay their fair share of taxes.[72] Seventy-one percent of Americans are also bothered "a lot" or "some" by what they must pay for income taxes (see Figure 2). However, polling research suggests that the lack of transparency and communication about line-item spending has much to do with the majority's attitude toward taxes. It isn't so much we hate paying income taxes, we're bothered more by not knowing what our money is spent on—especially conservatives on "big government."

The cost of health care for Americans remains such a high percentage of monthly expenses for some Americans that many weigh whether important health treatments are worth the cost—a difficult conundrum for all but the wealthiest Americans. Eighty-three percent of those polled by Pew Research in 2018 believed the cost of medical treatments made quality care unaffordable. Some other concerns raised in the same poll about medical costs are that Americans "rely too much on meds that may not be necessary" (68 percent) and that "prescription drug side effects create as many problems as they solve" by 59 percent.[73] Americans are becoming wary of the exaggerated costs of prescription drugs in the US and wary of the intense marketing in the industry.

With escalating healthcare costs, many Americans favor a single national healthcare system. In a July 2020 poll, 63 percent of US adults believed the government should be primarily responsible for providing healthcare coverage for all, a percentage that went up from 2019's polling.[74] This consensus is mostly driven by the attitudes of Democrats, with roughly a third (34 percent) of Republicans believing it was not the federal government's responsibility to provide health insurance to all Americans beyond Medicare/Medicaid.[75]

Fifty-four percent of Republicans believed in at least continuing the US government's role in Medicare/Medicaid coverage, with only 11 percent of those Republicans polled believing the government should have no involvement in health care coverage at all. And 63 percent of Republican-leaning voters also stated that medical insurance access should not be denied for preexisting conditions. Despite the reluctance of Republicans to want the US government involved in health coverage, it is difficult to believe that US Health Insurers would provide affordable health insurance to Americans with preexisting conditions. Obamacare ensures that health insurance may be practically affordable to many more Americans, though the cost of health care remains too expensive for many average American household budgets.

How can we improve economic equality and the costs of living with the consensus that we have?

The American economy is intricately linked to a global economic system where bull market optimism has always been the mantra for growth. However, going forward, bipartisanship has to be the mantra for transformation and progress in a global economic system in flux with new challenges emerging every day. Suppose we want to improve the US economy for the great majority of Americans. In that case, we have abundant examples of economies overseas that are successfully meeting challenges in addressing inequality and many examples of other nations still underperforming for their middle classes. The US now ranks 48th out of 167 countries with the highest income inequality as measured by the Gini coefficient, in the top third of countries with the highest disparities of income in the population.[76] Most countries with high levels of income inequality are, not surprisingly, the most impoverished countries still in the throes of postcolonial recovery. These are African and Latin American countries where the income differences between executive and working classes are quite profound, countries like Zambia (4), Namibia (2), Belize (14), and Colombia (9). But even large economies in relatively prosperous nations like South Africa (1), Brazil (17), and the economic zone of Hong Kong (9) have enormous income differentials brought on by the income rewards and pitfalls of a globally integrated economic system.

Though our income inequality has grown, the US, far and away, remains the world's greatest producing and consuming nation. Our gross domestic product is 25 trillion dollars annually—total domestic product defined as the market value of all final goods and services from a nation produced in a given year. Our GDP is about the same as the total of the third (Japan) to tenth (Italy) major producing countries combined. As a country, we are wealthy materially by any measure, so it is particularly frustrating for many Americans to be told their economy is "doing well" when they have little to no extra income remaining from their paycheck after paying high bill costs, food, and rent at the end of the month. We make good money comparatively in the world, but for a majority, expenses have outpaced the rewards.

Many countries have taken on the economic reforms that were initiated here in America to outperform us, where we once excelled.

Since Norton and Ariely's survey in 2010, Sweden's income inequality has remained low, but wealth inequality has grown because Nordic countries produce more millionaires per capita than any other nations. Six Nordic countries, with comparatively high tax rates, fully funded social programs, and fully funded higher education, occupy the top positions in the World Economic Forum's Global Social Mobility Index rankings.[77] One straightforward explanation of how and why social mobility is so high in Northern Europe is provided in George Lakey's book *Viking Economics: How the Scandinavians Got it Right – and How We Can, Too.* When Lakey asked Zoltan J. Acs, a former economist for the US Small Business Administration, why more Norwegians than Americans per capita become entrepreneurs, Acs replied:

> The three things we as Americans worry about—education, retirement, and medical expenses—are things that Norwegians don't worry about.[78]

Another economist cited in *Viking Economics*, Mark Zandi of Moody's Analytics, added:

> Thirty-somethings, a demographic usually productive of risk-taking and start-ups, are often held back by student loans in the US.[79]

The economic success and entrepreneurialism of younger generations entering the workforce is the engine that drives tax revenue in nations, not just in the present but for the foreseeable future.

Critically, the Scandinavian countries produce more millionaires from citizens who start with modest means. However, polling and consensus in the states indicate that Americans would not pay the income tax rates of Nordic countries. It should also be understood that Scandinavians are outproducing the world in social mobility as nations that valorize self-sufficiency through a strong Protestant ethic but also cultivate human social capital through higher education. The United States is a more culturally heterogeneous country than the Nordic countries, and there are many reasons why simply adapting social democratic reforms in the United States will not work. However, the means of increasing the purchasing power of US citizens and creating a US population more resilient to inflation is comparatively clear, and there is a political consensus to get it done. Increasing purchasing power means (1) increasing the salaries and income of Americans, or (2) decreasing the expenses of lower to middle-income Americans by lowering the costs of major expenditures like health, housing, and education, and commodities like food and energy. So how do we get there? First, we have to be sanguine with what has not worked, the dream versus the reality.

Thomas Piketty and Joseph Stiglitz conclude that one of the keys to fixing economic inequality and creating a more vibrant and sustainable economy in the US comes back to being smarter with redistribution to being productive with taxation. One of the enduring myths about the Scandinavian nations is that they are populated with citizens who want to give handouts to other citizens of the state. However, Nordic countries came to progressive taxation as nations that required all citizens to do their fair share of work, to be independent-minded, and to lift themselves whenever possible. But Scandinavian leadership also acknowledged and trusted the economic research that pointed to ways of increasing equality of opportunity by collectively paying for and controlling some of the structural expenses in the costs of living that have risen far above inflation: healthcare, higher education, child care, and housing. Populist policies made these countries more productive by ensuring a basic safety net so individuals could invest in new industries and innovation. The structural changes that came with neoliberalism in national economies like the US have, over time, essentially bought core nations (like ours) pools of cheap labor. However, over 40 years, industry worldwide has benefitted from automation, and greater production efficiency is the primary factor keeping any commodity prices down, along with healthy markets ensured by healthy competition for consumer spending.

The US economy from 1980-2020 shifted toward mega-conglomerate capitalism. Modern industrial nations had to lower corporate tax rates to invite international investment and production in an economy that benefitted monopolistic corporate mergers and extra capital for lobbying power in Washington. In 1952, corporations paid 32.1 percent of all tax revenue in the US. In 2017; they paid just 9 percent of our national tax revenue when Trump cut the nominal corporate tax rate from 35 percent to 21 percent, increasing the national debt and adding equity to buy up more small-scale commodity producers. In the US, stock buybacks are a common financialization strategy of major banks and corporations that has substantially increased corporate profits and dependence on interest income. Levying a tax on capital gains in the US, particularly those gains made through stock-buy backs may be one solution to increasing revenue, paying down the national debt, and helping to fund education, which should include kick-starting universal Pre-K— setting up every child on a path of opportunity from the get-go and enabling new parents to get back to the job market.

Joseph Stiglitz uses forty years of economic data to demonstrate that austerity measures, or cutbacks on spending for social or domestic incentive programs to pay down the national debt, only constrict national economies and do more economic damage to nations than the debt itself. The national debt must be paid down; it is a concern of most Americans and a tremendous liability to US creditworthiness. Polling data suggest that increasing taxes or levying new taxes is only popular so far as the wealthiest corporations and individuals are targeted, those who have increased their wealth substantially as the debt has risen. Polling consensus indicates that paying down the national debt could be accomplished by tightening up tax enforcement at the top, cutting loopholes, and taxing capital gains. In the long term, tax revenue could be increased by directly infusing increased tax receipts into economic programs that build up the middle classes, like adding to small business loan funding, funding occupational training, and providing grants for programs that directly increase educators in impacted occupational programs like nursing—smarter redistribution.

Big brands emerged in the US in the heyday of the 1950s and 1960s. Ten massive companies like Pepsico, Kellogg's, and General Mills now control the prices of nearly everything one can buy in the center aisles of a US supermarket.[80] Yet, beginning in the 1990s with microbreweries, consumers began to react to the blandness of rice beer and the nutritional deficits of processed foods. Small food and beverage producers in the US began to expand the inventory of available locally-made products such as honey and dairy products like eggs, milk, cheese, and even dining staples like fresh bread. Now, in some areas of the country, neighbors are beginning to set up trade networks to share products grown organically and sustainably from their land. There is a return to small-scale resource production that subverts the reliance upon international supply chains and processed food giants.

Monopolism in the food, petroleum, and health sectors has also lessened the incentive to lower prices because market competition has been weakened. Expanding localization efforts, whether it is building and allocating community gardens and rooftops and in vacant lots in urban settings, is one small, low-cost way consumers can take back some control of the supply chain, product-dependent home economics. Simple solutions and the movement toward *localization* can counter the worst effect results of food grown thousands of miles away and shipped around the world where planting a fruit tree in the backyard—where the climate is amenable—or putting an herb box in the window can produce food the way our great-- grandparents did—fresh, organic and cheap.

In 1980, at the height of union power, 23 million Americans were part of a union, and only 8 percent of the total wages in the US were received by the top 1 percent of the nation's wealthiest people. As union membership numbers decreased, so did economic equality. By 2007, only 16 million Americans belonged to a union, and by then, the top 1 percent of the nation's wealthiest people were collecting close to 24 percent of the total income of the nation. The US, among the world's top economic nations, has seen the greatest decline in union membership per capita and the steepest descent into inequality. As of August 2022, approval rates ranked by Gallop on labor unions have soared to 71 percent, from a nadir at 49 percent in 2009, and almost back to their highest approval ratings in the height of the depression at 72 percent (1936) and to their highest level since 1957.[81]

Americans *en masse* are looking more favorability on labor mobilization and fair wages than they have for a very long time. It is a good time to continue to unionize the workforce of America to keep wages in pace with the cost of living. Unions were a key factor in the sixty years of progress on economic equality from 1920 to 1980. Non-government organizations like One Fair Wage, a US national organization representing nearly 300,000 service workers, over 2000 restaurant employers, and dozens of organizations nationwide have been working to lift subminimum wages nationwide. In a Pew Research Poll from April 2021, 62 percent of US respondents supported raising the minimum wage nationally to $15 per hour. Eighty-nine percent of Americans feel that the current national minimum wage of $7.25 per hour should be lifted to represent a more reasonable living wage.[82]

We learned from the COVID years and the rise of dictators like Putin that dependence on the global supply chain is now a national security issue and a dangerous dependency. Economic inequality worldwide opens the door for populist uprisings and the usurpation of democracies by populist dictators who inevitably set back progress and propitiate violence. Fair labor practices are essential for sustaining democratic governance worldwide. This is one more reason that the US should lead the world in a transition to a more equitable economy. Our consensus is there, and our political will should follow.

Tax revenue and national budgetary consensus

What do the American people want tax dollars spent on? A Pew Research poll conducted in March of 2019 raised the question: "If you were making up the budget for the federal government this year, would you increase, decrease, or keep spending the same …percent)." The sectors of most support for an increase in national public tax revenue spending—by more than 50 percent of those polled—included education (72 percent), veteran's benefits (72 percent), rebuilding roads, bridges (infrastructure) (62 percent), Medicare (55 percent), environmental protection (55 percent), health care (53 percent), and scientific research (52 percent).[83] Areas where the most support for a decrease in spending would include military defense (23 percent), assistance to the needy in the world (28 percent), and assistance to the unemployed (23 percent).

A good size majority of US citizens in 2021 favored making college tuition free for all students: "Conservative/Moderate Democrats (81 percent), Liberal Democrats (89 percent), and Moderate/ Liberal Republicans (57 percent) were supportive of free college tuition at least "somewhat," with only one-quarter of the US population, Conservative Republicans, mostly opposed to free tuition.[84] If we reframed the education priorities around two years of free higher education or two years of free vocational retraining, this would move Republicans considerably toward a bipartisan consensus on free higher education—a positive structural trajectory toward increasing social mobility.

If we lowered the cost of higher education and health care costs and increased the availability of affordable housing—particularly for first-time home buyers—this would go a long way toward increasing social mobility in the US. Is there a consensus on where we should provide greater spending in the US? The value of higher education has come under scrutiny lately in the press and political climate. I think it is important to consider that higher education produces engineers and scientists, computer coders, medical doctors, nurses, and teachers for positions that need to be filled immediately in the workforce. The United States pioneered free public school education for the many. Higher education has been adapting to meet the demands of a 21st-century workforce even as those requirements are changing rapidly with AI technologies, but it needs to adapt further. Still, a degree in a higher education institution is far and away the surest pathway for economic mobility, even today. Funding and expanding vocational training in community colleges also directly translates to higher wages and opportunities for millions of Americans.

In coastal cities in the United States, we have seen an escalation of real estate prices that now render the cost of buying a home unrealistic for millions of Americans. Residents in the West have seen rents and housing prices rise most significantly. One solution to housing that will increase productivity, efficiency, and the time required for building millions of new homes in the US has reached maturity, modular home construction. Modular homes are no longer the cardboard cutouts they once were; they are far more energy efficient, cost and waste efficient, and only limited by the imagination of the architect who designs them and the design teams to create desirable options in their manufacture. Modular homes can also speed up production by up to 50 percent of the time to build a home and make homes that are highly efficient in R-values (insulation ratings) and consume less of the electric grid to inhabit (saving money and electricity). Local and state governments need only revisit and alter zoning and building restrictions to expedite construction.

In San Francisco, commercial vacancy rates are the highest they have been for years. City leaders now acknowledge that the vacancies may be permanent with more people working from home and the tech sector increasing layoffs. Ironically, many city workers need housing near those commercial vacancies. Hundreds of thousands of Americans are looking to purchase property or rent affordably near their workplaces, and educators/lower-income Americans working in expensive cities have to commute long distances where they can afford rent to go to work—as tens of thousands of vacant storefronts and office space remain empty and unused. Could this be an opportunity rather than a double-edged problem? Two legislative bills in California look to have transformative potential, California Senate Bills 6 and Assembly Bill 2011, signed by Newsom in September 2022. Both bills incentivize housing projects in commercial corridors otherwise zoned for large retail and office buildings to help California fill a multimillion-unit shortage in its housing supply. Both bills guarantee union-scale wages and promise an expedited construction process while keeping development close to city centers to help the state meet its environmental goals and avoid sprawl.[85]

The urban transformation process may be costly. Still, the potential for creating mixed-use inner cities in California that respond to an affordable housing shortage while filling empty and unused commercial corridors is a win-win economic plan helping to alleviate two important concerns of urban Americans—urban decay and the cost of housing. Taking what is already built to rebuild will revitalize inner-city communities and bypass NIMBY concerns that have held up construction in the suburbs. Creating mixed-use urban districts also makes use efficient use of under-utilized public transport corridors. Why not turn urban problems into opportunities? Global cities like Curitiba, Brazil, have accomplished much more with effective city planning for pennies on the dollar of what we spend in the US.

An increasing majority of Americans now indicate that healthcare costs are still unaffordable. The most recent Kaiser Foundation (KFF) Tracking Poll conducted in March 2022 found slightly more than half of the public (55 percent) hold a favorable opinion of the Affordable Care Act (ACA), while about four in ten (42 percent) hold a negative opinion of the law.[86] Views of the ACA are still largely partisan: nearly nine in ten Democrats (87 percent), along with six in ten independents (58 percent), view the law favorably, while eight in ten Republicans (79 percent) hold unfavorable views. Looking more closely at the KFF data, however, reveals that Republican, Independent, and Democratic-leaning voters desired a healthcare system that doesn't deny coverage for pre-existing conditions (72 percent overall) nor one that prohibits sick people from being charged more (64 percent). There is even consensus on requiring health insurance companies to cover the cost of most preventive services (62 percent).

The debate over national healthcare coverage was long and acrimonious. I would suggest that we work within the existing system to fix deficiencies in the Affordable Care Act (ACA) to continue to lower costs for all. We forget that the taxpayer now pays for emergency services for people admitted to emergency rooms who don't have health care insurance through Medicare reimbursement. The Inflation Reduction Act, signed in the summer of 2023, will allow Medicare to negotiate the price of only 10 of the most popular drugs and will not take effect until 2026. But at least a total ban on negotiating prices has been lifted. Before the bill was signed, a Kaiser Family Foundation found that 83 percent of Americans favored removing the ban on drug price negotiation, including 95 percent of Democrats, 82 percent of independents, and 71 percent of Republicans. This indicates that there is popular support for empowering programs like the ACA to engage in more price negotiation on behalf of the American healthcare consumer.

Toward a Now & Future Democratic Economy

Can we recognize that our perspectives on the economy differ, but it rewards us all to lift the middle classes in America? We have enormous consensus in the US for increasing social mobility in the US as long as we prioritize giving a "hand up" over a "hand out." Adam Smith was a moral philosopher but also a realist. He recognized that human beings were complex, generous, and cooperative, yet also materially self-serving when focused on personal or family welfare. At an individual level, Americans are a very generous people. So many first-generation citizens provide remittances to family and friends from the countries they've emigrated from, where a little more cash goes a long way. And in 2019, individual Americans donated $310 billion to charitable causes—most generously to religious groups, education, human services, foundations, international affairs, arts, and environmental causes in that order of plentitude.[87] This was nearly fifteen times as much as US corporations ($21 billion) or four times as much as national foundations. We also give more money out as a nation by GDP, almost twice as much in donations to non--profits as the next most generous nation, New Zealand. US citizens are generous by any standard and with clear limitations, generous with each other.

How much of the cause of inflation should be attributed to large corporations and big institutions, as the majority American public believes? Corporations were invented to pool money from individual investors, and their reason for being is to make money for their investors. The executive for a major corporation thinks daily about her investors by increasing efficiency and market share through consolidation. Only fair business practices and regulations, moderated by a representative society, keep corporations from trying to subsume competition and monopolization driven by lower overhead costs and increased profit margins. We have to accept that most wealthy people and wealthy corporations are motivated to conserve their resources, not risk them. But consumers are not passive victims in the game of capitalism. Consumers can elect not to pay the carry-on baggage fees of one airline to go with another. Our collective consuming choices modify the corporate product place—given a free marketplace where competitive choices are available.

We must also acknowledge that corporations, like social groups, are not all the same; their stakeholders fashion their value systems. Schreiber Foods, a dairy company headquartered in Green Bay,

Wisconsin; Graybar, an American wholesale electrical company based in Clayton, Missouri; and the publisher W.W. Norton & Company all have something in common: they are all employee-owned corporations. Many companies have now committed themselves to a new ownership model as stakeholder-focused companies that invite employees to take ownership of the company they work for and be a part of the decision-making process. We can also take ownership of our consumption, we can be more involved in our company's business practice, and we can be a creditor as well as a debtor with a bit of financial literacy.

Thomas Piketty reminds us that progressive taxation ensured the US government could fund massive civil works, like hydroelectric dam construction, the national highway system, and the Space Race, projects that propelled the US into a superpower with unparalleled infrastructure. He reminds us that overall the long trend, from feudalism and slavery, there has been economic progress, that economic equality has improved over a long duration. One hundred years ago, immigrants who arrived in the US in their lifetime could see how their labor translated directly into increased social mobility for their children and grandchildren.

According to the World Economic Forum, even in countries with the greatest social mobility, the Nordic countries, on average, it would still take two to three generations of lower-income citizens to attain a median income. Now, in the US today, it is estimated to take six generations on average; in China and India, seven; and in South Africa and Brazil, nine for the promise of equality to materialize.[88] The aftermath of World War II that followed a world financial collapse shook the world's established economic order. The idea of lifting the middle class took hold in the American economic ethos. To counter the excesses and exploitation embedded in capitalism, labor unions flourished in the United States. Increased union participation and leveraging labor power helped raise US economic equality for over sixty years.

Coming out of college, university graduates in coastal regions of the US face rental costs for a small studio apartment that could take up to 50 percent or more of their monthly wages. We have disincentivized so many young people, now concerned with simply attaining self-sufficiency more than realizing social mobility for themselves and their families. Renewed levels of high inflation and stagnating pay for 80 percent of Americans over the last forty years have withered aspirations for economic mobility for many in the US.

The Inflation Reduction Act of 2022 (IRA) invests in domestic energy production, infrastructure, veterans' welfare, and the ability of Medicare to negotiate drug costs with major pharmaceuticals. Programs that called for funding higher education and universal pre-K were cut from IRA, which would have substantially boosted social mobility; investing in the potential of Americans has always been key to US economic success. As every economic indicator provides, higher education or vocational training increases income; it directly impacts social mobility. Should we allow Americans of all ages to leave college with little or no debt or to train for a new career in high-demand fields for which we have to import labor: senior care, STEM fields, and automation technologies? Do we desire the US to have lower economic mobility and fewer innovators than smaller nations that focus more on their human capital?

When older Americans look nostalgically back to the US of the 1950s, 60s, and early 70s, I would submit that much of what they are feeling is the loss of purchasing power and the explosion of opportunities created by government financial stimulus in sectors like space technology, infrastructure and construction, and educational television. By worldwide standards, on paper, Americans still possess enviable purchasing power. Alexis de Tocqueville's paradox that social frustration grows more quickly as social conditions and opportunities improve may also be afflicting us, a decline in civic republicanism, in the pride of national spirit, an "affluenza" born of too many options and not enough satisfaction. As Jurgen Habermas and members of the Frankfurt School remind us, material culture is one small part of human existence. Still, our material status in a globalized economy seems to measure more and more of how we value each other and contributes to fierce political fights over taxation and economic fairness.

Frustration and concern with inflation and the cost of living have mounted in the US because the options we have long been given to get ahead are to work harder or longer hours, change our jobs, and work ourselves to the next economic level. However, statistics on labor hours indicate that North Americans are already working long hours. Our neighbors to the South in Mexico work longer hours than any other nation on earth. Many in the US, especially at the lower economic level, work as many hours as possible in repetitive gig jobs with little job security. Job security is now measured by having the luxury to give up one of the multiple jobs that so many find necessary to make a living. For many, working more hours, working harder, or finding time or money to train or educate to the next level just isn't an option.

Americans are asking themselves: How much more of my life can I spend dedicated to everyday labor, paid and unpaid? Have I got the best of what I can get in this economic system? Polls show that 90 percent of us desire a fairer distribution of wealth in the US. Americans are in a state of malaise because our trust in institutions, including our trade and monetary structures, seemed to have benefited only those in the executive classes. Most of us also agree that our economic system cannot be thrown out for some utopian socialist system, and the vast majority of Americans acknowledge that some economic inequality will always exist in our system. But it is within our power to continue to democratize our economic system "American-style" and excise our monopolistic and oligarchic tendencies in the US. We can forge a pathway toward a more democratic economy with our systems already in place, an economic system that favors entrepreneurialism and inclusion, competitive markets, and social welfare that lifts more than it hands out. A demopoly, if you will, propped up by a vibrant economy of clear and transparent rules, where everyone can take some ownership of their material future and where all can trust that their aspirations—with perseverance and hard work—will pay off.

One could—and many philosophers have—cast the material nature of human beings as either compassionate/generous or as self-serving creatures. We can be infused with idealism and collective spirit to be altruistic and generous, and we can also be pushed toward a self-serving nature, living in a material world of competitiveness and unequal rewards. Our views on economic fairness in society differ, but we have far more accord than differences. Polling data indicate that the difference between funding social programs, education, and other national spending hinges on a fulcrum point of difference: Democrats see the economic system, particularly economic inequality, more as a structural problem. Republicans see economic inequality as a personal choice, linking wealth with effort and opportunity. We all want Americans to fulfill their economic potential. Let's look at the data and ourselves and talk honestly about how we will get there.

Figures: Chapter 1—The Cost of Living, Economic Equality

Partisan differences in assessments of many national problems, but both Republicans and Democrats see the ability of the parties to work together as a problem

*% who say each of the following is a **very big problem** in the country today*

	Dem/ Lean Dem	Rep/ Lean Rep	Total
Inflation	52 ●	● 77	65
The affordability of health care	54 ●	● 73	64
The ability of Dems/Reps to work together	62 ●	● 63	62
Drug addiction	56 ●	● 64	61
Gun violence	38 ●	● 81	60
Violent crime	52 ●	● 64	59
The federal budget deficit	39 ●	● 72	56
The state of moral values	39 ●	● 69	54
Illegal immigration	25 ●	● 70	47
The quality of public K-12 schools	43 ●	● 51	47
Climate change	14 ●	● 64	39
Racism	14 ●	● 55	35
Condition of roads, bridges and other infrastructure	29 ●	● 37	34
Domestic terrorism	25 ●	● 41	34
International terrorism	23 ●	● 36	30
Unemployment	23 ●	● 23	24

Source: Survey of U.S. adults conducted June 5-11, 2023.

PEW RESEARCH CENTER

Figure 1. National economic issues were among the top concerns of Americans in a June 2023 poll, rating "inflation," "the affordability of health care," and "the federal budget deficit" as very big problems.

Americans' frustrations with the federal tax system

% who say each bothers them _____ about the federal tax system

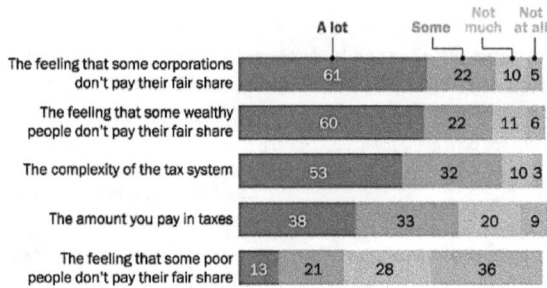

	A lot	Some	Not much	Not at all
The feeling that some corporations don't pay their fair share	61	22	10	5
The feeling that some wealthy people don't pay their fair share	60	22	11	6
The complexity of the tax system	53	32	10	3
The amount you pay in taxes	38	33	20	9
The feeling that some poor people don't pay their fair share	13	21	28	36

Note: No answer responses not shown.
Source: Survey of U.S. adults conducted March 27-April 2, 2023.

PEW RESEARCH CENTER

Figure 2. A majority of US citizens polled in April 2023 were "bothered a lot" that corporations and wealthy Americans don't pay their fair share of taxes.

Chapter 2

Social Justice, Balancing Two Issues

Should we live and learn from our history?

Flashback 1: March 3, 1991. Southern Californians watching KTLA that Sunday evening were about to be drawn into a national race struggle. Affordable personal high-quality video camcorders were just becoming available. One had been purchased by a plumbing salesman and amateur videographer named George Holiday, who was about to shoot the first-ever viral video. Just after midnight, he looked down from his apartment terrace at Foothill Boulevard and Osborne Street off "the 210" East of San Fernando Valley. His video camcorder plunged directly onto the well-lit street where a tall Black man with short-cropped hair and white pants lay flat on the pavement. He slowly rose into a crawl when police batons came down on his back and legs; a boot came down on his shoulder, then his back. Rodney King continued to try to rise back up to his knees.

With his friends, Bryant Allen and Freddie Helms, King had been driving his 1987 Hyundai Excel west on Interstate 210 in the San Fernando Valley north of Los Angeles. The three had spent the night watching basketball and drinking at a friend's house in L.A. At 12:30 AM, two officers of the California Highway Patrol noticed King's car speeding on the freeway. They pursued King with lights and sirens, and the pursuit reached 117 mph. King refused to pull over and later said he tried to outrun the police because he believed being charged with driving under the influence would violate his parole from a previous robbery conviction.[89] After approximately 8 miles, officers cornered King in his car. Holiday video covered the portion of King's arrest after he had been ordered to lie prone on the ground. According to court documents, King rose to his feet and collided with one of the officers when he was tased, and one officer, Powell, with whom he had collided, knocked King to the ground with his baton.[90]

For many who watched the video broadcast on local television stations and later on CNN, their thoughts echoed that of Black community activist Ameshia Cross, who stated, "I was waiting for someone to stop it…and the fact that no one came, and no one was willing to stop it" was deeply troubling.[91] Holiday's video complicated the world in an instant. It reinforced a prevailing idea that the LA police had become too militarized, that police training undertaken with perhaps the best of intentions—to protect officers and "neutralize" threats—had only found more ways to tactically dehumanize individuals. For many people of color, a jury trial that found the policemen innocent of excessive use of force charges also reinforced ideas for many in L.A. that the judicial system was structured to take care of their own first. The aftermath of the incident also raised other issues that loomed in the headlights: intersectional forces related to racism, the role of video cameras and new visibilities, the challenges posed in 21st Century law enforcement, and how drug addiction could erode a man in the prime of his life. We could not have known it at the time, but Rodney King's arrest also came at the peak of violent crime in America that hasn't been matched since.

Flashback 2: September 16, 1988. Rebecca Bell was a beautiful "lively seventeen-year-old" model student in her Indiana high school—according to Felicia Lowenstein, writer of the book *The Abortion Battle: Looking at Both Sides* (1996). "Becky never did anything wrong…Nobody worried about Becky—until she met her boyfriend."[92] When she turned seventeen, she found out she was pregnant and went to a local Planned Parenthood. There, she learned that a girl in Indiana could not get an abortion without parental consent. Though Becky loved her parents, she was deeply ashamed of what had happened and felt like she couldn't tell them she had gotten pregnant. Instead, Becky drove 110 miles to Kentucky to get an abortion in the nearest state that didn't have a parental consent law. She explained to her parents that she was going to a party. She came back to her parent's house at 1 AM, complaining that someone may have spiked her Coke and not feeling well, crying.

The next day was a Sunday and Becky went to work at a local grocery store as a cashier. By Wednesday, she had a fever and thought it was just the temporary aftereffect of the abortion. By Friday morning, Becky agreed to go to the hospital even though the doctors might have to disclose to her parents that she had had an abortion. She had greatly weakened by then, and when nurses attempted to day draw blood, they couldn't. Becky's veins had already collapsed. The hospital staff urged her parents to talk with Becky to find out more information. "Tell mommy what is wrong?"[93] urged her mother. Instead, Becky took off her love knot ring and said, "Forgive me for what

I've done," and "she seemed to die."[94] Within 24 hours, Rebecca Suzanne Bell died in the hospital in a small Indiana town "where everyone knows everybody, and they talk." It took months for her parents to piece together the story of their daughter's death about the parental consent law in Indiana. Becky's shame and silence are all too common emotions in abortion, her inner turmoil is now emblematic of a divided nation unwilling to see how ideological battles harm the most vulnerable people in our society, a legislative system that rewards polarization over compassionate discussion.

Two social issues have come into political prominence in the last few years, dividing the nation around ways in which politics and law intersect with deeply personal matters:

1. In June 2022, in a case known as *Dobbs v. Jackson Women's Health Organization*, the US Supreme Court ruled that the US Constitution of the United States does not confer a right to legal abortion.

The court's decision overruled both *Roe v. Wade* (1973) and *Planned Parenthood v. Casey* (1992), decisions that first created and then affirmed the right to legal abortion in the United States with exceptions. The *Dobbs* ruling returned to individual states the power to regulate abortion and has put the issue front and center of US national political debate for the foreseeable future. As we learned in early 2024, the *Dobbs* decision has had ripple effects, making *in vitro fertilization* (IVF) and medical abortions to save the life of the mother potentially illegal practices. The debate over abortion access is part of a longer, historical debate in the United States around the role of the state in the private sphere of Americans. And:

2. The death of African-American men like Rodney King, Trayvon Martin (2012), Eric Garner (2014), and George Floyd Jr. (2020) reignited debate over racism in America. Garner's last few words, "I can't breathe," became a slogan associated with the Black Lives Matter movement in the US.

Much of the debate centered around "woke" activism diminished with the suspension of Ron DeSantis' campaign in the runup to the Republican presidential primary—anti-diversity, pro-life legislation in Florida had been the centerpiece of his campaign rhetoric. When we consider national views on the topic of equal opportunity, racism, and diversity, the political gulf in the perception of these issues centers on new progressive and youth-led movements of the last few years. The perception of the Black Lives Matter movement, for example, is significantly differentiated by ethnicity, generation, and political affiliation. But "race" and racism also intersect with deeper currents in defining otherness throughout US history and with the role of the state to ensure equal opportunity for all.

Abortion and diversity in the US are issues of social justice because they directly impact the lives and liberty of historically underprivileged groups in the United States, including women, those born into lower-income families, and those ethnic groups who have faced discrimination in our nation. Social scientists have increasingly looked at issues within social justice as *intersectional*, meaning gender, race, and class are interconnected factors that play into the status and liberties of the individual and their families in America. Within these interconnected issues, Americans are confronting quickly evolving and highly personal questions. Is there a stage in the pregnancy where the rights from the rights of the pregnant woman shift to the unborn? Should these decisions remain with a woman and her doctors, or do we owe an obligation to the rights of the unborn to legally intervene, and at what stage? Is racism still a problem in America? Or is racism mostly a problem we have left behind us? How do our perceptions of racism differ? Have movements like Black Lives Matter brought Americans together or torn us apart? Can we find consensus and balance on publicly polarizing issues that intersect at the deepest level with our private lives?

Where do we believe we differ on legalized abortion?

From December 2017 into January 2018, a national poll sponsored by The Knights of Columbus and conducted by the Marist Institute for Public Opinion queried 2,517 people in the United States.[95] Unlike similar polls, the Marist Institute dove into some deeper philosophical questions on the issue of abortion, like "When does life begin?" More than half of Americans polled at that time, 62 percent, believed that life began within the first three months of a woman's pregnancy, and fully 47 percent believed life began at conception. Still, another 24 percent of Americans believed that life began only when a fetus had the "viability" to live "outside the womb" or that a person's life began at birth. These views represent the moral ambiguity surrounding the abortion issue, with both medical science and religion influencing the decision to have an abortion and new laws constraining the procedure. Almost half of Americans believe life begins at conception, that this is a scientific fact. Conversely, as many Americans believe, defining life at conception is a philosophical or religious belief.

Views on gender equality, beliefs on the starting point of life, how and where one is raised and chooses to live, and current religious

beliefs are important factors that influence policy debates and personal convictions on the issue of abortion. In 2018, 56 percent of those
polled believed abortion was morally wrong.[96] This percentage is lower
than it was in 2012, when 62 percent of Americans polled believed
abortion was morally wrong—a percentage that has been coming
down slowly since the *Roe v. Wade* decision in 1973. In a March
2022 Pew Research poll, 72 percent of Americans believed that "the
decision about whether to have an abortion should belong solely
to the pregnant woman" described their views at least somewhat
well.[97] However, a slimmer majority (56 percent) of Americans also
believed the statement, "Human life begins at conception, so a fetus
is a person with rights." Significantly, a "third of Americans hold
these seemingly conflicting views about the autonomy of pregnant
women and the rights of the fetus at the same time" (see Figure
1).[98] Americans are politically but also psychologically conflicted
on the issue—an ethical quandary between the rights of the mother
versus the rights of the life within her.

American public's support of abortion "for any reason" (without
restrictions) has only become substantially partisan since 2008. In
1977, four years after *Roe v. Wade* legalized abortion in the US, more
Republicans (39 percent) than Democrats (33 percent) supported
legal abortion "for any reason."[99] This might seem counter-intuitive
based on the polarization of the issue in the political parties today.
However, the US was a more conservative nation in 1977 overall,
and the Democratic Party had a majoritarian share of socially conservative Catholic parishioners in that day. Before *Roe v. Wade*, the
fewest restrictions on abortion by the state were in "blue" states like
New York, Washington, and Hawaii, followed closely by "red" states
of today, Alaska, and the entire Eastern Seaboard from Maryland
down to Florida. The shift in views on abortion can be explained

in part as a shift in religious/political demographics: opposition to abortion waned in Democratic Catholics, but opposition to abortion became a conservative Evangelical cause beginning in the 1980s.[100] However, in 1977, a majority of either party did not support legalizing abortion. Support for abortion "for any reason" by Republican-leaning voters increased by 1991 to 41 percent, went down to a low of 26 percent by 2012, and ticked up to 35 percent in 2022. For Democratic-leaning voters, support for legalized abortion went up slightly from 1977—10 percentage points to 44 percent by 2008—then surged up to 69 percent by 2021 on the road up to the overturn of *Roe v. Wade* in June 2022.[101]

Support for abortion also has a generational component. Seventy-four percent of those in a March 2022 Pew Research poll aged 18-29 believed abortion should be legal with some exceptions. For those Americans 50 years and older, the percentage drops to close to 54 percent.[102] The older one gets in America, generally the more conservative one polls on the issue of abortion. Though age and sex might connote some disposition on abortion views, the profile of who gets abortions in America and the reasons why people oppose or support legal abortion are more counter-intuitive. Only 39 percent of abortions performed in America are on women who have never had a child, and 61 percent of abortions in America are performed on women who have already had at least one child.[103] A common misperception is that a "typical" female who needs an abortion is a young single woman in her teens or early twenties. A more accurate portrait of a person seeking an abortion is a woman in her late twenties or thirties with a child or two who became pregnant when she did not want to, a mother already caring for children.

Where do we believe we differ on racism?

Institutional racism became an intense subject of national discussion after the deaths of Black men Trayvon Martin, George Floyd, and Eric Garner, whose deaths spawned the emergence of Black Lives Matter in July 2013—after the acquittal of George Zimmerman in the shooting death of Trayvon Martin. Zimmerman had accosted Martin, a young Black man, in an act of vigilante justice as a watch member of a neighborhood in Sanford, Florida. Zimmerman falsely suspected Martin had committed a crime. The Black Lives Matter (BLM) movement reached the height of its popularity in June 2020, just after the death of George Floyd, who died at the hands of Minneapolis police (suspected of using a fake $20 bill at a local grocery store).

In June 2020, a Pew Research poll registered 67 percent of the nation at least somewhat in support of the movement. But during and soon after the presidential election of 2020, support for the movement began to wane in White Americans as diversity, equity, and inclusion (DEI) came under fire from conservative media and politicians. In April 2023, 81 percent of Black adults stated they supported the movement, along with 63 percent of Asian adults and 61 percent of Hispanic adults. However, by 2023, only 42 percent of White American adults supported the movement, and they were far more likely than those in other racial and ethnic groups to describe the movement as "divisive" and "dangerous" (about four in ten White adults) compared with 30 percent or fewer among the other groups.

Differences on the Black Lives Matter Movement are, however, far more representationally polarized when comparing political parties' views on the issue, with 84 percent of Democrats and Democratic-leaners polled supporting the movement in June 2023 and 82 percent of Republicans and Republican-leaners opposing it. Significantly, "Democrats are more likely than Republicans to say the words empowering (42%) or inclusive (27%) describe the movement extremely or very well."[104] Republicans, in turn, are more likely than Democrats to say the words "dangerous"s (59 percent) and "divisive" (54 percent) describe the movement well. Whether you believe the movement is divisive or not, measured by polling data alone, hashtag social movements and DEI have helped to polarize the national electorate.[105]

However, the underlying locus of division on racism centers around how far racial equity in America has come since the civil rights movements of the 1950s and 1960s and what is needed to address systemic racism today. In 2021, Pew Research found that:

> Nearly eight-in-ten Black adults say a lot more needs to be done to ensure equal rights for Americans of all racial backgrounds. This includes 58 percent who say that in order to achieve this goal, most of the nation's laws and major institutions need to be completely rebuilt because they are fundamentally biased, and 19 percent who say needed changes can be made by working in the current system.[106]

Smaller majorities of Hispanic (59 percent) and Asian Americans (56 percent) adults say a lot more needs to be done to achieve racial equality. Still, significantly, only 30 percent of Hispanics and 24 percent of Asian Americans say laws and institutions are fundamentally biased and need to be completely rebuilt. Though the degree to which institutions are fundamentally biased against minorities differs among Americans of differing ethnicities, a difference in the overall perception of structural racism in America exists between White and Non-White Americans. The amount of structural bias registered by African Americans (58 percent) who believe laws and institutions need to be fundamentally rebuilt—compared with 40 percent of Democrats and 7 percent of Republicans—speaks to the weight and depth of the social inequality still perceived by a majority of African Americans in the US.[107]

One of the more contentious issues that have been brought to the fore in the last four years has been a reconsideration—mainly on the Right—of the way the history of American racial relations is taught in grade school. This is a reaction to a refocus on racial equality on the Left brought about by the Black Lives Matter movement and a concerted effort on behalf of publishers to seek out new and diverse voices in the production of fiction, including children's literature. Like many of the issues presented in this book, up until the last few years teaching about the history of racism in America since the 1970s has not been a politicized issue in our national discussion. In the same July 2021 Pew Research poll, respondents were asked to rate whether they believed "increased public attention to the history of slavery and racism in the US " was "very good," "somewhat good," "neither good nor bad," "somewhat bad," or "very bad" for American society.[108]

For all of the noise leveled against "woke-ism" in the American public sphere, at the end of 2021, only 26 percent of Americans overall believed the increased public attention to the history of slavery and racism was bad or very bad for the nation, with over three-quarters of Democrats believing it was at least somewhat good for the nation. Republicans were more divided on the issue, with 46 percent of Republicans who believed it was bad or very bad and another 25 percent of Republicans who believed it was at least somewhat good (29 percent were neutral on the issue). Polling numbers counter the accuracy of generalizations that paint Republicans as a uniform electorate against discussions or policies addressing social inequality. Among Black adults in the US, 75 percent stated the heightened public attention on racism was a good thing, with majorities of Asian (64 percent) and Hispanic Americans (59 percent) also believing so.[109]

What is "race," and should we abandon the term altogether?

To define the basis for racism in the US, it is important to clarify what we mean when we say one's "race" and why we still use a word that has been outmoded in the study of human beings—anthropology—for some years. In late March 2024, the United States Office of Management and Budget announced that the US government would revise how it categorizes race and ethnicity, adding the category of "Middle Eastern or North African" to forms such as the US Census to better reflect an increasingly diverse population.[110] For Americans who are biracial or who perceive their ethnicity as different from their race, demarking one's race or ethnicity can be confusing. Almost 44 percent of those who identified as Hispanic in the 2020 US Census, for example, picked "some other race" rather than the subcategories offered on the form, or they simply did not respond at all.[111]

The modern concept of race emerged as a product of global European exploration in the 16th to 18th centuries, as a way of defining others by skin color and physical differences, assigning cultural generalities to people as a whole, and linking cultural caricature to appearances. One definition embedded in the word "race," the idea in Western culture of linking people and their place of origin to a character of that region, is very old. The Greek philosopher Hippocrates of Kos (460-370 B.C.E), the "father of medicine," in his essay *On Airs, Waters, and Places* wrote:

> There are in Europe other tribes, differing from one another in stature, shape, and courage...Such as inhabit a country which

is mountainous, rugged, elevated, and well-watered, and where the changes of the seasons are very great, are likely to have a great variety of shapes among them, and to be naturally of an enterprising and warlike disposition; and such persons are apt to have no little of the savage and ferocious in their nature; but such as dwell in places which are low-lying, abounding in meadows and ill-ventilated, and who have a larger proportion of hot than of cold winds, and who make use of warm waters—these are not likely to be of large stature nor well proportioned, but are of a broad make, fleshy, and have black hair; and they are rather of a dark than of a light complexion, and are less likely to be phlegmatic than bilious; courage and laborious enterprise are not naturally in them, but may be engendered in them by means of their institutions.[112]

Hippocrates' views informed William Shakespeare's caricature of people of different lands, linking physical attributes such as "tawny skinned" and geographic climates to attributes of human character.

These Western markers of human societal difference are closer to what we would define today perhaps as an ethnicity—albeit a stereotype of ethnicity. Making caricatures of other ethnic groups is a common response to unfamiliar foreign cultures and languages. Ethnocentrism, or the tendency to look at other people primarily from the perspective of one's own culture or experience and, therefore, to believe in the inherent superiority of one's own culture, was as common in ancient societies as it is today. However, one could become "civilized," or part of the "real human beings," as Native Americans would say, if one acculturated to the ways of dominant society. For example, although ancient Greeks thought of themselves as superior and Europe's northern peoples as "barbarians," foreigners could learn the Greek language and culture and, through their acculturation process, shed their barbarity. Roman frescos depict dark-skinned men with curly hair, Northern Africans holding scrolls symbolizing scholarly pursuits. Skin color or physical attributes did not equate to innate cultural or mental qualities in ancient Rome. And though Shakespeare uses common perceptions of cultural caricatures of his age, the characters of his plays are nonetheless imbued with deep humanity and individual complexity—fully fleshed-out human beings.

The modern concept of "race," or more accurately, "the races," arose during the scientific revolution in the middle of the 1700s. European imperialism and colonization of the world triggered the inquiry into the physical and social differences among the various human groups Europeans encountered. Enlightenment naturalists George Louis Leclerc, Johann Friedrich Blumenbach, and the philosopher Immanuel Kant grappled to understand why people appeared to be so different around the world. In the third edition of his essay *De Generis Humani Varietate Nativa*, published in 1795, Blumenbach introduced a classification system that divided human races into quasi-different species: Caucasian, Ethiopian, Mongoloid, Malayan, and American races. Blumenbach's philosophical investigations provided us with the word "Caucasian," a racial group of lighter-skinned Europeans.[113] In his aesthetic, the superior beauty of people from the Caucasus region of Europe seemed a likely region for the origin of the human species and of the white race. It was believed that all of the world's peoples began as civilized white human beings but then degenerated as they were cast about in the world, replicating the biblical conception of the dispersal of human beings after the collapse of the Tower of Babel.

Degeneration theory, as it would be called, was part of several speculations on the evolution of human beings that later formed what anthropologists now view as a body of theory known as scientific racism. Western philosophers and proto-anthropologists coopted the terminology of race to speculate that the human race either degenerated from a white race or that the other races of people in the world evolved up to the white European race. A hierarchy of racial attributes outlined in scientific racism provided the unfortunate rationality for the colonization of native populations and the enslavement of Africans. As has been disseminated recently on Internet media, the enslavement of others has a long and broad history in human societies. Slavery was practiced in pre-contact tribes along the Northwest Pacific coast and, more notably, among the ancient Aztecs of Mexico, in historical Europe, and Africa. What made modern Western slavery particularly pernicious, however—exemplified in the antebellum South—was the ascription not only of cultural inferiority but also of biological inferiority of other races, therefore justifying the treatment of enslaved people as lesser than humans.

By the early 1920s, with early genomic, cultural, and linguistic evidence, theories that Europeans were a "master race" had been entirely disproven, even as the *eugenics movement* in the United States gained momentum. This movement promoted the idea that inferior groups of people or immigrants would infect the "quality" of white European genetic stock in the US. Today, we know that physical appearances are quite literally only skin deep. Light skin, for example, is a specific genetic adaptation to aid vitamin D production in pre-historic societies that moved into higher latitudes with less sun, and this adaptation toward lighter skin is fairly recent, only a few thousand years old. The ancestral populations of Europeans who immigrated into Northerly regions from Southern latitudes were all darker-skinned. The process of physical changes initiated by a few pieces of the human genome to adapt to environmental conditions is called a *clinal* change, defined as a "measurable gradient alteration of a species' single characteristic (or biological trait) across a geographical range."[114] What once was thought to be the "Caucasian race" originates from a complex panoply of peoples that contains large add-mixes of early Middle Eastern farmers and other ancient human infusions, including a small genetic add-mixture of Neanderthal genes.

Key to understanding why racism persists may well have been found in a Harvard cognitive psychological study that queried 61,000 participants testing for implicit stereotypes of different ethnic groups, determining how human versus animal-like they perceived people of diverse ethnicities. However, an overwhelming majority—over 90 percent—of the people tested explicitly stated that White people and non-white people are equally human. The experiment compared animal word associations—like wild and farm animals—and suprahuman word associations—like Gods and desert flowers—to associate unconscious bias between those with non-White physical ascriptions of ethnicity and those with White-physical attributes. The experiment's results "from over 61,000 participants is that White and third-party test takers consistently associated Human more with White people than other racial/ethnic groups." [115] One of the researchers in the study, Kirsten Morehouse, attributed these findings to the fact that white people are socially and economically dominant in the United States. [116] An unconscious bias that white Americans are "racially" superior, in some respect, to other prevalent ethnic groups in the US lingers in the subconscious of a majority of people they tested. Most likely as Morehouse suggests, because a higher level of humanness is associated with the dominant socioeconomic status of Whites in the United States. Economic success breeds an unconscious association with ethnic superiority.

Genetically, human beings are one species, a single "race" of beings less diverse genetically than a troupe of Chimpanzees living together in Central Africa. Differences that we see between ethnic groups on the genetic scale are smaller than the genetic diversity within any one ethnic group. The physical differences in our skin and eye colors, and hair texture are attributable to minute genetic variations. We see differences rather than similarities so acutely within one another because, neurologically, our brains are designed to see the subtlest variations in facial expressions and eye signals—and we see differences much easier than similarities. For millions of years, our evolutionary survival was predicated on interpreting the subtlest gestures from one another, honing our visual perception of the unusual or different.

Racism has taken on new meanings that involve other biases and class politics. Still, it is important to note that racism began with a dangerous and persistent cultural or biological framework of the inferiorization of others. The ascription of cultural inferiority to others has a long history in humanity tied to varying degrees of ethnocentrism and ignorance of another's culture. The biological ascription of inferiority, though proven invalid, has remained persistent because it has suited the purposes of colonialization, domination, and the genocide of marginalized populations. "Race," as a term, comes with immense baggage and an inaccurate speculative history that has long been proven invalid. So why do we continue to reference ourselves by "race?" It is deeply encoded into the native taxonomy of Americans, the way we commonly differentiate between each other and the parlance of ascription. The Harvard study, however, provides good evidence that the people of the United States are not a racist nation. Yet we harbor unconscious biases against other groups we don't know on a personal level, including Black Americans, Hispanics, Muslims, Gays and Lesbians, Jews, and Evangelical Christians, as a Pew Research poll from March 2021 suggested.[117]

Is critical race theory invading our schools?

Critical race theory (CRT) is a body of legal scholarship, with theories and approaches assembled in the 1970s and 1980s and focused on the role of US law in perpetuating racism. Critical race theorists look at common but discriminatory practices like *redlining* in real estate and draw from the work of several 20th-century legal scholars and the work of political philosophers like Antonio Gramsci, Sojourner Truth, Frederick Douglass, and W. E. B. Du Bois.

Redlining was a discriminatory practice in which lenders or insurers targeted majority-minority neighborhoods to inflate home and business loan interest rates. In redlining, city maps were colored in various colors to signify poor risk areas of investment in the urban landscape. Green and blue colors were used to mark out areas of the city on regional maps that were considered low-risk, yellow was medium-risk, and red-colored neighborhoods were considered high-risk. Red-colored areas generally housed the lowest-income, black, and brown peopled neighborhoods. The effect of redlining practices ensured a lack of investment in those neighborhoods that would forestall any new and updated building projects. It made denying home insurance easier or getting business credit harder, stifling small business development. Redlining was also instrumental in creating food deserts: supermarkets would hesitate to locate within these red zones, and residents would have to rely on food from liquor stores or travel out of their neighborhoods to fulfill grocery needs.

Research regarding the discriminatory practices sanctioned

by laws, or the lack of law, was informed by CRT. Still, critical race theory has not been used very often in the social sciences outside of criminal justice—though intersectional issues that incorporate US law are studied in-depth by some social scientists with criminal justice in focus. While the goals and directions in CRT are significant and laudable, the name itself is problematic in disciplines like anthropology. The name critical race theory could be misconstrued as a body of research that legitimizes the term "race," for example. CRT has also been misconstrued as theory and research that underlies all discussions on racism—it is not that either. Research on poverty, racism, ethnicity, and gender has been part of academia in some respect for more than a century. CRT is an important but small part of the body of research on racism, one that has been focused predominantly on racism in law.

Where and when did "Woke" emerge?

The first reference to "woke" can be found in the phrase "stay woke," popularized originally by Black American folk singer-songwriter Huddie Ledbetter, a.k.a. Lead Belly. He used the phrase as part of a spoken recited explanation to his 1938 recording "Scottsboro Boys," which tells the story of nine black teenagers, young men falsely accused of raping two white women in Alabama in 1931. In the recording, Lead Belly says he met with the defendant's lawyer and the young men themselves, and "I advise everybody, be a little careful when they go along through there [Scottsboro] "best stay woke, keep their eyes open." Aja Romano writes at *Vox* that this usage reflects "Black Americans' need to be aware of racially motivated threats and the potential dangers of white America."[118]

The idea that Black Americans had to be conscious of themselves while being wary of others' intentions was first written about by African American sociologist and historian W.E.B. Du Bois. In his autoethnographic work, *The Souls of Black Folk*, published in 1903, Du Bois described how African Americans had to live with and survive in a world of virulent prejudice, "always looking at one's self through the eyes" of a white Americans and 'measuring oneself by the means of a nation that looked back in contempt." [119] For Du Bois:

> After the Egyptian and Indian, the Greek and Roman, the Teuton and Mongolian, the Negro is a sort of seventh son, born with a veil and gifted with second-sight in this American world—a world which yields him no true self-consciousness but only lets him see himself through the revelation of the other world. It is a peculiar sensation, this double consciousness, this sense of always looking at one's self through the eyes of others, of measuring one's soul by the tape of a world that looks on in amused contempt and pity. One ever feels his two-ness—an American, a Negro; two souls, two thoughts, two unreconciled strivings; two warring ideals in one dark body, whose dogged strength alone keeps it from being torn asunder.[120]

The term "woke" began to be used derisively by Right Wing pundits to suggest the term was part and parcel of a new postmodern brand of progressivism that included *cancel culture*. While an argument can be made that postmodern progressivism has been overly focused on politically correct discourse, "being woke" derives from the hyper-awareness of Black Americans to racialized violence in the US.

A concise history of women's reproductive rights in the United States

1791-92 were two foundational years in women's history. In the political maelstrom of the French Revolution, two extraordinary women stepped forward onto the public stage to "declare" a new vision for the role of women in society.

Born in southwestern France to an upper-class family, Olympe de Gouges began her short but consequential career as a playwright in Paris in the 1780s before becoming an advocate for women's rights during the French Revolution. Her plays and pamphlets spanned a wide variety of issues, including divorce and marriage, children's rights, unemployment, and social security. A passionate advocate of human rights, she was also one of France's earliest public opponents of slavery. Gouges welcomed the outbreak of the French Revolution but soon became disenchanted when equal rights were not extended to women. In 1791, in response to the *1789 Declaration of the Rights of Man and of the Citizen* written at the beginning of the French Revolution, Gouges published her *Declaration of the Rights of Woman and of the Female Citizen*, in which she challenged the practice of male authority and advocated for equal rights for women including the vote.[121]

In 1792, one year after Gouges' publication, a keen observer of the French Revolution, Mary Wollstonecraft published *Vindication of the Rights of Woman*, which advocated for women's education. Together, the manifestos of Gouges and Wollstonecraft would help inspire the first Women's Rights Convention ever held at Seneca Falls, New York, almost sixty years later in 1848, attended by early women's rights activists Elizabeth Cady Stanton and Lucretia Mott.[122] The rhetorical style of the *Declaration of the Rights of Woman and the Female Citizen* was paraphrased in the first feminist manifesto, *Declaration of Sentiments*, formulated at the conference. It demanded for the first time the women's right to vote in the US.

A steady and implacable push for women's suffrage thereafter culminated in the signing of the 19th Amendment into the US

Constitution in 1920, which succinctly states: "The right of citizens of the United States to vote shall not be denied or abridged by the United States or by any State on account of sex." Significantly, the 19th Amendment would require politicians to consider women's political opinions and views, changing the focus and range of issues politicians would have to address to be elected for office—a sea change in American politics.

While women from 1848 forward in the US slowly progressed toward the vote, reproductive rights tracked in reverse. Before 1821, in the US, abortions were generally accessible to white women and performed by midwives and doctors. In 1821, The Connecticut General Assembly passed the first US law banning medicinal abortion, and by 1860, 20 US states had criminalized abortion procedures.

In March 1873, The Comstock Act passed in the US Congress, "making it a federal crime to sell or distribute contraception through the mail or across state lines."[123] Drafted by Anthony Comstock, a devout Christian known for his crusade against prostitution, pornography, and birth control, the statute defined birth control as an obscenity.[124] The illegality of preventing and planning parenthood led pioneer social justice advocate Margaret Sanger to open the first birth control clinic on October 16, 1916, beginning a slow march for women's reproductive autonomy in the US.

Sanger's life was shaped by the poverty of her childhood and the death of her mother at age 50, which Sanger understood resulted from the physical toll of eleven pregnancies. Sanger strongly believed that the ability to control family size was crucial to ending the cycle of women's poverty.[125] By December 7, 1936, a US Circuit Court of Appeals ruled in favor of an amendment to the Comstock laws in the United States vs. One Package, making it legal for doctors to distribute contraceptives across state lines.[126] Sanger had worked behind the scenes to ensure the amendment reached the court. The ruling paved the way for new advances in contraception since physicians could then mail contraceptives to patients throughout the country. In the late 1950s, with funding from International Harvester heiress Katharine McCormick, Sanger recruited researcher Gregory Pincus to develop an oral contraceptive. The "pill" was eventually approved by the Food and Drug Administration in 1960.

In 1967, Colorado became the first state in the nation to loosen abortion restrictions, allowing the procedure if a woman's physical or mental health were at risk, in the cases of rape or incest, and if the pregnancy was likely to result in birth defects. Eleven states soon followed suit.[127] On January 22, 1973, in the landmark case *Roe v. Wade*, the US Supreme Court ruled 7-2 that a woman's right to an abortion is protected under the US Constitution's 14th Amendment. *Roe v. Wade* struck down a Texas law banning abortions, effectively making the procedure legal nationwide. Significantly, however, it did not confer unlimited rights. The decision gave women full rights to an abortion in the first trimester, states could regulate the procedure in the second trimester, and states could ban abortion in the third trimester.

Roe v. Wade was overturned on June 24, 2022, when the US Supreme Court, in a 6-3 decision, ruled in *Dobbs v. Jackson Women's Health Organization* that the right of abortion laws be left up to the states. Trigger laws already in place in many states created a patchwork of restrictions on elective abortions across the US. In states like Idaho, elective abortions are illegal at any stage, as they are throughout the Mid-Southern States from Texas east to Alabama, with the Dakotas, Missouri, West Virginia, Tennessee, and Kentucky included. In coastal states like California or Georgia, Western states like Colorado and New Mexico, upper-mid Western states like

Minnesota and Illinois, and New England states, abortion is legal to varying degrees set by the stage of the pregnancy. The patchwork of laws on abortion nationwide has wrought havoc on much of the OBGYN medical community in the US.

It is important to note that abortion rates have continuously declined from a peak in 1980 of 30 per 1,000 women of childbearing age (15–44) to 11.3 by 2018.[128] In 2018, 78 percent of abortions were performed at nine weeks or less gestation, and 92 percent of abortions were performed at 13 weeks or less gestation—within the first trimester. By 2020, medication abortions accounted for more than 50 percent of all abortions.[129] Almost 25 percent of women will have had an abortion by age 45, with 20 percent of 30-year-olds having had one.[130] Reported in *The New York Times*:

> Six in 10 women who have abortions are already mothers, and half of them have two or more children, according to 2019 data from the Centers for Disease Control and Prevention. "One of the main reasons people report wanting to have an abortion is so they can be a better parent to the kids they already have."—Professor Upadhyay from the CDC [131]

How does religion play into views on abortion?
Religious faith is still very much part of the American social fabric. Three-quarters of the US population in 2020 still identified with a specific religious faith, and in 2007, 56 percent of Americans stated that practicing religion was important to them. [132] However, the number of Americans who claim no religious affiliation, the *nones*, has been increasing over the last sixty years. In 1965, only 9 percent of Americans claimed no religious affiliation. By 2015, the nones

made up more than 25 percent of the population, with an ever-rising population concentrated among Millennials (35 percent).[133] Compared to other wealthy Western nations like Australia, Germany, and Canada, however, America is more religious as a nation, with almost twice as many people claiming that religion is very important to their lives.

Religion plays a significant role in judgments of morality and support for abortion, but parishioners of religious faiths in the US vary considerably in their views on the topic. Some parishioners even dispute notions that religiosity itself might connote a particular belief in abortion access. In a YouGov.com poll completed in May 2022, those Americans who describe themselves as "strongly Pro-choice" included 81 percent of Atheists and 66 percent of Agnostics. In the same poll, 88 percent of Jewish respondents, 76 percent of Buddhists, 55 percent of Muslims, and 47 percent of Catholics in the US also described themselves as at least "somewhat Pro-choice." By percentage, only those who self-designated in the religions of Eastern Orthodox (50 percent), Protestant (57 percent), and Mormon (69 percent) as a majority stated they are at least somewhat Pro-life.[134]

Certainly, religious affiliation may roughly connote a stance on abortion, but even with the US Protestant population, there are considerable variations in views. Sixty-eight percent of Protestant Episcopalians in the 2022 *YouGov.com* poll self-designated at least somewhat Pro-choice, with 63 percent of Protestant Pentecostals self-designating as at least "somewhat Pro-life"—a more conservative stance on abortion than all other Protestant parishioners. Religious affiliation only connotes a tendency but not an absolute denominator of abortion ideology, and there are differences in views between religious women's and men's views. Measured across all Western Christian religious affiliations in the US, more women parishioners are inclined to state they are at least somewhat Pro-choice by differences of between 12 percent and 30 percent than men in those same religions. Women across all major Christian religions are considerably more likely than men to be Pro-Choice—in contrast to the differences between men's and women's views on abortion in the general US population, which varies only by 2-3 percent.

Statistically, those religions whose majority membership believed abortion should be illegal included Seventh-day Adventists (54 percent), Southern Baptist Convention (66 percent), Mormons (70 percent), and Jehovah's Witnesses (75 percent).[135] Surprisingly, one-third of all white evangelicals, among the most conservative groups, support abortion in most cases. Religion and abortion are not necessarily aligned with one's spiritual identity. There is individual non-conformity within "agnostics" on one end of the abortion ideological spectrum to evangelical Christians on the other. This also points to a broader 2020s political phenomenon in the US: there is a rising number of political and ideological independents in the US who defy generalizable orthodoxies.

What is the national consensus on abortion?

Support for legal abortion did not change more than a few percentage points in 25 years, according to Pew Research polling. However, in just two years, from May 2021 to May 2023, support for legalized abortion surged four points, increasing to 61 percent of those who broadly supported abortion rights. Opposition to abortion rights also ticked up to 37 percent and up 2 percent from 2021. Key to this change was the decrease in the "unsures," from 8 percent down to only 2 percent nationally.[136] News coverage of the *Dobbs* decision has forced the American public to take a side, and it has galvanized Democrats more fiercely. In the same 2023 poll, for example, 41 percent of Democrats stated "they will vote only for a candidate who shares their view on abortion," and this figure jumped from 25 percent in 2021.[137]

Despite the polarization around abortion, there is a large consensus of Americans who support legalizing abortion up to 3 months (66 percent), and 82 percent of the US population supports legal abortion to save the life of the mother. Crucially, according to medical practitioners I have interviewed, in most cases, three months should be enough time for a woman to take a urine test, determine if she is pregnant, and schedule and complete an abortion—so long as resources are available locally.[138]

So much of the length of term in pregnancy and the legality of abortion hinges on the underlying perceptions of the morality of abortion—concerns that have only amplified with modern medicine and the reduced term of pregnancy for an unborn child to live. In a June 2021 Gallup poll, 46 percent of US adults indicated that abortion was morally wrong in at least most cases.[139] Those who believed abortion is morally acceptable in the US, however, hit a new high in 2021 at 47 percent. Yet 20 percent of Americans who polled in favor of legalizing abortion up to three months of term still believe abortion is morally wrong. While the laws around abortion have forced Americans onto one side or another, abortion as a practice is still fraught with substantial moral ambiguity in the minds of almost half of the US population.

As far as abortion pills are concerned, according to the same 2021 Gallup poll, "While Democrats (73 percent) are more likely than Republicans (55 percent) and Independents (57 percent) to oppose banning medication abortions," a substantial majority (64 percent) of Americans oppose limitations on these drugs.[140] Still, a difficult faultline around the topic of what constitutes life and the rights of the unborn, on the one hand, and a woman's autonomy over her reproduction are highly charged views, among the most difficult to negotiate a policy as a compromise—and views on both sides haven't altered much for at least two decades. What has changed most noticeably since *Dobbs* is an upsurge in support for the legalization of abortion under clearly defined circumstances and for abortion access to be legally granted outside state boundaries:

> Seven in ten Americans (70 percent), up from 63 percent, support laws which would allow abortion at any point during pregnancy in cases of rape or incest. More than two in three residents (68 percent), up from 63 percent, support laws which provide safe haven for people seeking an abortion out of state. Forty-four percent of Americans support abortion laws which allow abortions up to 24 weeks when there is viability outside of the womb. This is up from 34 percent in May 2022.[141]

There has also been a swing in the proportion of more conservative-centrist Americans who now support legal abortion up to 6 weeks of gestation—40 percent, up from 27 percent previously.[142] Overall, two-thirds of Americans support legalizing abortion up to the first trimester, and 82 percent of the US population supports legal abortion at any stage of pregnancy to save the life of the mother.

What is the national consensus on racism?

When a bipartisan group of Pew Research poll respondents in July 2021 were asked: "When it comes to ensuring equal rights for Americans regardless of their racial or ethnic backgrounds," 71 percent of Republican-leaning voters responded that over the last 50 years, "a lot of progress" had been made, with only 25 percent acceding that only "a little" had been done.[143] Only 29 percent of Democrat-leaning voters in the sample acknowledged that "a lot had been done" to ensure equal rights in the last fifty years, with 61 percent acceding that a little had been done. Seventy-four percent of Democrat-leaning voters and 22 percent of Republicans in the same sample acknowledged that a lot more needed to be done—though 47 percent of Republicans acknowledged "a little" had to be done at this point to ensure equal rights. On racism, it is not the lack of acknowledgment that racism still exists that divides the parties; it is the consensus on how far the nation has progressed toward the elimination of racism that differs and how much further we have to go.

What is particularly relevant to consensus on racism in the US centers around the perception of law enforcement and racism. The exposure of law enforcement to body-cam footage and citizen journalism increased the everyday visibility of police during arrests. In an April 2023 Pew Research poll, "a majority of Americans say the increased focus on issues of race and racial inequality" from June 2020 to April 2023 did not lead "to changes that have improved the lives of Black people." However, half of Americans right after the death of George Floyd predicted it would.[144] Significantly, two-thirds of Americans in the same April 2023 acknowledged that "Black people are treated less fairly than White people in dealing with the police," and according to Pew, a:

> smaller but sizable share [of Americans] say Black people are treated less fairly when applying for a loan or mortgage (50 percent), in hiring, pay, and promotions (50 percent), when seeking medical treatment (44 percent), in stores or restaurants (41 percent), and when voting in elections (37 percent).[145]

While some of the GOP political candidates waged war against "wokeness," leading up to the 2024 US Presidential Election, journalist Susan Page, sourcing from a USA TODAY/Ipsos Poll in March 2023, found the majority of Americans viewed the term "woke" as a positive attribute rather than a negative one. [146] Fifty-six percent of those surveyed in the poll stated the term for them translated to being "informed, educated on, and aware of social injustices."[147] This perception includes not only three-fourths of Democrats but also more than a third of Republicans. The term "woke," however, is one of many cultural memes that have proven perceptually divisive, essentialized by far-Right media and politicians to represent a meaning more closely defined as "overly politically correct" to police the words of others. Overall, 39 percent of poll respondents believed the word matched a far-right political definition, a view of 56 percent of Republicans.

Looking at the broader picture of race and racism in the US, a fundamental consensus does emerge. In a July 2021 Pew Research Poll that queried whether progress on racism had been achieved, 15 percent of the total surveyed, a conservative portion of the US electorate, responded that ensuring equal rights in America had already been achieved. In the same poll, 7 percent of those polled, representing views from the far-Left, believed that no progress on race had occurred over fifty years to 2021. Though views on Black Lives Matter shifted somewhat in two years from 2021 to 2023, fully 93 percent of the respondents indicated that at least some progress on racism had been achieved in 50 years, including 91 percent of Democratic-leaning respondents. Eighty-four percent of respondents, including 69 percent of Republicans, acknowledged that at least "a little" still needs to be done to fix racism in the US (see Figure 2).[148] By a large majority, Americans believe we have progressed on racism, but at least "a little" work still needs to be done. What solutions might be suggested by consensus on racism in America?

What solutions have been floated around to fix racism and abortion policy?

Racial inequality has a long history in the US. Ethnic groups have faced discrimination in the internment of Japanese American citizens during WWII, the scapegoating and denial of property rights for Chinese-Americans, the squatting and de-facto seizure of Mexican--American and Native American lands by Western settlers, and the enslavement of African-Americans—all of these truths are a part of US history. How do we begin to repair all of the intergenerational losses that have been incurred as a consequence? Could we ever come to a consensus on how? In some cases, US and state governments have passed bills to allow for reparations. Norman Mineta, a California congressman in office from 1975 to 1995, was instrumental in spearheading the Civil Liberties Act of 1988, granting $20,000 to 82 219 Japanese-American survivors of internment during WWII.[149] A Japanese American himself, Mineta's family had been forced to leave their home and business behind when they were interned. In 1946, the US Congress also created the Indian Claims Commission, a government body designed "to hear grievances and compensate tribes for lost territories," awarding about $1.3 billion to 176 tribes and bands.[150] Reparation legislation and awards have precedence in the US.

Perhaps the single most significant unresolved case for reparations remains in Tulsa, Oklahoma, where a race-based massacre occurred on May 31, 1921. It was on that day that a mob of white Tulsa residents gathered outside a county courthouse where Dick Rowland, a young Black man, was being held over allegations that he had assaulted a young white woman. Rowland was exonerated, and mob violence followed:

> The rioters, including men deputized by the civil officials, eventually descended on Greenwood, a neighborhood so self-reliant that it had become known as Black Wall Street. Within two days, it was gone, and 35 blocks burned to the ground. Neighbors were dead or missing. Buildings were reduced to rubble. The toll was staggering: up to 300 dead, at least 8,000 suddenly homeless, and nearly 1,500 homes burned or looted.[151]

As of November 2023, lawyers for the two remaining survivors of Tulsa are arguing before the Oklahoma Supreme Court after a lower court dismissed their lawsuit earlier.

Reparation for the descendants of all those enslaved in pre-Civil War America has been proposed. Though a majority (63 percent) of Americans in a Pew Research February 2019 poll indicated that slavery's legacy still affects black Americans to this day at least a "fair amount," this acknowledgment has not yet fueled overwhelming public support for reparations.[152] Though 77 percent of Black Americans believe descendants of people enslaved in the US should be repaid in some way, only 30 percent of Americans in an October 2021 Pew Research poll believed they should be directly financially compensated.[153] Democrats are divided on the issue, and Republicans, by a large margin (91 percent), are not in support of reparations.

President Obama outlined the political difficulty of reparations on his podcast with Bruce Springsteen, "Renegades: Born in the USA." stating that though he believed much of the wealth of the nation was built on the backs of enslaved people, the "prospect of actually proposing any kind of coherent, meaningful reparations program struck me as, politically, not only a non-starter but potentially counterproductive."[154] President Obama's presidency has been used to justify the case Republicans make that progress has already been made on racial justice, and it is certainly true that many Black Americans have achieved their American dreams with substantial visibility in the US public sphere.

For those who do support repayment of some kind, what is considered the most useful method for reparation is insightful. A large majority favor educational scholarships (82 percent), financial assistance for starting/improving businesses (75 percent), and financial assistance for buying/remodeling a home (73 percent), all assistance focused on improving prospects for social mobility.[155] Social justice revolves around issues of discrimination based on ethnicity and gender, but it also intersects with class-based economic inequality. Solutions based on lifting the income and prospects of all Americans have the most traction in the US, and a disproportionate share of middle to lower-income Americans are black and brown. Civil court cases continue to redress wrongs inflicted upon those marginalized groups and individuals who have suffered intergenerational violence on a case-by-case basis. But the power of consensus in righting social wrongs of the past only reaches a critical mass occasionally. Consensus in polling data suggests that a majority of Americans support economic policies that would help build social mobility for black and brown people in the US. These economic investments include:

1. **Funding universal Pre-K which was floated early in Biden's presidency.** It is still an important objective. It would give all children, regardless of background a head start on the pathway to equitable learning and the confidence required to advance into positions of

responsibility later in life. A successful pathway through public schools depends upon early entry and preparedness, leading to equal opportunity aspiration.

2. **Building affordable housing for lower to middle-income individuals and families**, especially in mixed-use urban landscapes, will allow first-time homeowners to build intergenerational wealth in real estate and to thrive in the places they have called home all of their lives.

3. **Increasing and sustaining the income range at which Americans can be subsidized through Obamacare** up to 100 percent of median US income into the middle classes. This will cut expenses for healthcare and lift Americans around the nation, many more of whom in rural areas now have family members afflicted with drug dependencies—a rising concern in the US.

4. **Reducing the cost of higher education and vocational training** will also help adults, regardless of background and raise their prospects in life.

Affirmative Action began as an Executive Order enacted by President Kennedy and ended after the basic tenets of Affirmative Action were dismissed on June 2023 in a US Supreme Court ruling. Despite the cloud Justice Clarence Thomas painted over the achievements of the program to diversify institutions, Affirmative Action did increase diversity in significant ways. For one, it opened up the upper echelons of decision-making and executive-level power to a more representative group of Americans who are now able to assert their own experiences on policy within institutions, particularly higher education. College professors are far more representative of the diversity of the students they teach than they were sixty years ago. At the very bottom of the economic scale, most ethnic groups saw small to significant gains in poverty rates while Affirmative Action was in place.

Poverty rates among Asian Americans have greatly declined from 1989, dropping from 17 percent to equal the poverty rates of white Americans at 7 percent in 2021. While Hispanic Americans have seen a decline in poverty rates from a high of 31 percent in 1995 to 16 percent in 2021, and African Americans have seen a drop from 36 percent in 1984 to 19 percent in 2021. However, household incomes of White Americans are still around 160 percent more than that of Hispanic and Black Americans. In 2019, the average household income for Asian Americans had surpassed that of White Americans and nearly doubled that of other ethnic groups in the US. While the percentages of Hispanic and Black Americans with college degrees are as high as it has been, the numbers are beginning to drop once again—especially with male graduates—and statistically, White Americans earn a higher percentage of college degrees. Homeownership percentages of White Americans are at least 150 percent more than that of Hispanics or Black Americans.[156]

Some centrist conservatives, like former Discovery Channel host Mike Rowe, have argued through his Works Foundation that higher education in America is "lending money to kids who can't pay it back to train them for jobs that no longer exist." However, higher education produces teachers, engineers, nurses, and doctors, and those jobs do indeed exist and have immediate vacancies that need to be filled. Students most affected by the cost of higher education and vocational training are first-generation college students of any ethnicity, who, more than any other group, have to weigh college costs with family needs—hard and disruptive decisions toward advancing in life. Making public colleges or vocational training more affordable would lift all Americans, particularly Black and

Brown students. Those Americans without a college education are much more likely to fall out of the middle class in the US each year. Granted, higher education, particularly public institutions, also have to reform the structural inequalities that stifle the advancement of diverse and talented faculty: strip out unnecessary administrative costs, fix escalating top administration pay increases to the cost of living, and provide their "forever temporary" adjunct faculty, who do the bulk of instructional work, a living wage and at least some pathway for advancement based on merit

Finding consensus, moving forward on abortion

Rebecca Ball was not a front-page story. Hers was a story like so many that have been unreported about the horrors that prevailed upon women when surgical abortions were carried out in silence. Gradually, stories like hers came out of the shadows. For those going through an abortion, the process is most often heartbreaking—even when women and couples are convinced the choice is the best one for themselves and their families or if the abortion is necessary to save a woman's life.

The *Dobbs* decision by the US Supreme Court has enabled conservative-majority state legislatures to outlaw or greatly curtail legal abortion access. The decision has also fundamentally altered the relationship of women to their doctors, who now have to weigh if their hypocritic oaths contradict the law in the state. This puts profound tension in the very ability to practice medicine or to under-take life-saving procedures such as ending a potentially fatal ectopic pregnancy, one among many hundreds of scenarios that require a medical procedure that aborts a fetus to save the life of the mother. With such difficult issues at hand, the majority of Americans have determined that abortion should be a decision for the woman and her family, with some limitations. With increasing maternal mortality in the US, medical costs, and declining family planning access, the *Dobbs* decision has taken a difficult process full of psychological stress and intersectional health discrimination and made it worse.

Supreme Court Chief Justice John Roberts sought to find a compromise with his conservative justices to save some of the precedent in *Roe v. Wade*. Almost 7 in 10, 69 percent of Americans polled by July 2023 believed abortion should be legal in the first trimester.[157] To solve the abortion/prenatal care crises, the US Congress will have to step in and legalize abortion nationally; it is the surest way to alleviate the problems inherent in a patchwork of abortion laws across the nation. This would at least set a baseline for health practitioners to work within the law, and states could expand or loosen further restrictions based on consensus—similar to the actual ruling in *Roe v. Wade*. The opposite view from the Right, that legislation should be passed that makes abortion illegal after three months and states could determine for themselves to set stricter laws, has the support of less than one-third of the US electorate. Rather than *restricting* all states to a 3-month term for abortion, national consensus supports abortion laws that *allow* a woman's right to choose up until the end of the first trimester and for abortion to be legal in cases of rape and incest or to save the life of the mother at any point in the pregnancy term.

Sixty-five percent of Americans polled are now also concerned that abortion bans have made it difficult for doctors to care for pregnant women with complications.[158] Having a baseline of legality following the national consensus allows women at least a minimum autonomy over their bodies. It allows doctors the ability to uphold their medical and ethical prerogatives without worrying about being jailed or sued for basic medical practices. Americans are more dissatisfied with abortion laws than at any time a poll was used to measure the issue, with new majorities among Catholic and Protestant women saying the laws are too strict.

According to the Centers for Disease Control, about 53 percent of facility-based abortions currently are medication abortions, or abortions induced by a pregnant woman using about 200 milligrams of the drug mifepristone, followed one to two days later with 800 micrograms of the drug misoprostol. The success rate of this drug combination is 96.6 percent through 10 weeks of pregnancy. Because medication abortion is a relatively new practice, 24 percent of Americans are still "unsure" about its legalization. However, in April 2023, 53 percent supported the legalization of medication--induced abortion, and support will rise with more awareness of the procedures involved.[159]

The unfortunate irony of the original *Roe v. Wade* decision is that the ruling legalized abortion for up to the first trimester across the United States, allowed states to regulate the procedure in the second trimester, and allowed states to ban abortion in the third trimester, which is remarkably close to the majoritarian view of Americans on abortion rights in the United States today. In lieu of a reversal by the US Supreme Court, it falls upon the US Congress to reach a bipartisan consensus and ensure national reproductive rights for women through national legislation.

Why does "race" still divide us?

Bruised and battered, Rodney King got through his famous encounter with L.A.P.D. on March 3, 1991. One of the things I remember about him was that while he was recovering from a leg fracture and facial contusions, he made an articulate and sincere appeal to the public to cease the violence. He was awarded $ 3.8 million in a lawsuit against the L.A.P.D.. He was later found unresponsive in his swimming pool with small amounts of drugs in his system, never quite moving on from his addictions nor fully understanding how his life, along with George Floyd and Eric Garner's, would impact national consciousness in the future. In a Pew Research poll from February 2019, two-thirds of Americans polled believed Black Americans are treated less fairly than White Americans in dealing with police and by the criminal justice system.[160]

But views on racial discrimination since 2019 have grown more divided. In an April 2023 Pew Research poll, 53 percent of those queried stated that "not seeing racial discrimination where it *does* exist" is the bigger problem (down from 57 percent in 2019), but 45 percent of those polled believed "seeing racial discrimination where it really *doesn't* exist" as an even larger issue. This percentage is up from 42 percent in 2019.[161] Many Americans, particularly Republicans, believe it has become too common to call out all things and others "racist." Generalizations of others, if taken and held as characteristic of a whole group, are overly simplistic discriminatory framings regardless of one's political identity.

We must admit our shortcomings and human beings are innately ethnocentric. To varying degrees, we think of ourselves as rational and others as "crazy"—which seems to sum up the attraction for reality television in America. Locating our prejudices is about listening to one another, tracing back to where the logic of our prejudices derives, and bridging those gulfs in our understanding. In a world of cultural ignorance and unconscious biases, it is worth remembering it takes effort to undo our initial framings of others and to humanize our opposition. As a cultural anthropologist, I learned long ago that I had to acknowledge, even take joy, that my first impressions of others would be woefully shortsighted and that my unconscious prejudice of others was seldom reality.

The increasing politicization of racial inequality is also symptomatic of the overall decline in economic equality by the majority of Americans over forty years. For a very long time, blue-collar, working-class Americans were frustrated with an inability to enact societal change and victimized by the system; their frustrations were redirected by political opportunists toward scapegoating others as the cause for their economic insecurity. The internalized dejection of the underclasses adds fuel to the fire of prejudices. Historically, in the US, it has proven much easier for politicians to gain traction in working-class neighborhoods, with citizens already frustrated by long working hours and little pay, to blame one or some ethnic groups rather than solving endemic societal issues that may require hard work, intense negotiation, and compromise. We need to keep vigilant of this recurrent political strategy and call it out for what it is: scapegoating is a purposeful and strategic prejudice that distracts from unresolved and underlying societal issues like economic inequality.

Though "staying woke" comes from the concept of double consciousness, in a politicized public sphere, slogans of advocacy come to represent division. On its face value, "anti-racism" is a rational concept, but the term has the unfortunate context of being doubly negative and implicitly accusative to many. There are more inclusive concepts for teaching children the richness of diversity. One of the more unfortunate consequences of the current climate of polarization is that non-partisan organizations created to stand up against bigotry when ethnic violence was an everyday occurrence (like the NAACP) or to stand up for the independence of women when they had very little determination over their bodies (like Planned Parenthood) are now represented as highly partisan. Academics, politicians, and advocates who have worked their entire lives to end racism or support women's rights now find their life's work in support of vulnerable populations immersed in a polarized battleground.

Conservatives in the US are correct in assuming individuals in America are now more often considered for the "quality of their character," as Martin Luther King stated, as they were more generally by the color of their skin in previous generations. Americans, by and large, also acknowledge that the US continues to struggle with racism embodied in white supremacy and anarcho-terrorism, which perpetuate forms of caustic discrimination against one group or another. We are still coming to terms with systemic racism in America, particularly in the legal system, as the Innocence Project has proven with the number of black and brown men found determined to be innocent by DNA who were convicted of serious crimes by misidentification or over-zealous prosecution. In health, Black maternal mortality rates in the US remain disproportionately high. Most Americans realize forms of discrimination and prejudice still abide with us. We need to change the tone with one another to embrace our differences—and there are many.

Is it time to quit the word "race?" In 1998, the American Anthropology Association issued a short statement indicating that it had "become clear that human populations are not unambiguous, clearly demarcated, biologically distinct groups," and given the overwhelming genetic and archaeological evidence, the concept of "race" had no merit. The AAA pointed out that far more genetic variation in human beings is associated with culture groups (94 percent) than between culture groups (about 6 percent), which would have marked out so-called "racial" differences.[162] Black Americans, for example, have far more variation genetically within the group of Black

Americans than they have between other "race" groups. For many Americans who undertake genetic ancestry, the results are more often than not surprisingly diverse. The average African-American genome in the US, for example, is one-quarter European-derived. Latinos in the US carry an average of nearly one-fifth Native American ancestry and 6 percent African ancestry, and one out of eight White Americans in states like South Carolina and Louisiana have at least some African ancestry.[163]

Along with race terminology in our country, we are also still stuck with dualistic framings to define our differences—exemplified by the categories of difference I must use for this book. While there may be a "Black" culture broadly speaking in the US, one that derives from American and African roots, both Black and White identities have been artificially poised in opposition that need not exist. Social scientists acknowledge ethnicity, community, country, personal experience, and disposition are the primary factors in determining what makes each human particular and unique. It is ironic that "diversity" itself has become a politicized concept. We should all be able to celebrate our cultural roots and legacies, our ancestral families, and the historical roots of our identity. While "race" is exclusionary, inaccurate, and meaningless, "ethnicity" invokes a power of self-knowledge, a consciousness of the challenges that brought our ancestors to the US. Making the world post-racial means celebrating the diversity within everyone rather than stifling it.

So much of our race problem in America is attributable to income inequality and status in the US, an intersectional problem that involves gendered inequities as well. The deep structural problems inflicting Black and Brown people are predominantly intersectional. While Americans broadly see racism improving over the last 70 years, Black and Brown people continue to lag in social mobility measures like average household income, college education, and home ownership. Arguably, the biggest interectional problems that now confront the "races" in the US are attributable to forms of economic inequality, which disproportionately affects Black and Brown people in the US.

Figures: Chapter 2— Social Justice, Balancing Two Issues

One-in-three adults say both that human life begins at conception and that the decision to have an abortion belongs solely to the woman

% who say each statement describes their views ...

"Human life begins at conception, so a fetus is a person with rights."

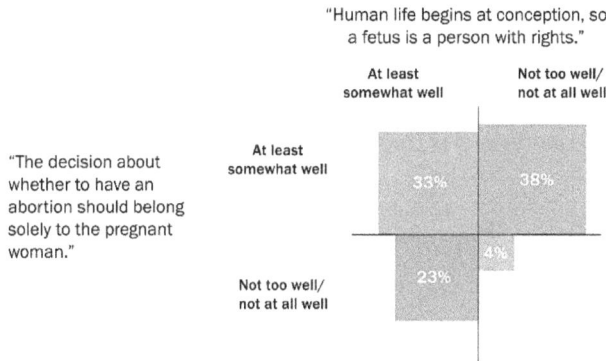

Note: Those who answered neither question are not shown.
Source: Survey of U.S. adults conducted March 7-13, 2022.
"America's Abortion Quandary"

PEW RESEARCH CENTER

Figure 1 - One-third of Americans polled believed life begins at conception, yet support the women's ability to choose

Republicans more likely than Democrats to see a lot of progress on race in the last 50 years; Democrats more likely to say a lot more needs to be done

When it comes to ensuring equal rights for all Americans regardless of their racial or ethnic backgrounds, % who say ...

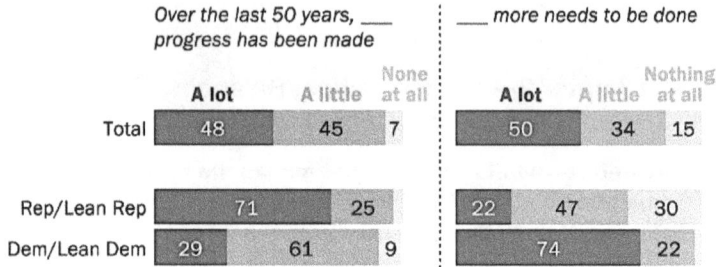

	Over the last 50 years, ___ progress has been made			___ more needs to be done		
	A lot	A little	None at all	**A lot**	A little	Nothing at all
Total	48	45	7	50	34	15
Rep/Lean Rep	71	25		22	47	30
Dem/Lean Dem	29	61	9	74	22	

Note: No answer responses not shown.
Source: Survey of U.S. adults conducted July 8-18, 2021.

PEW RESEARCH CENTER

Figure 2 - Party perceptions of progress on racism and more to be done.

Chapter 3
A Green and Prosperous Country

Bridging the two definitions for cultivating land

In the 2020 documentary film *Kiss the Ground*, Ray Archuleta, a conservation agronomist based in Kansas, delivers a simple and clear message: "Don't till the soil!"[164] He goes on to say he has been to every state in the US trying to convince US farmers that the key to successful harvests begins with the conservation of rich and organically alive soil. Archuleta worked for over thirty years in the National Resources Conservation Service, an organization created within the US Department of Agriculture to battle the problem of soil erosion that led to the Dust Bowl centered in Western Oklahoma in the late 1930s. A farmer himself, watching Ray Archuleta at work you may begin to forget that he is preaching soil conservation ecology to farmers in deeply red states, using his own experience working in big government as an asset rather than as a point of division. He is blunt and transparent with his information, pointing out seemingly impossible win-win scenarios for farmers to thrive economically while preserving land sustainably.

Thirty percent of all Iowa farmers now employ regenerative agricultural practices which have several components but start with no-till or minimum-tillage farming. Tilling land and churning the ground to make space for crops is an agricultural practice that goes back millennia, but it ruins soil over time. Tillage pulverizes soil, increasing greenhouse gases noticeably, destroying living fungal communities that process raw living matter into nutrients, and depleting water absorption sponginess in the soil, which leads to severe runoff during strong rains common in the Midwest.[165] In no-tillage farming, soil fertility is increased by leaving cover crops in place (like grass or beans that embed nitrogen), using crop rotation, and composting the soil with range animal manure—all of which preserves the soil in place and reduces the need and cost of insecticides and chemical fertilizers.[166] Because far fewer nitrogen and phosphorus compounds from fertilizer chemicals enter downstream rivers and produce dead zones by starving waterways of oxygen, waterways also benefit from no-tillage farming, keeping habitats healthy for fish and wildlife.

The farmers and educators from the organization Ray helped found, the Soil Health Academy, represent a diverse ranching and agricultural community from the heart of the US with a mission to bring the benefits of modern agronomic science home to his fellow farmers.[167] The Soil Health Academy also represents one of many grassroots organizations helping to bridge understanding between those who produce the food and resources the US depends upon, and the majority of Americans who now believe human beings are responsible for global warming and action is needed to alter unsustainable consumption practices.

In 2014, the Yale Program on Climate Communication con-ducted a national study that asked several questions, including "Do you believe human activities mostly cause global warming?" At the time, majorities in only 18 of the 50 US states believed this was true. By 2020, when the same study asked the same question, majorities in 46 of the 50 states of the union believed this was true. In six years, a significant threshold had been crossed in the United States. For the first time, a representative majority in US states believed human actions were primarily responsible for climate change. During those six years, 2014-2020, major forest fires scorched California, record flooding swamped the US Southeast, and across the states, all-time high temperatures in winters and summers were recorded. Recog-nition of climate change in the US has become more pervasive as weather extremes become more frequent and arrive at the front door of many Americans. Of those who say their community experienced extreme weather in the US, 89 percent, on average, believed climate change was a factor at least "a little" in the floods, seashore erosion, wildfires, or droughts that affected them.[168]

In Benton Harbor and Flint, Michigan, in 2021, lead-tainted water drew national attention to America's aging freshwater sys-tem.[169] Water quality and water pollution in the United States are the greatest environmental concerns of a majority of Americans.[170] Tangible in scope, environmental issues like ensuring clean drinking have broad-based prioritization in the US population. Other envi-ronmental issues are more politicized and represent a more divisive arena that frames environmentalists against resource extraction industries or farming/ranching communities. The US is highly dependent on fossil fuel energy and modern ranching practices, two big contributors to global warming. With such high stakes for the future of American society and ecology, do we have consensus in

America on policies that balance concerns over the national economy, energy production, resource extraction, and ecological conservation?

How do we perceive global climate change and going green in the US?

In a January 2024 Pew Research poll, 45 percent of Americans viewed "protecting the environment" as a top priority of the president and Congress to address in 2024. Another 36 percent of Americans in the same poll believed "dealing with climate change," and 46 percent believed "improving the energy system" should also be top priorities. Understandably, fuel and energy production costs became more critical with rising gasoline prices in the last few years, as more and more Americans struggled with the added costs of living with inflation.[171] And 68 percent of Americans, a substantial majority in a June 2023 Pew Research Poll, believed the US should not go all in on green energy yet but rather continue to use a mix of renewable energy sources, including oil, coal, and gas, along with renewable sources.[172]

Views on the urgency of combating climate change have also grown more partisan over the last ten years. Two-thirds of Democrats in a January 2023 Pew Research poll felt protecting the environment was a "top priority," along with dealing with climate change (59 percent). Still, only 20 percent of Republicans felt protecting the environment, and 13 percent believed dealing with global climate change was a top priority for Washington.[173] Republicans still also have mixed views on the causes of climate change. In an April 2021 Pew Research poll, 40 percent of Republicans believed human activity contributed "not too much" or "at all" to climate change, with 59 percent believed it contributed "some" or "a great deal."[174] However, in a 2018 CBS News Poll, 85 percent of Democrats along with

60 percent of Independents believed climate change was primarily human-caused.[175]

Significantly, the perception of global climate change, its causes, and the consensus of climate scientists are only now becoming clear to a great many Americans. According to a Yale-George Mason study, in 2018 only 1 in 5 Americans realized there is overwhelming scientific agreement that climate is caused by human activity—but this overall perception is destined to change over time.[176] By 2021, a survey of more than 88,000 research articles concluded: "high statistical confidence that the scientific consensus on human-caused contemporary climate change—expressed as a proportion of the total publications—exceeds 99 percent in the peer-reviewed scientific literature."[177] The scientific consensus that climate change is caused by human activity is overwhelming. However, perceptual differences in the urgency of solving environmental issues remain highly partisan and significantly generational as well.

For many Gen-Z and Millennial generation Americans, environmental issues are perceived as a top national concern expressed through activism, engagement on the problem, social media posting, and polling. Younger generation Americans are also more willing to adjust to green technologies and winnow out fossil fuel consumption altogether.[178] According to Pew Research, a third of Gen Zers and 28 percent of Millennials say they've done something in the past year to address climate change, such as donating money, volunteering, contacting an elected official, or attending a rally or protest.[179] Two-thirds of Gen Zers and 61 percent of Millennials said "they've talked with friends or family about the need for action on climate change in the past few weeks."[180] For 70 percent of Americans, global change is one of several important concerns for the nation, but for more than a third of younger Americans, global climate change is a top concern (see Figure 1).

Where do our understandings of the natural world derive?

The basis of politics and consensus on environmental issues in the United States derive from deep philosophical currents in humanity's relationship with the natural world. The Western view of this relationship derives from the melding of two orienting cosmologies: one rendered in the Old Testament, which placed human beings as a separate creation distinctly apart from the rest of the natural world. The other derives from ancient Greek philosophy—most notably from the Greek philosopher Aristotle (384–322 BCE). In the Western biblical account of the creation of the world in the Old Testament, flora was created by God on the 3rd day, fauna on the 5th day, and humans on the 6th day in God's image to "rule over the fish in the sea and the birds in the sky, over the livestock and all the wild animals, and over all the creatures that move along the ground."[181] The perception of human beings as different, created apart from the rest of the living world in Western civilization, became set in place with the spread of Judaism, Islam, and Christianity.

One of the surviving works of ancient Greek philosopher Aristotle, *History of Animals*, pioneered the work of zoology and was held up as the gold standard in the taxonomy of nature for nearly two thousand years.[182] Aristotle recognized humans as a living being of the natural world, he understood there were inherent connections of humans to other social animals like bees (at least in function), for example. For Aristotle, a human being's ability to reason and communicate also sets them apart from other beings of the world, the hallmarks of humankind. The biblical view of creation and Aristotle's views on the natural world become reconciled in the West by the Medieval school of philosophy known as Scholasticism to form *The Great Chain of Being.*[183] In this hierarchal story of cosmological origin, the chain of being places God at the top above angels, followed by human beings—understood to be both spirit and matter and the only creature possessing a soul as a consequence. Animals are placed below human beings in the chain, with the dominant animal, the lion, on top. Further down the chain, plants then minerals—from life to matter.

For more than a thousand years in the West, man was a creature of the earth in form—and sometimes in function—but also a living being created in the image of God. The Great Chain of Being, translated into feudal Medieval Europe, ranked human beings from those closest to God, the Monarchs, to those of the lowest stations, the peasants—who were closer to the beasts of the animal kingdom. The natural world was viewed as an extension of one of the many resources that God put into the hands of human beings. However, the rank-ordering of human beings above the animal kingdom was an ontological orientation that came late in human societal evolution. As Western city-states emerged more than five thousand years ago, animal and plant domestication, together with emergent justifications for inherited monarchial rule in urban settlements, ruptured the cosmological connection of humans to the natural world. The philosophy of the natural world that developed in the West helped to rationalize the impulse to exploit animals and plants with little regard for loss or extinction. This created tensions between early European colonists and the tribal nations of the New World they settled.

Professor Virginia Anderson points out key differences in natural philosophies between white American colonists and Native Americans in her book *Creatures of Empire: How Domestic Animals*

Transformed Early America (2002). Anderson points out that early colonists who held to the Great Chain of Being believed animals— and the natural world in general—"were property over which they had a biblically ordained right to assert dominion; they were an economic resource to be manipulated and exploited."[184] Central to the English settlement of America was the civilizing process of both inhabitants and untamed wilderness, replicating patterns that existed in the rural Old World for centuries. Anderson argues that "classifying animals not just in terms of their utility but also their market value added a new dimension to the relationship of dominion. Putting a price on animals symbolized the conversion of creatures into commodities."[185] For Anderson, the Native Americans that early colonists encountered, on the other hand:

> viewed themselves as part of, rather than distinct from, the natural world. In Indian languages, for instance, there was no word to distinguish "animals" in general from humans, simply words to identify separate species. Native Americans' relationship with animals was largely reciprocal, reflecting the belief that many creatures possessed their spiritual power.[186]

The cleavage between the natural philosophies of New World colonists and American Indian tribes revolved around the preeminence of human beings over all living beings, the anthropocentrism of Western views, and a distance in perspective that would grow with the industrialization of ranching and farming in the United States.

Industrialization – the beginning of greenhouse Earth and the shrinking of wild America

Industrialization in the Western world began around the year 1774 CE with the invention of the steam engine. Scottish inventor James Watt created the first powerful commercial steam engine, which began to be used on passenger ferries and train locomotives and to power drilling, mining, milling, and refining equipment. Farm equipment began to be steam-powered beginning in the 1890s, motorized tractors and threshers enabled one farmer to increase harvest yields considerably. Increased agricultural output would, for the first time in human history, easily surpass the growing needs of a populous nation. The over-supply of grain caused wholesale prices to drop, forcing many small farmers into debt and bankruptcy. This eventually shifted American agriculture away from small-scale agronomy that once defined the nation to large industrial-scale agriculture in the mid-1900s that could weather the cycles of commodity pricing easier. Blessed with abundant raw materials, including crude oil, coal, and iron, by 1890, the United States rose quickly to be one of the three great industrial giants, alongside the United Kingdom and Germany.

With the opening of the West, in one century, from 1800 – 1900, much of the abundant fauna of North America that had survived the Ice Age were either hunted or trapped to extinction or corralled into wildlife corridors in the Western United States. By 1900, the American buffalo, which numbered in the tens of millions in 1800, had been reduced to a few hundred animals. The American passenger pigeon, with numbers estimated to be in the billions around 1800, migrating North/South through the waterways of the upper Midwest, had been trapped for food into extinction. Across North

America, the megafauna that once inhabited America from coast to coast—beavers, mountain lions, wolves, and grizzly bears—became secluded to small populations in less-inhabited refuges; in the seas around the world, giant sea mammals like the North Atlantic right whale were hunted to be the brink of extinction for whale oil used for lighting lamps before the use of kerosene or electricity.

Industrial output in America began to change the air we breathe. In 1850, the global yearly output of greenhouse gases was about 4 billion metric tonnes (4.4 billion tons) a year, the year that sulfur dioxide emissions reached their peak in London, which had worse air than today's developing mega-cities from the pervasive burning of goal for trains, heating, and industry. Tonnage increased gradually to 13.5 billion metric tonnes by 1945. By 2021, with increased energy demand produced from coal-fired electricity production, annual greenhouse gas emissions grew to 54.6 billion metric tonnes annually, a four-fold increase from the end of WWII.[187]

Diminishing returns, man-made resource losses

From 1934 onward, the overall effects of one hundred years of industrialism, use of industrial chemicals, over-fishing, unsustainable farming practices, population growth, and westward expansion began to produce environmental problems that simply could not be ignored. The American Dust Bowl came in three time periods: 1934, 1936, and 1939-1940. Severe drought, but also intensive farming in seasonally dry conditions, helped to create the dust storms that blanketed the US prairie states centered around Oklahoma's panhandle. In response, the Civilian Conservation Corps planted a huge belt of more than 200 million trees from Canada to Abilene, Texas, to break the wind and hold the soil in place. Roosevelt's governmental soil agronomists also began to educate farmers on conservation and anti-erosion techniques, such as crop rotation, contour plowing, and terracing techniques that helped keep the topsoil from being blown away.[188]

Industrial fishing around the world has depleted and, in many cases, ended whole fishing industries. In the late 1800s, an entire fishing fleet lay at anchor at the mouth of California's Sacramento River, feeding San Francisco's population with fresh wild-caught salmon. Today, only a trickle of wild salmon hatchlings make the journey to the sea from one of two rivers along California's North Coast. In 1992, Northern Cod populations fell to just 1 percent of historic levels, due in large part to decades of overfishing, depriving more than 30,000 fishermen of their livelihood in Newfoundland.

Add to this the leaching of petroleum wastewater and nitrogen--heavy fertilizer runoff from farming and ranching in the United States and you have a storm of environmental factors that have decimated native fish stocks in North America. Tilling and the use of chemical fertilizers and insecticides continue to leave farm soils vulnerable to severe runoff and overall topsoil erosion. Some agronomists predict that soil in the US Midwest and California Central Valley will turn to sand, clay, or be too salinated to use by 2050. Improper forest management in the US West—and East Coast and Canada—taken together with higher sustained temperatures and drier seasons, has meant forest fires cover more acreage, burn more intensely, and do more damage to manmade structures and infrastructure.

Organic chemistry, plastics, and the synthetic revolution

By the 1950s, a century of investigation and experimentation in organic chemistry had created a safer world for human beings, with cures for syphilis, diphtheria, and pain with the first synthesized aspirin developed by the German company Bayer, and new and powerful petroleum distillates like gasoline and diesel fuels that would power transportation. Organic chemistry would also produce a substance synonymous with modernity, plastic, and new and powerful insect-killing compounds like DDT that would free human beings from the scourges of malaria by killing its disease-carrying vector, the Anopheles mosquito.

The first plastic made from the chemical nitrocellulose was synthesized by the English inventor Alexander Parkes (1813-1890). Other inventors like American John Wesley Hyatt (1837-1920) innovated viable ways of producing solid, stable nitrocellulose, which he patented in 1869 as "celluloid." Plastic is an organic polymer, or artificially created molecules anchored by carbon atoms that repeat in long chain-like segments, creating synthetic materials that are incredibly durable. Though it burns readily, plastic simply doesn't break down very easily in nature. Hyatt's new polymer filled a materials niche that replaced dwindling supplies of elephant ivory used for piano keys, billiard balls, and false teeth.[189] Produced into a liquid emulsion called collodion, celluloid would be made famous as the first widely available film and photographic stock.

In the 1950s, plastic polymers of yet many different configurations began to replace glass used in bottles, manufactured into synthetic fabrics like polyester and rayon. They are used famously in food storage containers such as Tupperware. In the 1970s, plastics also began to be heavily used in the manufacture of automobiles, musical recordings (records, 1930s), kitchenware, and one-use food packaging of all stripes. In 1950, 2 million metric tons of plastic were produced globally. By 1970, the amount of plastic produced globally jumped to 35 million tons annually. And since 1980, the amount of plastic has nearly doubled every year, from 70 million tons to 459.75 million tons of plastic produced worldwide in 2019.

[190] Roughly 12 billion metric tonnes of plastic are expected to pack landfills or natural environments (sea, land, coasts, rivers) by 2050.[191] The amount is staggeringly high. Already, river banks around SE Asia are caked with plastic debris, and oceanic island beaches are studded with microplastics and plastic containers, suffocating, entrapping, and filling the digestive tracks of marine mammals, albatross, and sea turtles. Plastic is now ubiquitously embedded in the fabric of our clothes, making our inexpensive garments both more disposable and non-biodegradable, adding to a mounting plastic pollution problem.

DDT, or the large chemical named Dichlorodiphenyltrichloroethane, came into widespread use during the later part of WWII when it was dropped on jungle habitats that US soldiers were entering to control mosquito and lice populations infesting and killing hundreds of soldiers a day with malaria and typhoid. Colorless, tasteless, and almost odorless, DDT was one of a host of synthesized crystalline chemical compounds produced in 1874 by the Austrian chemist Othmar Zeidler. Its insecticidal effectiveness was later discovered by the Swiss chemist Paul Hermann Müller in 1939, who was awarded the Nobel Prize in Physiology or Medicine in 1948 "for his discovery of the high efficiency of DDT as a contact poison against several arthropods." As the Nobel description summarized, however, DDT killed more than disease-carrying insects.[192]

Before her groundbreaking and incendiary critique of chemical pesticide use in *Silent Spring* (1962), Rachel Carson (1907–1964) was best known for her trilogy of books that detailed marine life with poetic descriptions that managed to combine scientific accuracy with a humanistic approachable narrative style for the masses. Her books on the sea and marine life were award-winning best-sellers in the 1950s. However, the book magazine *Reader's Digest* turned down an essay of Carson's that cautioned against the widespread use of chemical pesticides like DDT in 1945, so she shelved writing on such a dark and potentially controversial subject and concentrated her writing on finishing a three-book trilogy, a lyrical journey of the evolution of the ocean. In 1958, however, Carson's attention was drawn once again back to chemical pesticides when she received a letter from a friend, Olga Owens Huckins, who described the death of birds around her property in Duxbury, Massachusetts, after DDT was sprayed on her property.

Carson was not eager to take on the chemical industry, but she knew an important story needed to be told for public interest. She was not against the "wise use" of pesticides per se; she was against the widespread use of chemicals that were being applied liberally in nature without knowing any of the long-term consequences of the chemicals on the ecosystem.[193] She coalesced biological and medical research from hundreds of sources to argue that synthetic chemicals were being added indiscriminately to skin lotions, insecticides, paint, wallpaper, and food systems, and in many cases, those chemicals were being found to be poisonous to livestock and wildlife. She also interrogated the unquestioned potential unintended consequences of technological marvels of modern science and the dominance of human beings in altering the evolution of the earth and its life systems—a process of slow change and punctuated equilibriums in a journey on the order of billions of years. More broadly, Carson helped to enact a postmodern paradigm shift in US society that questioned the effect of modern human progress in science and technological development on the natural world.

Nature conservation and the environmental movement

Ecological awareness in the United States emerged long before Carson, with mystical naturalists like John Muir and environmental policy innovators like Aldo Leopold, who fundamentally shaped the ethos and science of wildlife management that followed. Both came to reject Western anthropocentrism, and they provided the philosophical themes that would form the basis for the environmental movements to follow.

American environmentalism derives its earliest roots from the end of the Enlightenment in Europe and a reaction to the dawn of industrialism in Europe and America. In 1836, the American philosopher Ralph Waldo Emerson (1803–1882) published his book-length essay titled *Nature,* where he laid out the foundations for what would later be called *transcendentalism*, a philosophical/ spiritual/literary view that the divine in God and salvation could be found in nature and everyday presence, in the goodness of life rather than in a distant heaven. Emerson was inspired to write his essay after a visit to the Muséum National d'Histoire Naturelle in Paris, where he could see the connectedness in the processes of life on earth firsthand. In *Nature*, Emerson asked and solved an abstract problem: Why do humans not fully accept nature's beauty? He concluded that people are distracted by the demands of the material world. Society, he believed, is retrospective, dependent on what history has gone before, and has lost connection with its original relationship to the mystical presence in the universe as a whole. For Emerson:

> Nature, in its ministry to man, is not only the material but is also the process and the result wind sows the seed; the sun evaporates the sea; the wind blows the vapor to the field; the ice, on the other side of the planet, condenses rain on this; the rain feeds the plant; the plant feeds the animal; and thus the endless circulations of the divine charity nourish man.[194]

The "Father of the National Parks," Scottish-born naturalist John Muir (1838-1914), came to his ideas about ecological and geologic processes after a trip to Yosemite Valley, where he was hired to build a sawmill for James Mason Hutchings—one of the early promoters and land developers of Yosemite Valley, and responsible for the attention Yosemite received as a place of wonder before the American Civil War. Yosemite also carries with it the profound stain in the history of the valley when, in December 1850, the new state of California funded a state militia to drive the Ahwahneechee American Indian tribe—steward of the land for hundreds of generations—from the park into reservations after skirmishes with settlers and miners.

Muir built a modest dwelling for himself and a fellow worker, part of which was over Yosemite Creek. For Muir, the landscape of Yosemite was overwhelming. He was driven to a sense of spiritual ecstasy, "scrambling down cliff faces to get a closer look at the waterfalls, whooping and howling at the vistas, jumping tirelessly from flower to flower."[195] He kept Emerson's *Nature* to read by his side, influenced by the philosopher's ideas of finding one's spirit in the solitude of nature. Emerson and Muir would meet in Yosemite, and he was "delighted to find at the end of his career the prophet-- naturalist he had called for so long ago... And for Muir, Emerson's visit came like a laying on of hands."[196]

Yosemite Valley was accidentally placed front and center in the creation of the US National Park System. Concerned by the impact of commercial interests, California Senator John Conness, a first-generation Irish-American, advocated to protect Yosemite Valley in a bill proposed in Washington D.C. During the bloody end of the American Civil War, he was able to help pass a bill and get it signed by then President Abraham Lincoln on 30 June 30, 1864. It granted

Yosemite Valley to the state of California as a free and open space for public use and enjoyment, predicated on the idea that idyllic, beautiful scenery should be spared commercial exploitation.[197] At the time it wasn't noted as a landmark decision, but it was the first time the anywhere land and the flora/fauna within it would be conserved as it was, and largely as it had been for future generations. Conness' idea of setting aside "unused land" in its virginal state also set a precedent for the 1872 creation of the first national park at Yellowstone in Northwestern Wyoming Territory.

After the founding of the Sierra Club by John Muir in 1892, a budding eco-tourism industry followed and blossomed during Teddy Roosevelt's presidency, who put forward an ambitious agenda of creating national parks. Attitudes in America about the natural world began to change, and the word "conservation" began to enter into the national dialogue. The US National Park system brought nature to the masses, a renewed connection with the wilderness that had been lost with a sweep of civilization that marched into the West. The industrial era propelled modern society into the machine age and burgeoning energy dependence, setting up a line of contestation between those who gathered energy resources and those who believed in conserving wild resources and habitats.

It has been estimated that half of the deforestation worldwide occurred in just one century, from 1900 - 2000.[198] The height of the deforestation of the temperate forests, found mainly in the northern latitudes of the world and Australia, occurred around the mid-century 1900s. Since then, reforestation in the Global North has outpaced deforestation. From the 1980s on, however, the world's tropical rainforests have been deforested at an alarming rate, losing more forests worldwide than an area half the size of India, according to Our World in Data.[199] Under the presidency of Jair Bolsonaro in Brazil, parkland reserves in Amazonia were overrun at pace by loggers and ranchers vying for new land to increase the supply of beef sold on the international market. Forests in Tanzania, Myanmar, the Philippines, and Indonesia have also been decimated in the last 20 years due to unstable governance, and in Indonesia's case, by the cultivation of oil palm trees, which are native to Africa. There has been an increasing global demand for inexpensive cooking used mainly in the Global South.

As the US entered into the century of science in the 20th Century, a new public discussion emerged that questioned the place of humankind within nature. At what point does using fossil fuels and the waste produced by convenient materials outweigh the costs of environmental deterioration and unsustainability? When will human beings begin to run out of the natural resources we have always been dependent upon? Will the motivation for preserving the natural world come down to decisions based on proactive ethical responsibilities or competitive survival mechanisms for dwindling resources?

Where is the consensus in the United States on environmental issues?

Most polls on environmental issues in the United States focus on questions of global climate change, and according to a March 2021 Gallup poll, 65 percent of Americans are at least concerned a "fair amount" about the effects of global climate change through the amplitude of concern is partisan:

> Majorities of Democrats, ranging from 51% to 69%, say they are worried a great deal about all six of the environmental threats, while no more than 40% of Republicans say the same. The party

groups diverge the most in their concern about global warming, with 68% of Democrats and 14% of Republicans highly concerned.[200]

Climate change is an abstract quantity to measure compared to other more direct health-related environmental concerns like clean drinking water or overall pollution in watersheds, rivers, lakes, and reservoirs.[201] Over eighty percent of Americans registered at least a "fair amount" of concern, and a smaller majority of Americans have a "great deal of concern" for polluted water. Certainly, heightened storm damage along America's coasts, record floods and heat, and severe drought conditions that have lowered watersheds and impacted the supply of fresh water are being recognized more broadly as results of global warming. However, the specific tangible effects of climate change are reaching the consciousness of a majority of Americans more slowly, as polling data indicate, as is the level of urgency for legislative action that once propelled clean water and anti-pollution initiatives.

Americans are also more concerned about the loss of tropical rainforests and the extinction of plant and animal species worldwide. At least 70 percent of Americans registered "a fair amount" concern for these environmental concerns, with an increasing share of the populace, 45 percent in 2022, greatly concerned with plant and animal extinction around the world. Air pollution also continues to concern Americans, with 73 percent of United States citizens registered "at least a fair amount of concern," even with decades of improvement in air quality in the US with gas emission laws that winnowed out lead and other toxic substances from the air.[202]

Prioritization polling numbers on air pollution may rise in the wake of a new report that has been written up. In April 2024, the American Lung Association published its "State of the Air Report," which found that "despite decades of progress cleaning up air pollution, 39 percent of people living in America—131.2 million people—still live in places with failing grades for unhealthy levels of ozone or particle pollution."[203] Many of the cities on the list of the most air polluted are situated in California, where wildfire pollutants have made air quality in summer months heavy with smoke particles, and the Los Angeles basin continues to have the most days of unhealthy ozone levels. However, US levels of air pollution, overall, have been decreasing since 2001.

There is a considerable amount of consensus in the United States registered on four actionable paths moving forward on national environmental policy:

1. When asked in a Pew Research poll taken in January 2022, nearly seven in ten Americans believed we should prioritize the development of alternative energy, such as wind and solar, over the expansion of oil, coal, and natural gas production.[204]
2. The same majority of Americans favored the US taking steps to become carbon neutral by 2050.
3. Almost three-quarters of Americans believed the US should participate overall in international efforts to help reduce the effects of climate change.[205]
4. Two-thirds of Americans polled also believed we should keep a mix of fossil fuel and renewable energy sources as we transition toward green energy.[206]

Where the resistance lies in the transition to renewable energy is in the perceived cost to consumers, which tempers attitudes about the speed of energy transition. In June 2023, Pew Research found that if the US greatly reduced energy production from fossil fuel sources and increased production from renewable sources, 59 percent of Americans polled believed air and water quality in their local area would be improved. However, 44 percent believed it would make the prices paid for everyday goods more expensive, and 42 percent believed it would increase the price of home heat and cooling as well. Republicans are considerably more skeptical about the costs of the renewable energy transition (see Figure 2).[207] Forty percent of Americans feel it would make it harder for the US to produce most of its energy inside of the country, versus 43 percent who say it would make it easier—we are perceptually divided on the outcome of the energy transition to energy independence.[208]

Americans, by and large, are concerned with the additional costs that green energy may bring to the cost of living, even as they see potential benefits in air and water quality, increased job opportunities in new green energy sectors, and decreasing frequency of extreme weather events when global warming is brought under control.[209] Though the importance of environmental issues is among the top policy concerns for Democrats, 42 percent of Republicans believe it is one of several important concerns, and other issues take higher precedence in the nation currently.

Even as the debate around global climate change in the US and prioritization and policy is debated and laundered through political debates, citizens of other countries have more consensus on climate change as an urgent issue. "In general, a smaller share of US adults are concerned about the personal impacts of climate change than are people in other advanced economies," Pew Research concluded after a Spring 2021 survey. A median of 72 percent of the citizens of 17 advanced economic countries expressed at least some concern that climate change will affect them personally, versus 60 percent in the US, in a Pew Research poll taken in September 2021.[210] More citizens in the United States also believe the Paris Climate Accord and other international policies "will harm their own country"— 33 percent in the US versus 24 percent in populations of the nineteen countries.[211] One of Pew Research's key findings is that the US is the most divided politically on environmental issues among the nineteen wealthiest nations in the world.[212]

Most Americans aged 18-29 are deeply concerned with global climate change and ecological degradation. They are impatient to see more policy progress on issues that help ensure a long, healthy, and fruitful future ahead of them. Younger adults are more enthusiastic about alternative energy in wind and solar, and the use of electric cars. Nearly half of those polled aged 18-29 state they are "very/ somewhat" likely to purchase an electric vehicle versus 38 percent of the general US populace.[213] Gen Z and Millennial adults are also engaging with climate change content on social media more than older generations, and seven in ten younger adults (18-29) record they feel anxious after reading news on climate change. In light of global environmental projections for 2050, their concerns are under-standable and rational.[214]

Where can we move forward on environmental and energy legislation?

Resistance to moving decisively on environmental legislation stems from a few conceptual challenges. How and where to take definitive action on environmental problems that are multi-scalar, complex, and seemingly daunting? Can we go green in a way that doesn't increase the costs of living for Americans, with the necessary electric charging infrastructure in place to keep Americans working? It is important to try to concisely review the environmental challenges confronting the United States to better clarify where and what solutions may avail themselves:

Excessive fossil fuel emissions in transportation and from coal-fired electrical plants are creating global climate changes that include sea level rise, melting ice caps and habitat loss for Arctic fauna, ocean acidification, and will include worldwide climate refugeeism in the future, and internal migration from low-lying areas in the United States.

1. **Modern and unsustainable consumption patterns** are increasing plastic pollution, food waste, and air pollution. Agriculture dependent on tillage and chemicals, and unsustainable groundwater extraction for energy production, agriculture, and housing, will soon increase food/water insecurity and increase costs for food and fresh water.

2. **Biodiversity and wild food resource losses** are being created through deforestation, the spread of invasive species, and habitat pollution. Overfishing has decimated once abundant wild fish numbers, and soil degradation in the US Midwest and Central California will lead to reduced productivity and desertification in the farm belts. Soil runoff has led to reduced fish and shrimp numbers downstream.

3. **Meta-environmental factors** continue to hamper environmental remediation like poor governance and consensus building, and missed communication opportunities across stakeholder communities (between farmers, ecologists, and fishermen, for example). An

increasing human population, particularly in the Global South, puts stress on all natural and food resource systems and remains a difficult global challenge to ecological sustainability.

Excessive fossil fuel emissions

Breaking down greenhouse emissions in the United States, the transportation sector accounts for 28 percent of total emissions, followed by electric power generation from coal and natural gas (25 percent), industry (23 percent), commercial and residential (13 percent), with agriculture and ranching following at 10 percent.[215]

The transition to going green is underway in the transportation sector; greenhouse emissions are being lowered worldwide with electrically powered cars, trucks, and trains. The US semi-truck manufacturer Freightliner is already selling an all-electric semi, model name *eCascadia*. It can pull up to 82,000 lbs. of freight.[216] Efficient and more powerful electric-diesel train locomotives are replacing older diesel locomotives in the United States and Europe. In 2022, Union Pacific began buying all-electric locomotives to begin rail testing for their fleet. Electric air travel has been the hardest transportation niche to transform to green, but small electric commercial planes are already being produced.[217] In October of 2022, the startup company Eviation began to put their sleek battery-powered aircraft that can carry nine passengers through flight trials. It is proving itself quiet and worthy, reliable transport for short hauls of about 250 miles.

Scaling up wind and solar energy production in the US will reduce greenhouse gases in the energy production sector and help supply the added demands of electricity that green transportation and industry will require. By 2022, the US had over 70,000 wind turbines in service, producing 435 terawatt-hours of electricity, about doubling in output every two years since 2000. Solar power is growing in the US as well, likewise rising exponentially in output every year in the United States since 2011.[218] Two-hundred four terawatt-hours of electricity from renewables were produced in 2021, bringing the share of the share of electricity from solar, wind, biomass, and geothermal sources up to 11.3 percent of the total electrical production in the United States.[219] Other countries have made a fuller transition toward renewable energy, including most of the South American countries that have invested in large hydroelectric plants.

According to the U.N.-affiliated International Renewable Energy Agency, which supports countries worldwide in their transition to a sustainable energy future, by 2021, eight countries received 100 percent of the electrical production from renewables, including Costa Rica, Paraguay, Nepal, Iceland, and Ethiopia.[220] Our neighbor to the North, Canada, has 67.5 percent of its energy deriving from renewable sources, and our competitive countries like China are at 28.6 percent and expanding their renewable energy sector at a fast pace. Almost all of the European Union has scaled up the percentage of energy deriving from renewables, surpassing the percentage output of the US, with Norway at 99.1 percent in 2021, followed by Andorra (93.3 percent), Luxembourg (89 percent), and Demark (79 percent). Though the United States produced fully 11 percent of the total global renewable electricity by 2021—a huge output—our demand for electricity is also voracious in the most productive (by GDP) country in the world.[221]

With more than four times the potential wind energy in the fifty states to supply all of the electrical demands of America and parts of the Western US bathed in near year-round sunshine, the potential for renewable energy production in the United States is enormous. General Electric is working on a giant off-shore wind turbine set to be even larger than the working mammoth turbines already in use. It will stand at over 800 feet in height and will be powered by 345-foot blades. The new turbine could potentially max out at 18 megawatts per hour in production. If one of these produces electricity at about 60 percent efficiency for a year, it could power a small town of 12,000 residents.[222] Build about 30,000 or more of these turbines, and we could power all of the homes in America.

Going green in the United States will cut down the overall water use in the United States, especially relevant to communities that require massive amounts of power in drying ecologies. According to the EPA, the total water use in the United States is far and away dominated by thermoelectric electrical production (mostly coal-fired), about 39 percent, and agriculture/ranching, which uses 41 percent of the total water in the US. Increasing the percentage of regenerative farming in the US will decrease the agricultural demand for water—allowing cover crops to work as a sponge holding water and soil in place, providing cleaner runoff for healthy fish habitats. Though thermoelectric production does recycle about half the water used, with global climate change, some regions of the United States are predicted to have less precipitation. Replacing electrical systems that boil immense amounts of water to operate with solar and wind energy production will cut water use substantially.

The United States is very fortunate to have the raw ingredients, sun, and wind to power clean energy. We also now have a large source of lithium for batteries found in the geothermal brines near the Salton Sea in California. The United States currently holds about 4 percent of the world's supply of lithium but is mining only half that.[223] Demand for lithium is expected to increase six-fold between 2020 and 2030, and the US Department of Energy in July

2023 announced $10.9 million for ten projects across nine states to "advance innovative technologies to extract and convert battery-grade lithium from geothermal brine sources in the United States."[224] The "lithium rush" has already begun in Australia and Chile, two countries with 22.3 percent and 43.7 percent of the world's reserves of lithium, respectively.

The good news for consumers and producers in the United States is that corporations, non-profits, individuals, and scientists are already at work trying to address ways to sequester more carbon to reduce greenhouse emissions and lower the costs of green alternatives. The Nature Conservancy, for example, is dedicated to planting one billion world trees around the world, a noble aspiration with enormous popular support—ninety percent of Americans favor planting more trees to absorb carbon emissions. Research has also shown that urban regions where green spaces are planned and emplaced (some even on rooftops) bring down the urban heat islands considerably and, in so doing, lower the costs and electrical grid demand for cooling overall. Though global deforestation has been occurring since humankind began clearing forests for agricultural and ranching use 10,000 years ago, seventy-four percent of global deforestation has occurred in just 300 years.[225] Since the 1980s, temperate forests in the global North have increased in acreage, while accelerated deforestation in the global South over the last forty years has substantially decreased overall forest coverage around the world.

Biodiversity and food resource losses

Production and consumption of beef, soybeans, and palm oil account for 60 percent of the products causing tropical forest deforestation. With most soybeans grown as food for livestock, consumer demand for less expensive beef and fried foods now accounts for about half of tropical deforestation.[226] Deforestation of tropical forests for raising beef impacts tropical forests doubly hard by decimating habitats within the ecosystem and by reducing forests to grasslands—which are only viable for feeding cattle for one or two seasons before the soil is depleted. It is one of the most unsustainable resource practices in the modern world. Returning land to its natural state is the best way to ensure the sustainability of our ecosystems, but using land everywhere that is already designated for ranching doesn't have to be destructive and unsustainable in practice. There are ways to limit greenhouse emissions, preserve some ranchland habitat for wild animals, and feed human beings from the meat produced.

In the Southern Mexican state of Chiapas, some ranchers whose lands lie along the tropical lowland savannah belts have turned to holistic ranching techniques like rotational cattle grazing—moving cattle around to limit grazing time on a given acre, preserving tree shoots and forest recovery. They also halt the use of seasonal burning. This departure from tradition does not affect the yield of meat or milk produced. Still, significant soil health is conserved through these tropical latitude ranching techniques, and natural forest corridors are kept open for wild species to move through.

Now, in the US, regenerative agricultural and ranching practices are getting a foothold with more than 30 percent of Iowa farmers who have already moved to such practices. Regenerative farming focuses on topsoil conservation and relies on several sustainable land-use techniques that include not tilling the soil—which destroys the natural biome of worms, fungi, and nutrient-producing living matter. Cover crops like wheat stalks and weeds are mowed by machines or trimmed instead by grazing farm animals that fertilize the land naturally. The land is then seeded with crops like soybeans that restore nitrogen to the soil. The benefits of regenerative farming are that it preserves moisture in the soil by limiting the "baking" effect of bare land, prevents topsoil runoff by creating a spongy top layer of soil to absorb torrential rainfall, and preserves the organic processes that healthy soils depend upon—evidenced by healthier crops requiring less insecticide and fertilizer and improved soil test results.

Regenerative farming also improves biodiversity by promoting richer and more diverse plant, bird, and insect populations by planting a diversity of crops and trees and introducing small-scale ranching, mimicking, to some extent, the sustainability already built into the natural landscapes. Since close to 80 percent of the fresh water in the US is ultimately used for agriculture and ranching (via evaporation, absorption, animal consumption, and processing), regenerative farming is more sustainable in a world of climate change where more violent floods will follow longer droughts. Preserving ground moisture will be significantly more important to sustainable agriculture in the coming years.

Modern unsustainable consumption patterns

Consuming sustainably in the US means transforming our recycling habits in the US and enacting policies that hold the plastics industry more accountable for an ever-escalating problem of un-recyclable products and containers. Recycling grew steadily in America over forty years but has now plateaued. As of 2018, about 67 percent of paper and paperboard was being recycled, 28 percent of glass, 50.4 percent of aluminum cans (all aluminum at 34.9 percent), and 99 percent of lead-acid batteries.[227] The US consumer with recycling disposal agencies has slowly increased the percentage of what is recycled or composted in the US from 10.1 percent in 1985 to 32.1 percent in 2018. Our waste being landfilled has decreased in America from 94 percent generated in 1960 to 50 percent in 2018. Still, much of this is due to waste being combusted for energy—beneficial to energy production and landfill overuse but not so beneficial to greenhouse gas production.

Still, far too much fully recyclable material is ending up in landfills, where it takes vastly more energy to produce finished products from scratch. Even after forty years of effort, the US is not nearly as efficient as countries like Germany, which recycles around 99 percent of its aluminum cans. Filling landfills with aluminum and not recycling is especially wasteful because it takes only 5 percent of the energy to reproduce aluminum into new products than it does to produce new products from raw ore. Every single restaurant, shopping center, and waste disposal company should provide clear and identifiable pathways for recycling metals and glass, those "forever recyclable" materials.

Plastics are, unfortunately a whole other problem. According to the Environmental Protection Agency, only 9 percent of plastic in the US is recycled. Even with widescale recycling efforts and burning for energy production, the amount of plastic reaching landfills went up 404 percent from 1980 figures to 27 million tons a year in the US (2018).[228] The problems with recycling plastic, it turns out, are many. The PBS news program *FRONTLINE*, titled "Plastic Wars," sets the stage during the late 1980s when the plastics industry came under fire for producing so much undegradable material:

> Facing heightened public concern about ever-increasing amounts of garbage, the image of plastics was falling dramatically. State and local officials across the country were considering banning some kinds of plastics in an effort to reduce waste and pollution. But the industry had a plan, a way to fend off plastic bans and keep its sales growing. It would publicly promote recycling as the

solution to the waste crisis — despite internal industry doubts, from almost the beginning, that widespread plastic recycling could ever be economically viable.[229]

It was not. In the last forty years in the US, less than 10 percent of all plastic made has been recycled. When the plastics industry came under fire in the 1980s, the Society of the Plastics Industry (SPI) introduced the Resin Identification Code (RIC) system, which divided plastic resins into seven different categories. Grouping plastics into seven resin groups would help recyclers to sort plastics efficiently. Plastic containers and items that are recyclable are now embossed with one of these code numbers on the bottom, a number encircled by a triangle of chasing arrows. The purpose was to "provide a consistent national system to facilitate recycling of post-consumer plastics."[230] As recounted on *FRONTLINE*, the plastics industry promoted recycling heavily anyway, counting on a simple strategy: "If the public thinks the recycling is working, then they're not going to be as concerned about the environment," stated Larry Thomas, who formerly headed the SPI.[231] Since then, after undergoing some minor variations, the RIC has been recognized as the worldwide standard plastic classification, a system, unfortunately, that only masks an immense plastic waste problem driven by unrecyclable plastic resin products.

About 79 percent of all plastics produced are one of six+ commodity plastics. In reality, only two plastics are ever consistently recycled in volume: #1 Polyethylene terephthalate (PET or PETE) used in soda bottles and widely recycled, and #2 High-density polyethylene (HDPE or PE-HD), used in milk jugs, the easiest plastic resin to recycle. #3 Polyvinyl chloride (or PVC) is used predominantly in the construction industry, #4 LDPE (Low-density polyethylene) is used for plastic bags, and #6 Polystyrene is generally recycled in the United States only in very limited capacities. #5 Polypropylene used in Tupperware containers, yogurt containers, and hangers is recycled but also not at a large scale. #7 designated "all other plastics" used in everyday consumer products are generally not recycled at all. That leaves #3 PVC, #4 LDPE, #6 Polystryene, and #7 "all other plastics" as products currently engineered to dispose or to burn—a more toxic air-polluting remedy at this point.

The recycling of plastics has proven problematic in several other ways. For example, plastic degrades through the recycling process so that only one or, at best, two generations of recycling are possible. Also, dyes or colors and other added chemicals in the plastic make sorting and recycling not cost-effective, and one of the primary reasons countries like China and Turkey have stopped accepting our plastic waste to sort and recycle for themselves: it simply isn't cost-effective. So, we are at an impasse with plastic and recyclables. We can keep filling up landfills with plastic and fill our oceans with more plastic than fish (which is projected to happen in 2050). Or we can support policies that curb the production of plastic resins that are not recyclable.

Scientists are at work trying to produce biodegradable plastics, and some of this is now being made from corn-based plastic into eating utensils and bags. These products could be scaled up and prices lowered. But Americans have simply become over-reliant on the miracle product of plastics with its endless permutations, colors, and resins. To limit plastic waste we can scale down plastic packaging diversity: make plastic containers more uniform and prioritize using recyclable resins #1 and #2. If the food industry and shippers could limit commodity plastic containers to simply black or opaque (and make the cardboard wrapping packaging materials the place for marketing), this simple step would make recycling easier and more cost-effective—streamlining the cycle of plastic utility from production to reuse. Ultimately plastics have to be developed that have much shorter degradable life-spans. This work has begun, let's demand its progress. Majorities in both parties favor industry doing more to stem environmental problems they have helped to initiate.

A majority of Americans, 58 percent (including 53 percent of Republicans), support mandatory recycling. Still, if we offered more "carrots" than "sticks," we would have more success bringing the percentage of recycled material up. It has been estimated that of people in the US with incomes below $40k, less than half are even offered curbside recycling.[232] Lower-income retail areas and shops are also less likely to offer recycling bins: we need to make recycling cost-effective and universally available. Providing a small rebate, however small on the amount recycled in one's trash, may be a way of helping to level the field and incentivize the lower-income green system.

Organizations across the US, like The Recycling Partnership, are working on solutions to the plastic crisis, but it only takes one highly motivated individual to make a difference.[233] Boyan Slat, a young man who founded an NGO called The Ocean Cleanup, is currently experimenting with a barge-like system that strains plastic from rivers.[234] Slat is directly working from research indicating that 1,000 of the world's most polluted rivers are responsible for roughly 80 percent of the world's plastic pollution. As of early 2024, his plastic garbage "Interceptors" have been deployed in Asian Countries—responsible for 81 percent of the plastic emitted into the ocean—Indonesia, Malaysia, Vietnam, Thailand, and in high emitter countries like the Dominican Republic. His company was also preparing to deploy in Los Angeles, California.[235]

Discussion - Creating a green and economically prosperous world

For years, beginning with the Nixon Administration, a mantra in the US has been energy independence. Once gained, energy independence would allow Americans to not be beholden to foreign petroleum cartels like OPEC, the Middle-East-based organization that sets wholesale prices for oil, manipulating the free market for their own national interests. But the US has quietly reached that goal. With fracking, the US now produces as much petroleum as it needs. And yet, we have continued to see gasoline prices fluctuate erratically, which has been explained as an absence of petroleum refining technology that can process the light, sweet crude that comes from fracking. Overseas oil remains cheaper—even with shipping costs—than domestically produced crude.

Saving our ecosystem as it is and conserving resources is both a liberal and a conservative cause. On the one hand, environmentalism is ideologically centered around more than a century of liberalism. Eco-advocates from John Muir to the young American Indian activists Keyen Singer Green and Nizhoni Toledi, members of the Confederated Tribes of Umatilla Indian Reservation, have worked diligently to reconnect the natural world with the human world in the great circle of life. Creating a sustainable environment and ecosystem while incentivizing a new, more sustainable industry has also been a conservative ideology. While the US has good reserves of natural gas that we are taking advantage of, we are not *conserving* our resources, which will run out given time. Having fossil fuels in place while transitioning to an American-based renewable energy system is conservative because this process *conserves* our resources. Not doing so isn't conservative, it is reckless.

Most Americans now believe our abrupt climate change is due

to human activity, but the environmental needle has moved even further toward conservation in the last few years. Nearly 7 in 10 Americans believe climate change is occurring, and 74 percent of Americans support efforts to address climate change internationally. With declining purchasing power in the United States, it is also understandable that many Americans fear environmental initiatives will not pay for themselves, that there will be a cost in jobs, and that energy prices will be more expensive. Inflation has reduced all but the wealthiest Americans' purchasing power in the last few years, and families can hardly conceive of spending more money on expensive electric cars. The US majority as a whole only slightly favors mandatory legal measures that prohibit or restrict emissions or make recycling mandatory.

However, providing incentives or rewards for sustainable consumption like money for recycling, cash rebates for buying electric cars, or subsidizing solar or wind farms are popular and easy policy options for politicians representing contested districts. Nationally, a consensus on environmental progress is being manifested in myriad ways by thousands of environmental non-profits, renewable energy producers, and even large corporations like General Mills, who are beginning to see the rewards of buying produce from regenerative farming. Green technology is already in place and need only be scaled up to meet the eco-challenges of today.

Choosing between the low energy prices and the greening of the planet is a false choice on at least two fronts. The Infrastructure Investment and Jobs Act (IIJA), enacted by a bipartisan coalition of the 117th United States Congress in November 2021, provides funding for hardening and updating the energy grid. Still, practical electrical transportation cannot go mainstream in the US until electric vehicle charging stations are in place. Prices for electric cars and trucks, along with the cost of residential electricity, all come down. The electorate is in favor of green energy technology if there are price incentives involved, like rebates on solar installation or grants for community energy production projects. Small and large-scale solar and wind investments and projects in the United States can put more energy on the grid, so long as the grid infrastructure is in place to handle smart energy flows. It is already happening; the American electorate can make sure it rolls out smoothly and promptly.

In the 1950s, the Eisenhauer Administration used national tax dollars to build an interstate highway system that brought the products of small and large companies to bigger pools of consumers, an example of government working to promote commerce for many millions of producers. The electrical grid, more than one hundred years old, is falling apart, creating wildfires, unable to handle the demands of a world heating up. The time is overdue to rebuild the system from the ground up, to encourage new commerce, and to update an electrical grid put in place over 100 years ago that we will become increasingly dependent upon.

Energy and economic policies of the last forty years have stifled free enterprise, and consumers in America are so beholden to oil companies and production that they, like the banking industry, have become too big to fail. Worldwide, big oil received $500 billion in subsidies in 2020, and this escalated to a record $1.3 trillion in 2022 as the government tried to mitigate the impact of the Russian oil embargo.[236] Energy production is being used as a strategic geo-political tool. Vladimir Putin has already weaponized the world's energy supply, but he and other dictators and human rights abusers have been doing so for years. Consumers around the world are now and will become increasingly beholden to dictators around the world who believe they can leverage gas and oil prices for the violence and power consolidations they undertake. Why not use the abundant power of the sun and wind in America and put ourselves in a position to leverage peace and democracy on the rest of the world?

Predictions of a human environmental resource catastrophe have been part of Western discourse for over two hundred years. In 1798, an English economist named Thomas Robert Malthus (1766 –1834) wrote An Essay on the Principle of Population, in which he theorized that an increase in a nation's food production improved the well-being of the population. However, improvements in wealth and status were only temporary because more production led to still more population growth and added dependency on a limited system, and this would perpetuate poverty. In Malthus' thinking, population growth would only outpace agricultural production, causing famine or wars for resources, resulting in poverty and necessary Draconian measures that would force world societies to depopulate. His ideas flew in the face of popular views in 18th-century Europe that saw the quality of life in societies as improving and even perfectible. His idea became known as the "Malthusian trap."

His theory has been resurrected in books like *The Population Bomb* (1968) by professors emeritus Paul R. Ehrlich and Anne Howland Ehrlich. Increased efficiencies in agriculture and ranching in the 20th Century eased some of the more dire prognostications of Malthus. Still, increased food production has come at a cost to the environment and soil health that is unsustainable. We are at a tipping point where we can choose to transition toward sustainably using the land and sea, slowing *The Sixth Extinction* (2014) event as environmental journalist Elizabeth Kolbert has described:

Over the last half a billion years, there have been five mass extinctions when the diversity of life on Earth suddenly and dramatically contracted. Scientists around the world are currently monitoring the sixth extinction, predicted to be the most devastating extinction event since the asteroid impact that wiped out the dinosaurs. This time around, the cataclysm is us.[237]

From 1979 to 2015, China implemented a One-Child Policy restricting families to one child in the hopes of stemming the looming overpopulation crises in China. The policy did slow population growth overall, but now China and other countries like Japan, Italy, and the US are facing another crisis: an aging population bubble of boomers requiring medical and earned entitlement support, with deposits into the system made by a smaller proportion of working-age Americans. Countries with the greatest population growth around the world are centered now in the Global South, Sub-Saharan Africa, and South America. Population growth in the Global North is slowing overall. Reaching a human population tipping point on earth, in which there are simply not enough resources to feed everyone, is still a looming concern, with the world population projected to be nearly 10 billion by 2050. However, the key to keeping population growth in check resides with empowering and educating all the women in the world—among the United Nations Millennium Goals. Where women and men are provided the means for reproductive self-determination, infant mortality, and unwanted pregnancies are lowered as well.

In January 2015, 26 of the 38 members of the International Anthropocene Working Group published a paper suggesting that the first atomic bomb blast at the Trinity test site on 16 July 1945 was the starting point of a whole new geologic epoch.[238] Significant about this date is that it marks a moment when humankind harnessed the power of the universe on earth, demarcating humankind's final dominance over the elemental forces in nature. This new era of *late industrialism* can also be a time for renewal and change, for environmental/economic transformation pointing "toward the possibility of another world taking shape…as people retrofit broken systems, build flexible coalitions and work creatively with time."[239] Research of the last fifty years has opened up innumerable vistas on the interconnectedness of the environment with human sustenance. Worldwide, consensus has grown for taking action on environmental sustainability.

More than one-third of Gen Z adults say climate change is a top concern

% of U.S. adults who say addressing global climate change is _____ to them personally

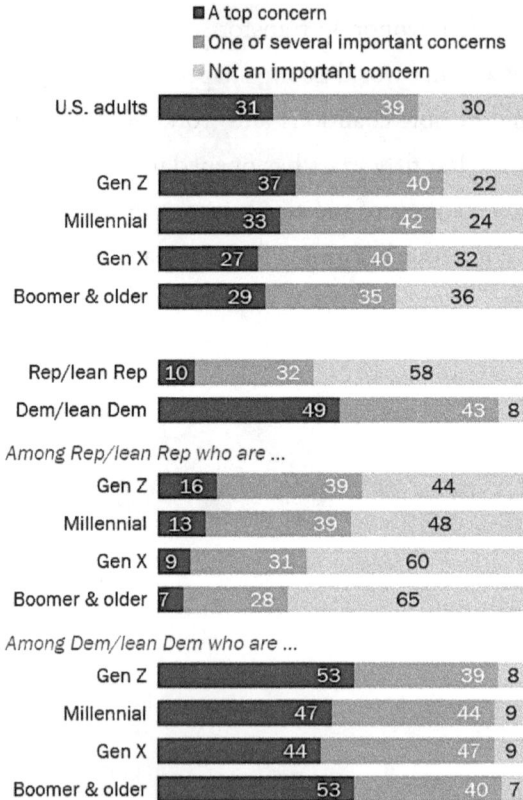

- ■ A top concern
- ▨ One of several important concerns
- ▢ Not an important concern

	A top concern	One of several important concerns	Not an important concern
U.S. adults	31	39	30
Gen Z	37	40	22
Millennial	33	42	24
Gen X	27	40	32
Boomer & older	29	35	36
Rep/lean Rep	10	32	58
Dem/lean Dem	49	43	8

Among Rep/lean Rep who are ...

	A top concern	One of several important concerns	Not an important concern
Gen Z	16	39	44
Millennial	13	39	48
Gen X	9	31	60
Boomer & older	7	28	65

Among Dem/lean Dem who are ...

	A top concern	One of several important concerns	Not an important concern
Gen Z	53	39	8
Millennial	47	44	9
Gen X	44	47	9
Boomer & older	53	40	7

Note: Respondents who gave other responses or did not give an answer are not shown.
Source: Survey conducted April 20-29, 2021.
"Gen Z, Millennials Stand Out for Climate Change Activism, Social Media Engagement With Issue"

PEW RESEARCH CENTER

Figure 1 - Climate change more of an important concern for younger Americans

Americans think an energy transition would have a more negative than positive impact on consumer prices

If the U.S. greatly reduces energy production from fossil fuel sources and increases production from renewable sources, % of U.S. adults who say it would ___ each of the following in their local area

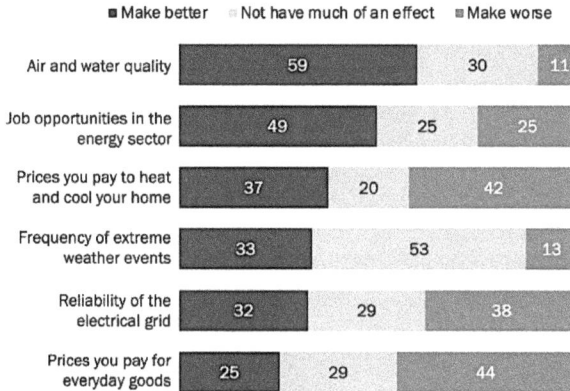

Legend: ■ Make better   ▫ Not have much of an effect   ▪ Make worse

	Make better	Not have much of an effect	Make worse
Air and water quality	59	30	11
Job opportunities in the energy sector	49	25	25
Prices you pay to heat and cool your home	37	20	42
Frequency of extreme weather events	33	53	13
Reliability of the electrical grid	32	29	38
Prices you pay for everyday goods	25	29	44

Note: Respondents who did not give an answer are not shown.
Source: Survey of U.S. adults conducted May 30-June 4, 2023.
"Majorities of Americans Prioritize Renewable Energy, Back Steps to Address Climate Change"

PEW RESEARCH CENTER

Figure 2 - The perceived negative costs of the energy transition

Chapter 4
Criminality, Guns, Immigration, and "The Other"

What can we learn from our ancestry?

A remarkable insight is provided in Chapter 10 of the book *Never Forget Our People Were Always Free: A Parable of American Healing*. In this chapter, author and former head of the National Association for the Advancement of Colored People (NAACP) President Ben Jealous invites readers to look "Beyond Black and White." He recounts his days growing up as a biracial individual on the Monterey Peninsula, California, in the late 1970s and early 1980s, acutely aware of the racial divides surrounding him. Jealous recounts a story of a "white guy" who showed up at the intake desk of a black non-profit mental health clinic called the Village Project in Monterey County, committed to putting a person's "culture at the center of therapy."[240] The experience of getting therapy was challenging for new clients who were asked about their background, including race, ethnicity, and religion. New clients may have had their pastors and their families invited into sessions. While the Village Project was dedicated to helping Black citizens in the region, it was ultimately committed to serving anyone in need. The White man was taken aback by the intake process and the questions asked:

> 'I'm White. I'm just White," The man stated when asked about his race, recalled Jealous. "I need some help. Can I get some help?" He didn't want to talk about his race. He didn't want to talk about his ethnicity. He didn't want to talk about his culture. He just wanted somebody to listen to his problems.

Mel Mason, a seasoned therapist, took up the man's case and noticed him using a non-English term when he became frustrated, a term he had learned from his father and grandfather. Mason looked up the word and discovered it was an expletive used in Od Irish Gaelic, and addressed the man in need:

> That saying is Old Irish, which means that the men in your family, your father, your grandfather, ultimately hail from Ireland. You're Irish. And for the rest of the weeks we're in therapy together, your assignment is to figure out what it means to be Irish and what that means to you.

As Jealous recalled, this sent the "man's head spinning. His entire life, he had simply been White. White, White, White, Wonder Bread White." Though the United States is a melting pot or a salad bowl nation, depending on how one sees it, whiteness and blackness have subsumed ethnic identifiers in America since the categorization of different biological races became assumed in the late 1700s. Most significantly, however, the labels of white and black disconnect us from the far-away cultures from which America was built, from the cultural mosaic of our origin. As Jealous points out, not knowing our ancestry ultimately disconnects us from ourselves, "us" from our ancestral "them."

Nowhere in the US are two historical personages more inextricably linked to the gulf between the American majority, the "us," versus the minority of "them" in America than in the personage of the criminal and the immigrant. When someone is accused of a crime, our legal language references "the people" versus "you." Seeing those words on a charging document is normally the first moment someone accused of a crime realizes they're being isolated from the great sea of humanity. And our laws clearly define those who we are—American citizens—and those who are not: the undocumented immigrants. We reserve our harshest sanctions and separateness in the US society for violent criminal behavior, especially for murderers and gun violence perpetrators who have saturated our public spaces and our public sphere of news and information.

Together, rising incidents of mass shootings, broadening media coverage of violent crime, and surging numbers of immigration encounters at the US-Mexico border have raised security concerns overall in America, especially among Republican voters. In a June 2023 Pew Research poll, gun violence and violent crime registered as the fifth and sixth most urgent problems in the United States. However, the level of concern on each issue was registered differently by party affiliation. Eighty-one percent of Democrats polled believed gun violence was a very big problem, versus 38 percent of Republicans, almost two-thirds of whom nonetheless believed violent crime in the US was a very big problem. About half of Democrats polled also believed violent crime in America was still a very big problem in America. In early 2024, immigration concerns surged among Republicans, with 76 percent of those poll believing immigration should be a top priority for Congress and the president in 2024, with Democrats' concern remaining relatively level from 2021 through to early 2024—despite increased mainstream news coverage—with 39 percent of those polled believing immigration was a top priority concern for the coming year.

More than any other issues in the United States, national concerns and public perception of gun violence, violent crime, and immigration are dictated to a great extent by newsworthy events that garner media attention, the persistence of media coverage, and the magnitude of the problems as they are portrayed. This chapter briefly examines the nature of human violence, the causes of gun violence, and the trajectory of gun laws in the United States to see how current US consensus intersects with policies and provisions to lower violent crime and gun violence. Similarly, this chapter examines the history of immigration policies and attitudes in America, untangling some of the myths associated with immigration to try to provide some answers for why immigrants come to the US and when the problem of illegal immigration began. For many Americans, the challenges their ancestors faced coming to and settling in America are buried in long-forgotten stories, in the painful uprooting process that many of our great-grandparents endured.

As Ben Jealous and other writers like Alex Haley have notably queried in their books, underlying these problems are deeper questions in the collective psyche of Americans: Who belongs in our society? How do we separate those who we believe have abrogated their rights as a citizen, and how do we reintegrate them? In considering violence, gun violence, and illegal immigration, should we interrogate deeper questions about what pushes people to ignore the restraints of law and order to be more informed about what solutions might arise with the consensus that we have on these hot-button issues?

How do Americans view immigration, gun rights, and criminality?

Immigration Perceptions

Like our views on violence in America, the perception of illegal immigration is partisan. In a Pew Research Center poll taken in June of 2023, after border encounters had slowed, only 25 percent of Democrat-leaners polled stated illegal immigration was a "very big" problem, versus 70 percent of Republican-leaners.[241] This 45 percent perception gap in the seriousness of the problem has been one of the largest gaps in perception between our two political parties. But Gallup polling in January 2024 suggested a turn in the overall perception of immigration in the nation with rising immigration encounters at the US Southern border, and as the issue became front and center before Congress in February 2024. According to Gallup:

> The percentage [of Americans] who are dissatisfied out of a desire for less immigration has risen sharply over the past two years, increasing from 19 percent in 2021 to 35 percent in 2022 and 40 percent today. This is still not as high as it was in the first few years after the 9/11 terrorist attacks when it ranged from 44 percent to 52 percent, but is the highest since 2016.[242]

Polls taken before and after the inauguration of the Biden Administration speak to politicized perceptions of border policies. In August 2019, when immigrant encounters had already begun to increase along the border, 58 percent of Republicans polled believed the US government was doing at least a somewhat good job of dealing with the increased number of people seeking asylum at the border, with only 15 percent of Democrats perceiving so. By April 2021, these figures flipped with a Democratic president in office; only 13 percent of Republicans believed the US government was doing at least a "somewhat good job," with 42 percent of Democrats believing so.

Some of this difference can be accounted for by partisanship, blaming the US president of the opposite party for immigration failures. However, polling numbers from 2021 mostly reflected a new awareness that overall encounters at the US-Mexico border had increased, and the infrastructure to handle the masses of people claiming asylum was being strained. Testimonies of border city mayors and border state governors and legislatures began to address the scale of the numbers more visibly by February 2023. Some of the factors that began to strain the system included the lack of infrastructure and personnel to process asylum seekers and safety issues in allowing undocumented people on the streets. Part of the problem at the US/Mexico border is a humanitarian crisis of immigrants who have been stripped of their savings by a more organized immigration "broker" in the new *Coyote*. Immigrants leave family behind and out of touch, and frequently, they are victims of violence (especially women) during their travels North.

Gun ownership and violent crime perceptions

Perceptions that violent crime is rising are among the top reasons why people buy a gun or would consider buying their first gun—the need for self-protection. Seventy-two percent of gun owners cite protection as a "major reason" they own a gun, with hunting (32 percent) and sport shooting (30 percent) also cited as good reasons to own a gun (see Figure 1). Significantly, 81 percent of gun owners state they feel safer owning a gun, and just 12 percent worry about the safety issues with having a gun in the home.[243] Concerns over personal safety are now the leading pull for owning a gun among first-time buyers, but it wasn't always so. When similar polls were taken in 1999—and violent crime was more prevalent nationally—an *ABC News/Washington Post* poll cited hunting as the top reason given for owning a gun by half the respondents, and only 26 percent cited "protection." Fully 47 percent of non-gunners, which equates to about 50 million Americans, "could see [themselves] owning a gun in the future."[244]

Increasing concern over public safety is not just a factor of 24/7 news broadcasts that report violent incidents in the US or an aging and more fragile American population who believe the world is generally more unsafe. In a study first published in 1993, sociologists Joseph F. Sheley and James D. Wright found that the primary reasons cited by juvenile offenders for owning a gun were also for self-protection.[245] The sheer ubiquity of guns in America, estimated to be 400 million in the United States, many of them including assault-style weapons and ghost guns, may have created reciprocal gun dependency, "if you have one, I should own one as well," gun ownership as a safety equalizer. A majority of Americans in June 2023 (60 percent) of Americans polled believed gun violence was a very big problem, and upwards of 83 percent believed it was at least a moderately big problem. As of June 2023, almost two-thirds of Americans also believed the level of gun violence would only increase.[246]

In 2018, 55 percent of Republicans polled perceived crime had risen from the previous year in 2017, when violent crime had actually fallen. In 2019, violent crime in the US was at near 32-year lows, but in 2020, violent crime went up slightly to 2010 levels, at 1.27 million reported incidents, according to Statistica.[247] This was 73,000 more incidents than in 2014, but 2014 recorded a forty-year low in violent crime. Gallup has noted that the misperceiving rising national violence has become a pattern in the United States. In the election year 2020, when a Republican president was in office, 73 percent of Democrats believed crime was rising, 18 percentage points above similar polling in 2016. Though immigration encounters have risen substantially in the last few years, the scale of the problem of both immigration and violent crime as it is perceived rises and falls in American voters proportionately with political cycles. More voters tend to believe violent crime is on the rise if the opposite party's president is in office.

In 2014, deaths by homicide per capita in the US were trending at a 54-year low, but by 2019, deaths by homicide increased slightly to the same moderate levels measured in 2002. In 1980, homicides accounted for 10.4 deaths per 100,000 people, at their 75-year peak.[248] Violent crimes, including homicide, aggravated assault, and gun assault, increased significantly from a short duration from May to June 2020 by 37 percent in 20 large US cities. Though violent crime rates are considerably lower than their high point registered in 1992, homicides temporally surpassed a forty-year high in 2020 and 2021.[249] The factors that increased violent crime during and right after COVID were all exasperating issues created by "job loss, illness, death, isolation, financial insecurity…partisan conflict, the proliferation of dangerous conspiracy theories, extremist ideologies, and future economic or political instability," according to criminologist Michael Pittaro.[250]

Suicide rates in the US have risen from a low in the year 2000 to the highest rates seen since WWII, surpassing levels documented in 1977, yet significantly lower than the rates recorded during The Great Depression in America—an unfortunate comparison considering our national depression rates have increased as well, and gun suicide account for 55 percent of all gun-related deaths.[251] Increased suicide rates by gun were the prevailing reason why firearm deaths rose to record national levels in 2020 and 2021, and death by suicide remains one of the leading causes of death in the US.

Should we excavate some of the deeper issues on immigration, violence, and gun ownership?

Are human beings naturally violent?

Is criminal behavior part of a disposition that a criminal is born with—their "nature"—or is criminal behavior formed through social environments and development through "nurture?" A tipping point comes to those who transgress laws and rules, a decision that may come to them explicitly but is usually implicit: Are the potential gains for transgressing laws, codes, and rules worth the risk? Granted, criminal behavior generally entails not thinking things through, acting impulsively, and not considering the consequences of transgressing laws. However, policies and programs committed to ending violent crime depend upon how we view the human potential for violence, how criminal behavior is understood, and whether such behavior is reformable or mostly incorrigible. Without asking deeper questions about criminal behavior, it is difficult to determine whether our penal system works to simply warehouse the wrongful or if it is effective at halting self-destructive behavior and reintegrating wrongdoers into society. Without asking deeper questions, we cannot begin to craft law enforcement and penal systems that work to lower violent crime and criminality.

In 1975, the French philosopher Michel Foucault published a book titled *Discipline and Punish: The Birth of the Prison*. The book documents the reasoning and moral logic behind the transformation of criminal punishment from torture and public execution—punitive procedures common hundreds of years ago—into the modern Western penal system. Countering established narratives of progress and reform, Foucault argues that the development of the modern penal system was not transformed out of humanitarian concerns; it was altered by an emergent bourgeoisie class concerned with exerting social morality, control, and uniformity on the criminal. For Foucault, this was accomplished by creating surveillance-oriented institutions that claimed reform-minded goals and equality before the law but, in fact, rationalized and sanitized the segregation of a criminal caste, isolating miscreants from public view or public consciousness:

> The development and generalization of disciplinary mechanisms constituted the other, dark side of [civilizing] processes. The general juridical form that guaranteed a system of rights that were egalitarian in principle was supported by these tiny, everyday, physical mechanisms, by all those systems of micro-power that are essentially non-egalitarian and asymmetrical.[252]

Foucault's discourse and arguments questioning the logic and efficacy of 20th-century institutions became a key part of what is known as *poststructural theory* in the social sciences, critical reflections on the efficacy and rationality of institutions created to further societal progress. During the Obama Administration, questions regarding law enforcement and the prison system began to bubble up in the consciousness of the general public, poststructural discourses had become mainstream. For the first time in a long time, Americans began to ask if tougher laws decreased crime or if the United States had created a law enforcement system that perpetuated discrimination along the lines of class and race.

The development of the Western justice system extends back to the European Middle Ages when the role and rights of individuals within the authority of the state began to be acknowledged and clarified in steps and sometimes by sea changes in outlook. The right to trial by jury was first inscribed in the *Magna Carta* c. 1215 CE as such a sea change, though it took many years to codify as a normal practice in law. The execution of King Charles I of England in 1649 and the subsequent violence and losses of the English Civil War (1642 to 1651)—which pitted Royalists against supporters of the English parliament (Parliamentarians)—led to another such sea change. The civil war severed the hierarchal social structure embedded in the Great Chain of Being that presupposed a natural hierarchy in society, with monarchs atop the chain, aristocrats lower down, and commoners at the bottom. English philosophers Thomas Hobbes (1588-1679) and John Locke (1632–1704) began to question how authority over others is justified and exercised and why rational human beings would voluntarily consent to give up their natural freedoms to be ruled by others. The philosophical conversations that followed would later be defined as *social contract theory*.

Thomas Hobbes kick-started the discussion on social contract theory in his book *Leviathan,* published in 1651. Hobbes began a thought experiment that imagined an original *state of nature* when human beings lived in a prehistoric world. Colored by the events of the English Civil War, he wondered how one of the most civilized nations in the world could have engaged in a blood bath in the name of religious liberty and against the abuse of monarchial power, only to end up at the close of the war with another autocratic ruler and a divided country with even less religious liberty. A view of ancient society similar to the Edenic vista painted in the Old Testament was soured. Hobbes imagined that humanity in the state of nature was primitive and self-serving and that human lives were "solitary, poor, nasty, brutish and short."[253] Hobbes justified rule by *leviathans* (monarchs) in nation-states because, without such supreme authorities, the innate qualities of human nature would drive society into lawlessness and anarchy. In an implicit *social contract* of law and order, citizens surrendered some of their rights to the monarch in society to ensure order and to prevent such chaos. Hobbes' view of humanity, loosely translated into modern politics would be considered conservative, and his views on the potential of humanity as realistic or cynical, depending on your perspective.

Writing just after the end of the English Civil War, the philosopher John Locke turned Hobbes' argument on social contract theory on its head and came away from the English Civil War with a different view of the social contract. He proposed that man in the state of nature was not wicked, per se, and that ancient people lived in a state of peaceful independence. To Locke, the human mind at birth was essentially a blank slate, a *tabula rasa*, and human behavior derived from the world human beings encountered and absorbed. He argued that in the state of nature, where human beings in primitive societies lived without strong laws and punishment, people would not necessarily act lawlessly. For Locke, human beings were still subject to the laws of God and nature—and sources of natural laws and natural rights. He argued that monarchial rule is not a bargain to exchange power for social order; monarchial rule is authorized only by the consent of the governed, and when kings usurp their authority, revolution against the state may be called for.

The conversation between Hobbes and Locke put into question the fundamental nature of human beings: Are we evil and self-serving beings requiring structure and correction to keep us in line, or are we virtuous beings with altruistic tendencies capable of self-rule? Do the codes and laws of society hold our natural impulses in check, or does the pressure of keeping up in society turn us into self-serving survivalists?—two fundamentally different worldviews on where criminal behavior originates. These contrasting perspectives determine how to build a justice system that prevents violence and protects the public from criminal behavior. Our attitudes about human nature also determine how we create a prison system that prevents criminals from reoffending and lowers crime and incarceration rates.

The basis of gun rights in America

The Second Amendment of the United States Constitution is shortly worded and, because of its generality and brevity, has been subject to diverse and perhaps overly expansive interpretations:

> A well-regulated militia, being necessary to the security of a free State, the right of the people to keep and bear Arms, shall not be infringed—Second Amendment to the United States Constitution.

The Amendment specifically links owning a firearm to maintaining a militia, for one, and therefore to the defense of the country from outside invasion or potentially from usurping tyrants. Significant in the wording of the Second Amendment is the wording "well-regulated," that the right to bear arms is subject to regulation and order but "shall not be infringed." It assures citizens that the federal government will not impede gun ownership as a right within states, while leaving the door open for local governments to regulate firearms as they choose. This reasoning follows US Supreme Court discussions and decisions over the Second Amendment throughout the 19th and 20th Centuries.

The right of an individual to bear arms draws us back once again to the end of the 17th Century, to the English Bill of Rights instituted in 1689. During that formative time in English history, the English Parliament asserted considerable power over the new monarch, William of Orange, compelling the country toward a constitutional monarchy. The right to bear arms was originally an *obligation* to bear arms rather than a right. The landed gentry under the rule of Late Medieval Barons in England were obligated to own firearms and defend territory when needed. The Bill of Rights in Great Britain extended the right to bear arms to all "Protestants…for their defense suitable to their conditions and as allowed by law."[254]

The Bill of Rights also removed the word "guns" from the list of items the poor were forbidden to own—as designated in the Game Act of 1671.[255] Essentially, the motive behind allowing citizens to own guns was to send a message to Monarchs that their power was not absolute and that they could not unjustly mobilize an army against the populace or Parliament. For Americans in the 1780s, firearms were not by themselves thought of as an extension of personal freedoms but rather as necessities of daily living. Before the American Revolution, firearms and gunpowder were often housed in depots away from living quarters of residences, owing to the dangerously flammable and explosive nature of gunpowder. The Second Amendment did not prohibit storing firearms in safe locations, common practices before the American Revolution.

For a very long time in the US, gun laws and gun regulations were created through local ordinances in state laws and generally left to local communities to set rules and regulations for firearms. The Old West, generally depicted in movies where everyone wears a sidearm and duels are common, does not depict common scenarios. In fact, gunfights were comparatively rare, and gun restrictions and firearm ordinances were common. Dodge City, Kansas, is more commonly known as the cowboy epicenter of the Old West, lying at the end of the Chisholm Trail, where cattle were loaded onto railroad cars bound for the slaughterhouses in the decade from 1875-1885. However, Dodge City formed a municipal government in 1878 that passed the first law prohibiting the carrying of guns in town, likely by civic leaders and influential merchants who wanted settlers to move there, to bring families and invest their time and resources in the town—according to Stephen Aron, a professor of history at UCLA.[256] The most famous gunfight in the Old West, the gunfight at the O.K. Corral, was caused by Billy Clanton and the McLaury brothers not turning in their guns at a local hotel or a lawman's office, which was required by Tombstone, Arizona, law in the Old West town at the time.

For most of our history, gun laws and gun rights in the United States were perfectly compatible: Only in the last few decades have the two become locked in a zero-sum relationship, where a gain for one side is seen as a loss for the other. Prolific and varied historical gun laws make clear that the default firearm policy in American history was the regulation and restriction of guns and other weapons in societal arenas.[257]

For a long time, the federal appellate courts and the Supreme Court of the United States held the opinion that the Second Amendment remained among the few provisions of the Bill of Rights that did not fall under the due process clause of the 14th Amendment, which would make gun rights an issue of national rights. In the 1886 US Supreme Court case *Presser v. Illinois*, the Court held that the Second Amendment applied only to the federal government and did not prohibit state governments from regulating an individual's ownership or use of guns.[258] As Robert Spitzer, an author of six books on gun policy in America and a political science emeritus at SUNY Cortland has pointed out:

> As I have learned from my research on early gun laws, weapons regulation in early America went even further, extending to three broad types of laws spanning nearly 300 years of American history. First, laws restricting weapons carrying were enacted, extending to guns, fighting knives, and clubs throughout the 1800s. These laws criminalized concealed weapons carrying in 50 states (including territories that later became states), open weapons carrying in at least 29 states, and even long gun carrying in at least 22 states. Second, at least 36 states laws passed laws that criminalized public weapons brandishing and display. Third, at least 47 states enacted laws providing for the licensing of some of these activities.[259]

The current polarization over gun rights began with the passage of the first and most high-profile federal gun control efforts, the Brady Handgun Violence Prevention Act in 1993, which kickstarted a national discussion about gun rights and new decisions by the US Supreme Court affirming the right to bear arms. The prevalence of mass shootings in the United States since 1993 has only amplified the debate between Second Amendment advocates and gun control advocates, who now include an expanding pool of victims of gun violence.

Immigration policy in the United States

One of the abiding contradictions in the history of the United States is the fact that while we are an immigrant nation, our history is tainted with highly prejudicial immigrant policies. US immigration laws and policies have vacillated between welcoming and restrictive from the establishment of our nation.[260] In 1776, Thomas Paine published a political pamphlet, *Common Sense,* which provided the rationale for a US/Great Britain separation. But he also reminded American colonists that "Europe, and not England, is the parent country of America. This new world hath been the asylum for the persecuted lovers of civil and religious liberty from every part of Europe."[261] America, for Paine, would be made stronger by the rabble of its diversity, by those who shared our aspirations for liberty. The United States Congress has also prioritized immigration policies around the interests and well-being of long-established residents over those of immigrants and bowed to the pressure of social movements reasserting native-born American rights or *nativist movements*. Highlighting some of the vacillations we have had on immigration laws and policies:

- The US Congress passed its first bill restricting American citizenship in the Naturalization Act of 1790, a law that restricted US citizenship to "free White person(s) of good character." Native Americans, indentured servants, Muslims, and enslaved people were among the groups denied citizenship.[262] The requirement meant "that immigrants seeking lawful residence and citizenship were compelled to convince authorities that they fit within the statutory definition of whiteness."[263]

- The Fourteenth Amendment, approved in 1868, opened up citizenship to people born within the United States regardless of "race," but it excluded Native Americans living on reservations.

- The US Naturalization Act of 1870 extended naturalization laws to "aliens of African nativity and to persons of African descent" while also revoking the citizenship of naturalized Chinese Americans.[264]

- Only 12 years later, The Chinese Exclusion Act was signed by President Chester A. Arthur on May 6, 1882, prohibiting all immigration of Chinese laborers for ten years. The law made exceptions for merchants, teachers, students, travelers, and diplomats. Still, it was the first and only major US law ever implemented to prevent all members of a specific national group from immigrating to the United States.[265]

Nativist attitudes in the US have not always been restricted to the immigration of non-white people. The *Know Nothings* was a nativist political movement that formed in the United States in the mid-1850s to counter what its members believed to be the empowerment of Catholic hierarchies and populaces in the United States. Irish and German immigrants were made suspect in a conspiracy theory that held Catholics in the US were going to subvert the civil and religious liberties of native-born Protestant Americans.

Irish immigration to the US provides a useful historical backdrop for examining some of the forces that push people out of their homeland and the pulls that attract them to come to the United

States. Catholics in Ireland were gradually dispossessed of their lands in wars waged against them by Great Britain beginning in Queen Elizabeth's reign and heightened during the years of the English Commonwealth under Oliver Cromwell's leadership. After Cromwell's campaign in Ireland, the Catholic-owned land situated in the conflict was confiscated under the Act for the Settlement of Ireland of 1652 and given to Scottish and English settlers and Parliamentary soldiers. The percentage of land owned by native Catholic citizens went from 70 percent to 30 percent in just five years.

By the time of the Irish Potato Famine (1845-1852), most Irish had become tenant farmers on their original lands. With a blight affecting potato crops, Irish farmers were deprived of their produce and could not afford rents or basic subsistence. What potato crops remained unaffected were exported to Great Britain under gunpoint by the middlemen of absentee British landowners. It is believed in one year, 1847, roughly 1 million Irish died, and another 1 million emigrated abroad, causing the country's population to fall by 20-25 percent.[266] Many Irish immigrants landed in New York City and Boston in wretched health and were perceived as a blight on the infrastructure of the cities. In 1850, the Irish-born population topped 1 million in the US and doubled in the years from 1860–1890, when the total number of Irish-Americans reached 13 percent of the total US population.[267] The "push" factor for Irish immigrants was deciding between starvation and beginning a new life in a land that "pulled" immigrants in search of more promising circumstances. However, resistance to the volume of Catholic immigrants in middle 19th century America was strong enough nationally to create a single-issue anti-immigrant political party in the Know Nothings.

In 1907, US immigration reached its peak. It has been estimated that three-quarters of New York City's population in 1910 was first-generation Americans. Congress followed the numbers with more immigration-restricting legislation, including:

- The Immigration Act of 1917, which established a literacy requirement for immigrants selecting for professional classes of immigrants,

- and the Immigration Act of 1924, which created ethnic quotas limiting immigrants from the Mediterranean region, Eastern Europe, and Asia.

By 1942, labor shortages in World War II prompted the United States to form a Bracero Program with Mexico—a neutral country during the war. The Bracero Program allowed Mexican agricultural workers and laborers to enter the United States on a work visa program. This program lasted until 1964 and helped the US fill an emergency labor shortage. Many of the immigrants eventually went back to Mexico, but the long-term connection to the US enabled many of the Bracero worker's offspring to emigrate north. After World War II, the US passed the first refugee and resettlement law to allow Europeans permanent residence in the US, many of whom had to leave all their possessions behind during the war or risk internment and death. Finally, in 1965, the Immigration and Nationality Act formally ended the national origin quotas set into law in the 1920s, ending explicit immigration discrimination in the USA.

Modern US immigration policy began in 1986 when Ronald Reagan signed the Simpson-Mazzoli Act. The Simpson-Mazzoli was a bipartisan Act that granted amnesty to more than 3 million immigrants living illegally in the United States. The act required employers to verify their employee's immigration status and made it illegal to hire or recruit unauthorized immigrants knowingly. The act also legalized certain seasonal agricultural undocumented migrants and undocumented migrants who entered the United States before January 1, 1982, and had resided here continuously. It also waived overstaying penalties, fines, or paying any back taxes due. Candidates were required to prove that they were not guilty of any crime, had been in the country before January 1, 1982, and possessed at least a minimal knowledge of US history and government and the English language to be granted amnesty.[268]

In 1987, Reagan used his executive authority to legalize the status of minor children of parents granted amnesty under the immigration overhaul, announcing a blanket amnesty on deportation for children under 18 who had a parent or parents legalized under the Act, which affected an estimated 100,000 families. The Simpson-Mazzoli Act also established financial penalties in the future for those employing undocumented migrants. Lawmakers believed that the employment restrictions would reduce undocumented migration. They introduced the I-9 form to ensure all employees presented documentary proof of eligibility to accept employment in the US. While the Simpson-Mazzoli Act temporally decreased illegal immigration, it did not decrease the population of undocumented immigrants, which rose by 5 million individuals from 1986 to 11.1 million undocumented immigrants by 2013.[269]

To counter the rise in illegal immigration and help settle the immigration issues arising in the US, in 2005, the US House of Representatives passed the Border Protection, Anti-terrorism, and Illegal Control Act of 2005 with bipartisan support, and in 2006, the US Senate passed the Comprehensive Immigration Reform Act of 2006. Neither bill became law because differences could not be reconciled in conference committees. Both bills, particularly the Senate bill, would have solved many of the current issues of immigration and undocumented people in the US today.

On January 28, 2013, another bipartisan group of eight Senators, known as the"Gang of Eight," announced principles for comprehensive immigration reform (CIR). Some of the policies envisioned by the Senators included:

- A pathway for citizenship for illegal immigrants already in the United States—contingent on certain border security and visa tracking improvements.

- Business immigration system reforms, focusing on reducing current visa backlogs and fast-tracking permanent residence for US university immigrant graduates with advanced degrees in science, technology, engineering, or math also known as the STEM fields.

- An expanded and improved employment verification system for all employers to confirm employee work authorization.

- Improved work visa options for low-skill workers, including an agricultural worker program.[270]

On June 27, 2013, the United States Senate approved Senate Bill S.744, known as the Border Security, Economic Opportunity, and Immigration Modernization Act of 2013, in a bipartisan 68-to-32 vote. The immigration reform bill was sent to the US House of

Representatives but was never brought to the House floor for debate by the Republican-controlled House for an up-or-down vote, and the Bill died at the end of the 113th Congress.

US Presidents have conducted executive actions that have alleviated some of the worst effects of an unresolved US immigration policy. In November 2014, President Barack Obama signed an executive order that enabled about half of undocumented immigrants to legally live and work in America. In March 2020, President Trump enacted Title 42 as an emergency measure to block immigration based upon the COVID emergency, as US-Mexico border encounters had begun to rise precipitously for the first time in 16 years by 2019. President Joe Biden kept the emergency measure in place until May 11, 2023. Facing lawsuits from immigrant rights groups to Title 42, further restrictions to immigration were put in place, like denying asylum status to immigrants who hadn't first applied to another country for protection and criminalizing reentry into the US for up to five years without that filling in hand.[271]

Ultimately it is the responsibility of the US Congress to solve the border crises. Article 1, Section 8 of the US Constitution grants the US Congress the responsibility "To establish a uniform Rule of Naturalization," determining how immigrants can become citizens. If a US President signs an executive order to limit immigration and or to revoke asylum statutes, their orders are at best only temporally actionable, lasting only as long as lawsuits arise and temporary stays in-laws are granted. Most likely, the US Supreme Court would invalidate any permanent presidential actions on immigration policy because writing immigration policy and law is one of the explicit roles of the US Congress written into our Constitution.

Where are Americans on Immigration, Gun Laws, and Violent Crime?

Gun violence and violent crime by the numbers

It is hard to define when or if gun violence has increased since the data in the US over the last forty years tracks violent crime (which most often involves guns) but does not track the use of guns in violence specifically. For years, since a high point in the last fifty years in 1992 when the FBI reported 1.93 million violent crimes in the US, violent crime numbers fell in the US to a little over 1.15 million cases in 2014 nationally.[272] Since 2014, an uptick in violent crime peaked in 2020 with 1.31 million violent crimes reported, but this number has come down once again.

Accounting for the uptick in violent crime in 2020 was a rise in the national murder rate per 100,000 people, which rose during the COVID-19 lockdown by nearly 30 percent nationally, according to Ames Grawert and Noah Kim, researchers working for the nonpartisan Brennan Center.[273] "Assaults increased as well, with the rate of offenses rising by more than 10 percent."[274] The researchers conclude that both increases are connected to a broader surge in gun violence, with more than 75 percent of murders in 2020 committed with a firearm "reaching a new high."[275] Big cities that report data on shooting incidences, such as New York, saw significant increases in gun violence as well. Grawert and Kim also conclude that despite politicized claims that this rise was the result of criminal justice reform in liberal-leaning jurisdictions, murders rose roughly equally in cities run by Republicans and cities run by Democrats, and red states actually saw some of the highest murder rates of all.[276]

Looking back at the broader picture of reported violent crimes in the states by the numbers, one would expect that the states with the largest populations would record the most violent crimes, and this holds for California, Texas, Florida, and New York. However, looking over the forty-year trend from 1979 to 2020, violent crime rates in blue states have actually come down slightly in California, substantially in Illinois and New Jersey, and overwhelmingly in New York, while violent crime rates have doubled in Texas, risen somewhat in Pennsylvania and Florida, and risen substantially in pro-gun rights majority states of the US including Tennessee, Arizona, North Carolina, and Georgia.[277] The surge in violent crime did not reflect an overall rise in crime nationwide in 2020 during the COVID lockdown; all property crimes except motor vehicle theft came down nationally, for example. After the lockdown, property crime rebounded in inner-city locations in the US, with organized looting rising. Between the first quarters of 2021 and 2022, the number of property crimes jumped in 62 of the 100 largest cities with available data.[278]

Though the incidences of property crime are modest compared to the early 1900s, certainly, the incidences of mass shootings, which understandably consume the fear of Americans, have become far more common in the last twenty-five years. Up until 1999, with the Columbine High School Massacre in Colorado, mass shootings in the US were an anomaly, with generally three or fewer a year reported in the US going back to 1982. In 1999, there were five mass shootings, and the perpetrator profiles of the Columbine shooters would be a barometer for the profiles of mass shooters to follow. The perpetrators were young men who had been bullied and had already gotten into trouble with the law for stealing equipment out of a van. One had created a violent gaming website that was reported by a classmate's mother. With hindsight overviewing the mass shootings of the last twenty years, the Columbine shooters fit the first profile of many young, troubled men to come.

Even though assault weapons had been banned with the signing of The Brady Bill, and been advocated for by Ronald Reagan and other high-profile Republicans, and signed into law by President Clinton in 1994, assault weapons never stopped being built. Gun manufacturers slightly changed the profile of their assault weapons, taking off bayonet brackets, flash suppressors, and folding stocks while keeping in place large magazines, small-sized semi-automatic designs, and pistol grips "so that the trigger can be pulled quickly while the gun is pointed from the hip"—characteristics of the Uzi submachine gun.[279] The Columbine shooters used friends to help buy guns for them since they were underage and purchased many of their guns at gun shows, taking advantage of gun registration loopholes. Both young killers used legal guns, which nonetheless fell into the hands of underage and illegal gun owners.

Mass shootings began to rise in frequency in 2012, and as President Obama tried to reinstate the Brady Bill, which had been allowed to expire in 2004, gun purchases increased, mostly by those who already had guns. The years beginning with 2017 through to the beginning of 2023 registered the five worst years for mass shootings in America. In 2020, for the first time, firearms were the leading cause of death for children and teens in the US, surpassing deaths by car crashes, drug overdoses, and cancer, according to research published in The New England Journal of Medicine.[280] In 2010, handguns surpassed rifles as the gun of choice, consistent with polling information that indicated the leading reason to buy a gun is for personal security.

While the incidences of property theft have remained level for years in most categories, and retail and car theft have increased only slightly within cities, the value of the thefts has increased substantially, indicating a rise in the serialization of theft of organized theft rings, making targets of higher value. While violent crime and property theft have not nearly increased to the proportions seen in the early 1990s, the cost of theft and the rise in mass shootings have elevated the perception of violence in America. But more generally, mainstream media coverage focused on violent crime has also contributed to a perception that violent crime is rising. As John Gramich, an associate director for the Pew Research Center, has pointed out:

> The public often tends to believe that crime is up, even when the data shows it is down. In 22 of 26 Gallup surveys conducted since 1993, at least six-in-ten US adults said there was more crime nationally than there was the year before, despite the general downward trend in the national violent crime rate during most of that period.[281]

Older voters are far more likely than younger voters to see violent crime as a key election issue. Three-quarters of registered voters aged 65 and older stated violent crime was a very important voting issue for them in the 2022 midterms, compared with fewer than half of voters under 30 (44 percent).[282] However, older Americans reflect the same gravity of concern for violent crime as Black voters, reflecting populations that are particularly vulnerable, by age and geography, respectively, to violent crime. These are concerns that younger or suburban voters may not inhabit to such a degree.

Polling and consensus on gun laws and restriction

In June 2022, the US Senate passed the Bipartisan Safer Communities Act, the first gun control legislation enacted by Congress in 30 years. It was a modest, though bipartisan bill that enhanced background checks for gun buyers between 18 and 21 years old, incentivized states to enact "red flag" laws that enable firearms to be temporarily confiscated from people deemed dangerous, and provided hundreds of millions of dollars for mental health and school safety. It also extended to dating partners of potential gun buyers, a federal law that prohibits domestic abusers from purchasing guns.[283]

In a poll conducted in June 2023 by Pew Research, 60 percent of those polled still believed gun violence was a very big problem (up from 53 percent in mid-2018), including 38 percent of Republican-leaners. Seventy-nine percent in the same poll at least somewhat favored increasing the minimum age for buying guns to 21, with an even larger majority (88 percent) who believed in barring people with mental illness from purchasing guns.[284] Two-thirds still favored banning high-capacity magazines that hold more than ten rounds, and 64 percent favored (re) banning assault weapons in America. Few Americans were in favor of allowing people to carry concealed weapons without a permit (24 percent) or shortening waiting periods for guns to be purchased legally (30 percent).[285]

Causes of gun violence and mass shooting

In February 2022, the National Institute of Justice published some of the results of a database compiled over 53 years of people who had committed public mass shootings over the last half-century. People who have committed public mass shootings in the US over the last half-century were commonly troubled by personal trauma before their shooting incidents, nearly always in a state of crisis at the time, and, in most cases, engaged in leaking their plans before opening fire. Most were insiders of a targeted institution, such as an employee or a student. Except for young school shooters who stole the guns from family members, most used legally obtained handguns in those shootings.[286]

Sadly, suicidal thoughts were also a predictor of mass shootings, particularly among younger shooters, with K-12 students found to be suicidal in 92 percent of cases of mass shootings by underage assailants. While mental illness is often cited as a cause of mass shootings, psychosis only played a minor role in one-third of shootings and a major role in only 10 percent of cases. Around 70 percent of shooters knew at least some of their victims, especially in school and workplace violence.[287] Three-fourths of mass shooters used handguns, with the other fourth using assault rifles, and, in the majority of cases, shooters obtained their guns legally. In the case of K-12 school shootings, over 80 percent of shooters stole their guns from family members. The overwhelming majority of mass shooters were male, with a mean age of 34. Over half were white, and most had prior criminal records and histories of violence, with over 25 percent of shooters having a history of domestic violence.[288] One in five shooters studied past mass shootings; many were radicalized online. Over half of all mass shooters died on the scene, either at their own hands or at the hands of law enforcement. With so many shooters dying in the act of murder and shootings broadcast regularly on mainstream news, ideations of "suicide by cop" have increased with mass shooters.

With this data in mind, will the Bipartisan Safer Communities Act work to curb gun violence? What more can be done with the consensus that we have on gun safety measures nationally? Certainly, the Bipartisan Safer Communities Act would have potentially helped bring public consciousness to the people aiding the two young perpetrators of the Columbine Massacre, especially the "incentivizing" provisions for reg flag reporting with the ability to disarm someone temporally deemed a threat to public safety. The millions of dollars in the bill to promote mental health programs, strengthen school safety measures, enhance background checks for young adults between 18-21, and to close down the loopholes for being able to buy guns for another person would have also helped. However, incentivizing communities and creating a strong baseline of laws are two different matters. Also, although the ATF has been trying to close gun show loopholes (as of September 2023), purchasing guns without licensing or accounting for a new owner is still fairly easy. National politicians will have to weigh the influence of a large majority of Americans who want further restrictions on gun sales. Seventy-nine percent of the US electorate still favor increasing the minimum age for buying guns to 21. Two-thirds of Americans believe in banning high-capacity ammunition magazines, and this follows polling in law enforcement agencies that support banning high-capacity magazines. "The high-capacity magazine is what takes it to a whole other level of carnage," said David Chipman, who served 25 years as a special agent for the Bureau of Alcohol, Tobacco, Firearms and Explosives. "It's the primary driver for why we're seeing more mass shootings more regularly."[289]

The perpetrators of the Columbine Massacre were forced to carry multiple weapons because, at the time, The Brady Bill had outlawed high-capacity magazines. What is often recounted in mass shootings is that perpetrators are killed or interrupted during changes in their bullet magazines, preventing more carnage. Sixty-four percent of Americans favor banning assault-style weapons. Still, most estimates put the number of these weapons owned at about 20 million in the US, mostly purchased since the lapse of the Brady Bill. Banning assault-style weapons at this point in the US would mean creating a system for surrendering those guns, like a buy-back policy, for example. It would be easier to require training or licensing of such weapons through local ordinances and state laws. Gun controls set by cities and communities are as old as the Old West in the United States, but imposing firearm restrictions and licensing requirements has greater traction in urban versus rural communities.

Consensus on US immigration

A Pew Research poll in January 2024 had "defending against terrorism" and "dealing with immigration" rising as issues demanding priority for national politicians. The two issues are driven by rising Republican concerns and linked through conservative media broadcasts.[290] As Pew report stated:

> Throughout Biden's presidency, the share of Americans citing immigration as a top priority has increased 18 percentage points—from 39 percent to 57 percent—with the change coming almost entirely among Republicans and Republican-leaning independents. Republicans have also grown more concerned over terrorism, especially in the past year (see Figure 2).[291]

Democrats and Republicans differ on the causes of the influx of immigration, with more Democrats believing a "major reason" for emigration is due to violence in home countries (79 percent). More Republicans stated a "major reason" for emigration is that US immigration policies make it easy to stay in the US once they arrive.[292] Democrats and Republicans also describe the problem of immigration differently, with 76 percent of Republicans believing immigration should be a top priority for the president and Congress in 2024 with only 39 percent of Democrats viewing immigration similarly. Some conservative media and former president Trump have been disseminating the idea that an influx of international terrorists is mixing in with immigrants crossing the border. While US security agencies have been on a heightened alert status after October 6, 2023, according to *Politifact*, such claims are mostly unsubstantiated. They quote Alex Nowrasteh, a vice president for economic and social policy studies at the Cato Institute, who studied attacks or planned attacks in the US from 1975 through 2022 by 219 foreign-born terrorists. Nowrasteh notes that "During the nearly five-decade span, four were from Palestine, and the most recent attempted attack was in 1997." Nowrasteh told PolitiFact that, as far as he knew, none of the attackers were part of Hamas. The largest group executing an attack on US soil came from Saudi Arabia—the 9/11 terrorists.[293]

In the political debate surrounding national immigration policy, other myths have circulated that seem particularly hard to correct. To clarify:

- Immigrants, including illegal immigrants, are much less likely to be incarcerated in prisons, convicted of crimes, or arrested than native-born Americans.[35]

- Before the recent flood of immigrants across the Southern border of the United States, most of the undocumented immigrants in the US did not cross the border; rather, they flew into the US and overstayed their visas.

- The great majority of dangerous drugs entering the US are concealed in trucks and not carried by immigrant "mules."

- Most immigrants crossing want to be captured to apply for asylum and stay in the US while their case goes into the courts. As conservative journalist David Frum asserts in a February 6, 2024, article in the *Atlantic Monthly*, we *are* enforcing the US-Mexico border using current immigrant laws; the problem is the laws themselves. They have to be changed.[294]

Most Republicans (72 percent) believe expanding the border wall along the US border would improve the situation at the border, with only 30 percent of Democrats expressing this view.[295] Though expanding the border wall has been used as a solution for the border crises, there are vast spaces along the US-Mexico border where building a wall is either impractical or not cost-effective. Increased spending money on border security would better be allotted to surveillance technology, including more drones with night-vision and building more border guard stations along the border. Modernizing scanning technology at well-trafficked border crossings could limit the number of dangerous imports that come into the country, like fentanyl, and limit the export of assault weapons and ammunition legally purchased in the US and exported to cartel members in Mexico.

Solving the immigration problem/crises

While the prioritization of border issues falls mostly along partisan lines, a large majority of Americans polled in late 2023 believed the US government was doing a bad job handling the immigration influx; the immigrant surge has become a great bipartisan concern overall. Democrats and Republicans have consensus on causes and solutions as well; majorities in both parties believe a large number of immigrants seek to enter the US at the Southern Border for better economic opportunities here in the US and bad economic conditions in their home countries. Half of Republicans and three-quarters of

Democrats believe boosting resources and hiring more immigration judges for quicker determinations at the border would improve the situation at the border.

On February 4, 2024, the text of a $118 billion immigration US Senate was unveiled, which came about as a bipartisan agreement between Senators James Lankford, R-Okla., Chris Murphy, D-Conn., and Kyrsten Sinema, I-Ariz. The bill would have been the most aggressive border security and migration overhaul in decades before it was turned down for a vote by the US Republican-led House of Representatives. It would have raised the standard for getting asylum, sent away those who didn't qualify, and expedited cases for those who did.[296] Though a bipartisan working group created the Senate Bill, many of the amendments to immigration that Democrats have long sought were omitted: like provisions that naturalize "Dreamers," providing amnesty to undocumented Americans who came to the US as children or male immigrants who have registered with Selective Service or served in the US military, be of good moral character, and have proof of residency in America for five straight years. The Senate Bill provided mostly bipartisan and Republican-leaning solutions to the border crises, including a new and greatly expedited system for processing asylum requests that would move the process into the Department of Homeland Security. It also included provisions for:

- A new standard for asylum seekers: they would have to establish "clear and convincing" proof that they have a credible fear of persecution if they stay in their country.

- Earlier rejections from asylum if the person has a disqualifying criminal history, if they were living safely in a third country before seeking asylum, or if they could safely relocate to their original home country.

- A new emergency authorization for the DHS to shut down the border if the average migrant crossing numbers reach 4,000 per day over seven days.[297] The bill also expanded the allocation of work visas. It provided more money to the US Immigration and Customs Enforcement and Customs and Border Patrol to make new hires, which would help to bring more manpower to the border in remote areas of crossings.

Emergency measures instigated by the Trump and Biden Administrations that have included sending National Guard personnel to the border and plans to open 100 regional processing centers, along with temporary work-visa measures for those immigrants in the US awaiting asylum hearings, have been necessary temporary measures. Sending Cuban, Venezuelan, Haitian, and Nicaraguan national refugees back to their home countries if they haven't first applied for asylum to any of the countries en route is also a necessary addition. Most of the countries pushing emigres out in large numbers are currently wracked by decimated economies and—except Cuba—violence-torn geographies. The crisis of immigrant numbers at the US-Mexico border that began in 2019 is only one small part of a global refugee crisis that now (and for the foreseeable future) requires international diplomacy, cooperation, and more stringent and decisive intervention to shore up democratic rule and more inclusive economies.

How can violent crime and gun violence be lowered?

Is a violent criminal born, or are they made? If it is mostly the latter, then jails and prisons serve as institutions to inculcate violent criminal behavior deeply into the habits and cognitive patterns of a criminal, and often for life. Criminal science and criminal psychology have progressed 100 years in advance of our carceral institutions in the United States—our prisons *are* that old, and our penal system that antiquated.

The first arrest of a violent criminal generally follows from someone not thinking clearly at all about the consequences of their actions. Often, it is an impulsive reaction based on the schema or cognitive map that the assailant has created for themselves and clung to as a mechanism for survival. Violent criminals are often the victims of intergenerational violence, and teenagers who act out deserve more of our attention, intervention, and mentorship at the first symptoms of a destructive trajectory. According to psychologist Lisa Firestone, violent people are often driven by self-deprecating, self-aggrandizing, and/or aggressive voices.[298] Self-deprecating voices may follow years of abuse, feelings that they as a person are "unlovable, and that no one will love or care about them." According to Firestone, these voices promote isolation and harden thinking around survival machinations. They attack other people and see them as rejecting. All of these voices encourage a person not to want anything from anyone else. An example of these voices is: "You will have to take care of yourself because no one else will. Don't expect anything from anyone; you will only be disappointed."[299]

Self-aggrandizing voices can be a precursor of violence as well because they promote a view that a person is superior to others and deserves to be treated as such. They support an inflated self-image that functions to compensate for deep-seated self-hatred. When the aggrandized sense of self is threatened, for example, by slights or perceived disrespect, a person may react violently to regain the aggrandized self-image. Research links violence in adolescent behavior to inflated self-esteem or vanity, for example. According to Firestone, the inner voice of such thinking might be voiced as: "You are so much better than them. How dare they talk to you like that!!" Overtly aggressive voices also contribute significantly to violence. These voices directly encourage taking violent action. They convince a person that acting out aggressively and violently would be an appropriate or even pleasurable release. An example of these voices is: "Violence is the way to go. Just smash them; you'll feel better."[300] Often, a lack of remorse follows violence in a person influenced by destructive voices.

It must be stated here that a mind full of negative voices could well be symptomatic of mental illness and not predictive of violent behavior. But starting from the cognitive profile of a violent criminal, incarceration systems like those in the US warehouse dangerous individuals in a system that only builds on the sociopathy of violent behavior. At every stage of their internment, living continually on the razor's edge of danger in a very violent prison landscape, destructive voices are only amplified, feeding violent and paranoic inner thoughts and voices. The US incarceration system functions implicitly on the dangerous misperceptions that violent criminals will never be set free or that they will enter society and within one day adjust to the expected norms of personal conduct in modern societies—having lived through years of warlike landscapes where violence is at best subdued outwardly but never resolved internally, psychologically.

Though genetic studies on criminal behavior have revealed specific genes associated with regulating neurotransmitter levels that may be tied to the small group of antisocial repeat offenders, the biggest predictor of violent criminal behavior statistically arises from living in areas of the country where residents "experience multiple forms of disadvantage, from poverty to disease to segregation to joblessness."[301] Poor and historically disadvantaged communities bore the brunt of the surge in violence in 2020, but the structural conditions for violence have been in place in disadvantaged communities for decades. Combining impoverishment and a lack of education or vocational training with the psyche of worthlessness that this cultivates is a potent cocktail for violent behavior. Inner-city programs like Baltimore's Safe Steet program, established in 2007, have successfully brought down the level of inner-city violence. US community-based programs like the Safe Street Program offer outreach services by social workers and former gang members who mediate disputes that could lead to violence. They intervene to offer social services, mentorship, and other support services to lower the risk of violent and impulsive actions—particularly among youths. Stopping the trajectory of incarceration before it begins in teenagers is the best of all outlooks for the prevention of violent crime.[302]

Incarceration rates in the US have gone down slightly since 2008, when we had 2.3 million people incarcerated in the US, and at 755 people per 100,000 people, one of the highest incarceration rates in the world. However, as of July 2023, the incarceration rate in the US is still the sixth-highest globally, only behind countries with authoritarian cartels ruling the country like El Salvador, Turkmenistan, and Cuba. The US still has the most people incarcerated of any country, with 1.767 million inmates, higher than China, with more than four times the US population. If the efficiency of incarceration can be measured in the degree to which inmates who leave stay out of prison, the Nordic and German systems of incarceration have us beaten, hands down. The key paradigm shift to their methodology is that their penal systems are at work getting their prisoners to transition successfully to outside society on day one of a prisoner's internment. Their approach emphasizes education and self-awareness and provides inmates with the tools to recognize their behaviors and reconnect themselves to the community while preparing for their exit.

The best, most efficient solution to violent crime is to prevent violent behavior from re-emerging in an individual offender and to intervene proactively at the first signals of criminal behavior. This is what Nordic and German penal systems are focused on and why recidivism, or repeat convictions, has come down in their countries. Their system is expensive, but I believe it could be adapted in the US with provisions that would enable inmates to help pay for their confinement, a self-sustaining model of restorative justice. In such a model, prisoners work for a living, at first within the confines of the prison and later in supervised and monitored work release programs. Prisoners would receive a decent wage in a humane work environments in jobs that help pay for a victims' fund, help pay for the expenses of their incarceration, and create a modest trust fund for their family support and for themselves to be administered by a trustee to help the transition to work and housing with small allotted dispersals on exit.

California's inmate firefighting program, which trains and employs incarcerated felons to fight wildfires, in many respects, fulfills a visionary model for reincorporating convicted criminals into society. Inmates undergo careful selection filters, but part of the technical firefighting training also includes mental health and addiction counseling.[303] While the wages are minimal, the social-psychological benefits of turning outcasts and miscreants in society into first responders in defense of community property is a priceless step in social reintegration. In California, Governor Gavin Newsom signed a bill in 2020 allowing courts to have the discretion to expunge criminal records of inmate firefighters. Many states in the union still keep criminal misdemeanor convictions permanently on public records, limiting job opportunities for those who have made youthful mistakes. Criminal courts and judges should have more discretion for expunging criminal records.

With few exceptions, the US system of incarceration ranks among the most wasteful, inefficient, and certainly the most expensive in the world. It remains so because the political liability of sounding soft on crime prevents any progress toward reforming the system in any meaningful way, enacting real changes to the US carceral system that have proven to decrease crime and violence.

What can be done about gun violence in a US awash in guns?

There are stark differences in views on whether gun ownership does more to increase or decrease safety in the US, with 49 percent of Americans polled stating it makes us safer to own guns and 49 percent stating that it makes us less safe. However, the question that should be asked is, "Safe from what?" Guns don't make people safe from their demons as they contemplate suicide. The injuries from a self-inflicted gun wound to the head are much harder to treat over the long term than a potential drug overdose or other means to commit suicide. We have built a world of guns in the US. In 2022, at least 45 percent of households in the US held one gun in possession. With 400 million estimated guns in the US, we have 1.2 guns for every man, woman, and child, about 2.6 guns per household on average in gun-owning families. Certainly, incidences of mass shootings, which have become far more common in the last twenty-five years, raise the level of concern for self-protection and reciprocal defense. It is understandable that 47 percent of non-gun owners "could see themselves owning a gun in the future," according to a Pew Research poll in June 2023.[304]

Criminal violence statistically has been halved nationally from the last high point in 1993, but firearm deaths in the US in 2021 were at an all-time high. Suicides by gun and "by cop" in mass shootings have also risen dramatically. In 1993, the peak year for criminal violence in the last forty years in the United States, homicides by firearms and suicides by gun were nearly equal in number. By 2007, the rate of suicides by firearms in the US began to rise from 16,883 cases in 2006 to 26,328 in 2021 nationally—a 64 percent rise. In 2021, suicide by firearm accounted for 53.9 percent of all deaths in the US by firearm, higher than homicides by firearm in 2021, which were 42.9 percent of all firearm deaths in the US.[305] While concerns about personal safety have risen in the US due to mass shootings and a sudden rise in shootings in some cities like Chicago and Los Angeles, statistically, having a gun in proximity while suffering suicidal thoughts produces more fatalities in the US than violent crime does.

Are background checks and new gun restrictions and policies within states working to lower gun violence? Statistically, yes. Measuring over the years 1981 to 2021, states that have enacted more gun restrictions, California, New York, Massachusetts, and New Jersey, have seen forty-year declines in firearm deaths, while states that have minimized gun restrictions, like Texas and Florida, have seen steep increases in firearm deaths during that same time. Three Red States that have loosed up gun restrictions, Mississippi, Louisiana, and Alabama, now have the highest homicide rates per capita by state, and 10 of the 14 states with the highest homicide rates are in Red States with lax gun ownership laws.[306] It is hard to argue statistically having more guns and easier access to guns has made the US any safer from gun violence. More guns, in fact, have generally raised homicide rates in the US in states with fewer gun restrictions. The majority of people in the US support more comprehensive background checks (88 percent) that close any loopholes in the system from gun shows and mandate waiting periods to take possession of guns. The majority also support a ban on high-capacity ammunition magazines (71 percent). The states that have enacted such restrictions have, by and large, seen a dramatic decline in firearm homicides.

Discussion – Who are "us," and who are "them?

Does gun ownership make the US safer, or do more guns make the US less safe overall? Americans are divided on this philosophical, factual query. However, a larger question pivots around who is entitled to own a gun and the conditions of risk that gun ownership places on a community. Fewer Americans believe someone convicted of a violent crime should be allowed to own a gun, nor anyone under 21 years of age without adequate training and supervision. Is America made safer with someone who is a danger to themselves and others owning a gun? No. Are Americans made safer in a household with someone who has gun training and is a responsible gun owner? Potentially, yes. Both positions are rational.

I belonged to a gun-owning family growing up; my uncles, cousins, and older brothers all owned guns. On my ninth birthday in Texas, I was gifted my first gun, a coming-of-age ritual in West Texas. About the same time, my twelve-year-old brother was also gifted his first rifle from my uncle. I was taught by both friends and family to respect the power of guns. As a teenager, my brother ended up taking a National Rifle Association gun safety course—which is how I was first introduced to the NRA. It always struck me as odd that someone would want to purchase an assault weapon since the weapon was useless for hunting, tearing flesh from prey rather than leaving small punctures. Justifying the need for an assault weapon for safety reasons when a double-barreled shotgun with buckshot and the destructive potential of a small canon always seemed over-wrought to me. Are military weapons too really needed for home defense? Polled in June 2023, 64 percent of Americans were in favor of a national assault rifle ban.[307]

Should we be more sanguine about the destructive potential of firearms, and what the statistical evidence is telling us? One myth that has been widely held onto about gun violence is that gun violence is a problem in metropolitan regions of the US and not in rural communities. It is true that rural areas in Wyoming, Vermont, Maine, Idaho, and Utah have some of the lowest homicide rates in the nation. Rural residents in those states don't favor stricter gun laws, and homicide data validate their views on gun ownership rights and safety. However, in the Southeast US, gun homicide rates in rural counties now outnumber those in urban counties within those states. Gun homicide rates in rural areas in Arizona and North Carolina have outpaced their large metropolitan counterparts. Gun homicide rates in rural Arizona were 14 percent higher than they were in the state's large metropolitan areas from 2016 to 2020.[308]

The most successful way to limit firearm casualties is to initiate sensible gun policies that follow the consensus of community members themselves, including input from law enforcement and surgeons—those who see the consequences of gun violence firsthand. Gun safety courses could be mandated for anyone 21 and under wanting to purchase a gun, or to anyone, period. Community ordinances could mandate how citizens buy and store weapons: using gun safes with households with children, or restricting firearms in public arenas. Red Flag gun hotline phone services with real enforcement and psychological screening are set to be put in place. More than any other action, intervening with someone in possession of a firearm who is going through a personal crisis or in a period of elevated hostility is the best preventative measure for preventing gun violence. This view conforms to conservative soundbites that tout "guns don't kill people, people kill people"—undeniably true.

It is no coincidence that the US is seeing a spike in asylum registrations from immigrants from Venezuela, El Salvador, Mexico, and Honduras, some of the countries with the greatest intentional homicide rates internationally and easy availability of firearms. Other countries like Japan, which have very strict gun control laws, record very few gun-related deaths because there are simply fewer guns in their society; only one person in every 300 owns a gun in Japan. However, there are countries like Switzerland, Norway, Portugal, and Canada where gun ownership is common. Gun-related homicides in those countries is low because gun safety training and gun law restrictions have been put in place. It is not incompatible to have a society awash in guns, with high gun ownership and low gun homicide. Polling evidence suggests African Americans who live in metropolitan districts want stricter gun regulation. We forget that the ability for "life and liberty" is not only expressed as an aspiration in the US Declaration of Independence, but it is also a fundamental right expressed in the 14th Amendment of the US Constitution. Communities have the fundamental right to see that the lives of their residents are not unnecessarily put at risk in public spaces. Gun ordinances invoke gun safety measures used by town folks in the Old and not-too-wild West.

Is the answer to criminal violence longer sentences? Twenty-eight states have some form of habitual offender law that creates much longer sentences for "persistent offenders." In California, the three-strikes law did not decrease serious crime or petty theft rates below a level expected based on preexisting trends.[309] The US has 5 percent of the world's population but 20 percent of the world's incarcerated population. The three strikes laws are an admission that some people don't deserve another chance and aren't worthy of saving, but isn't it also an admission of the structural failure in the stated goals of our prisons, a *recidivism fatalism*? Why should one of the most advanced democracies in the world lock away so much of its population and maintain a system that has disproportionately affected black and brown people in the US?

If one asks medical personnel in the US, they will tell you gun violence is also a human health problem. Similarly, for social scientists, crime is also a human development problem where criminality is enculturated in geographies of structural violence, where opportunities for social mobility are limited and good mentorship is difficult to find. Incarceration systems, like those in Germany and the Scandinavian countries that take the evidence of criminologists and cognitive psychologists seriously and apply their methods for altering such behaviors are seeing less recidivism and less crime. Looking globally, the research data point to a clear correlation in geographies of great economic inequality to higher crime rates and higher levels of suicide. In a highly competitive market system that clearly distinguishes its winners from the losers, equal opportunity is not only a moniker for fairness and equity, it also sets the conditions for a more peaceful, less violent society. Something as simple as universal pre-K, augmented funding for inner city K-12 schools, free vocational schools, and retraining fostering mentorship programs already in place in the US will go a long way toward decreasing the factors producing structural violence in our communities.

The question that underscores immigration, violent crime, incarceration, and gun rights comes back to: How do we view the value of community in the US? The most effective, long-lasting way to deprogram self-deprecating thoughts in the criminal mind is to re-introduce community, to transition inmates out of their physical and mental silos of hatred and ambivalence for others. Taking people out of their silos is what Ben Jealous documents in *Never Forget Our People Were Always Free: a Parable of American Healing*. We have the technology in genetic research companies to reconnect with our immigrant great-grandparents, retrieve our family connections, to build community from the past into the present. Part of us are them, and part of them are us.

Nearly three-quarters of U.S. gun owners cite protection as a major reason they own a gun

% of gun owners saying each is a ___ why they own a gun

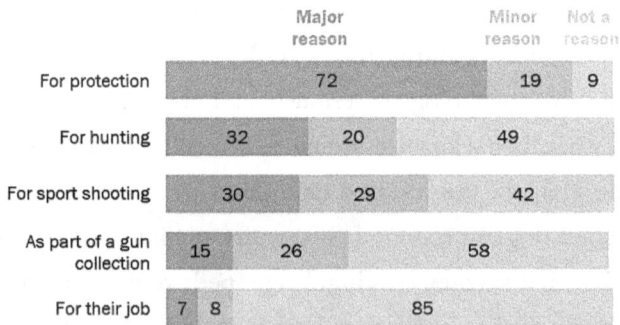

	Major reason	Minor reason	Not a reason
For protection	72	19	9
For hunting	32	20	49
For sport shooting	30	29	42
As part of a gun collection	15	26	58
For their job	7	8	85

Note: No answer responses are not shown.
Source: Survey of U.S. adults conducted June 5-11, 2023.

PEW RESEARCH CENTER

Figure 1 - Buying a gun for self-protection is now the most important reason cited for gun ownership

Since 2021, immigration concerns have surged among Republicans while holding steady among Democrats

% who say ___ should be a top priority for the president and Congress to address this year

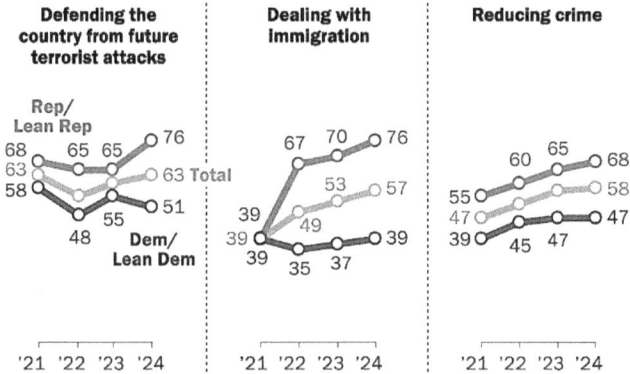

Defending the country from future terrorist attacks

Rep/Lean Rep
68
65 65 76
63
58 63 Total
55 51
48 Dem/Lean Dem

Dealing with immigration

67 70 76
53 57
39
39 49 39
39 35 37

Reducing crime

60 65 68
55 58
47 47
39 45 47

'21 '22 '23 '24   '21 '22 '23 '24   '21 '22 '23 '24

Source: Survey of U.S. adults conducted Jan. 16-21, 2024.

PEW RESEARCH CENTER

Figure 2 - Immigration, reducing crime, and terrorist attack concerns rising chiefly among Republicans

Criminality, Guns, Immigration, and "The Other" | 215

Chapter 5
Politics Beyond Division

Democracy As Usual?

In March 2022, something unexpected occurred at the sparsely attended budgetary meeting in the small West New Hampshire Town of Croydon.[310] About two-thirds of Croydon residents voted for Republican candidates in the US Presidential Election of 2020. Statewide, New Hampshirites pride themselves on independent thinking, political moderation, and libertarian-leaning state policies. Residents approved the town budget and moved on to the school budget, slated at $1.7 million. Then, a resident known for his Free-Stater "low-tax" views stepped up to the microphone, expressed his view that the school budget was a "ransom," and proposed cutting it to $800,000—reducing it by more than half.[311] Unexpectedly, residents in the poorly attended meeting voted 20 to 14 in favor of the proposal, and the budget passed.

But soon, the proposal's ramifications became clearer to town residents, especially those with children who would have to make up the shortfall, paying thousands of dollars to pay for their children's school budget and working extra hours to cover the costs. Slashing the budget meant upending students' educational continuity with the time and expenditure required to reallocate costs. Each student's educational trajectory had already been drastically affected by the COVID-19 pandemic. Some of the town's residents opposed to the measure mobilized to try and find a way to reverse the proposal.[312] In a surprising show of concern and political participation, on Saturday, 7 May 2022, nearly 60 percent of the Croydon populace came to the town hall to cast a new ballot to overturn the proposal 377-2.

While Croydon remains a good example where citizens of both parties came together across political lines to solve an imminent crisis, nationally, the gulf in trust and communication between Democrats and Republicans has reached a new and dysfunctional level. Twenty percent of Americans in a Pew Research poll conducted in 2022 believed division in society and government leadership was the single most important problem facing the country. About four out of five Americans thought their fellow citizens had too little confidence in each other.[313] From 1994 to 2022, the number of Americans who viewed both parties unfavorably rose from just 6 percent to 27 percent. Political ideologies have shifted since Obama's election, with new political movements like the fiscally conservative Tea Party emerging, though party branding has become more ideologically entrenched. The percentage of the US electorate self-designating as "independent" has increased to 42 percent, rising 10 percent since 2008. Individually, Americans have become more independent and less comfortable touting the party line in a new political landscape defined by its divisiveness.[314]

Thus far, I hope I have established that we do have a surprising amount of consensus in the United States on some of the most controversial and hotly debated issues confronting us. However, we have an even more existential problem ahead of us: empowering the consensus we can demonstrate. More citizens in the US now feel that our governmental deliberative process itself is broken, leaving any solutions to solving big problems or even discussing the issues at hand meaningless, a non-starter. In this chapter, I would like to ask some basic questions about these concerns and look at the polling data to help gauge the health of American democracy. Why is the consensus of the majority of Americans ignored in Washington? What hinders consensus-building in the US today?

What are our perceptions of political division in the US?

Though the US electorate has been characterized as engaged in a national contest of intense partisanship, polling data on Americans' attitudes about the state of politics in the US reveals a national electorate in transition, with inter-party divisions fracturing orthodox party ideologies. In an August 2002 Pew Research report, nearly four in ten Americans expressed a desire for more political parties, which just about matches the rising numbers of Americans who now self-identify as Independent.[315] One of the drivers of this transition is declining trust in the overall systems of national politics and politicians and polarization exhaustion registered in the national electorate of the past few years.

Polarization in the national electorate followed increasing negative perceptions of other party voters after the 2020 national election, with partisan media fanning the flames of division. In a July 2022 poll, 83 percent of Democrats believed that Republicans were close-minded, dishonest (64 percent), immoral (63 percent), and unintelligent (52 percent). Similarly, 69 percent of Republicans believed Democrats were close-minded, dishonest (72 percent), immoral (72 percent), and lazy (62 percent) (see Figure 1).[316] Polling suggests a widening perceptual division between party electorates, brought on by the socio-silo effect of increasingly mainstream Right/ Left news and information. However, widespread dissatisfaction with either Trump or Biden in the run up to the 2024 presidential election reflected not only the age issues of the candidates but also evolving interparty/generational divisions and growing dissatisfaction with the two-party system. As Pew Research noted in August 2022, half of all younger adults (18-29) said they "wish there were more parties to choose from."[317]

Overall, trust in the US government has gone down in America. As early as March 2018, 61 percent of US citizens polled supported the idea that "significant changes" were needed in the US government's fundamental "design and structure" to make it work today.[318] The percentage of citizens who believed that the US Government does what is right "most of the time" has declined significantly since 1965—when it was at a high of 77 percent—to 20 percent by May 2022.[319] This decline in trust was brought about by several historical factors, such as the national crises that emerged with the Vietnam War, Watergate, administrative justifications for the second Iraq War, and sustained political gridlock during the Obama years. Overall confidence in the US government has risen for brief periods, notably immediately after the crises brought on by 9/11, when overall trust in government rose to 60 percent as Americans mourned for those lost and national solidarity was galvanized. As our country has grown more staunchly partisan since the 1960s, trust in government in any one poll is notably higher among those whose party controls the presidency.[320]

There has also been a marked change in the political outlook of liberal Americans in recent years. Frustrated by what Democratic voters perceived as losses from political maneuvering on the Right, by 2018, Democrats became less willing to compromise on key issues. In the past, and as recently as the summer of 2017, Democrats were far more likely than Republicans to have positive views of elected officials who make compromises (69 percent). By the summer of 2018, only 46 percent of Democrats and 44 percent of Republicans supported elected officials who compromise with people they disagree with.[321] Now, Democrats have become even more frustrated with the erosion of liberties that specifically target their ideology—like women's right to choose. By the summer of 2018, Democrats' perspectives had hardened with the selection of Right-leaning US Supreme Court choices when 78 percent of Democratic respondents believed their side loses more often than wins.

A divided United States has ramifications for democracies worldwide and overall global security. Though the world went through unprecedented democratization beginning in the late 1980s with old Eastern Block countries, democratic rule has proven fragile in countries like the Philippines, Ukraine, and Israel. For many years, the US has represented a sanctuary for political expression for the rest of the world. Political dissent is part of the US's founding DNA, and our tolerance for division is still one of our great strengths. In a global attitudes survey undertaken by Pew Research in the Spring of 2017, majorities in 38 countries viewed representative democracy (78 percent) and direct democracy (66 percent) as a "good" way of governing a country versus rule by a strong leader (26 percent) or rule by the military (24 percent).[322] But polarization has grown in the US, and the threats that hold together American democracy are more fragile than they have been perhaps since the time of the

American Civil War. In this time of voter polarization and distrust in governance, it is worth reviewing what lessons we can learn from the formation of ancient democracies in their search for a sustainable government system and what lessons we can learn from our own political history.

What can we learn from ancient democracies?

Anthropologists who have studied modern tribal societies have noted the high levels of participation in community-level decision-making and the delicate balancing of individual power at the band level of social organization. A generalized form of egalitarianism in ancient tribal societies is presupposed in popular books like Jared Diamond's *The World Until Yesterday* and Yuval Harari's *Sapiens*. The presumption is that hierarchal rule in societies only emerged when societies grew in size with resource dependence on monocrop agriculture—beginning nine thousand years ago in the ancient Middle East. However, in a recent book titled *The Dawn of Everything,* anthropologists David Graeber and David Wengrow suggest that egalitarianism in all tribal societies of the recent and ancient past was far more culturally variable and nuanced than once presupposed. Some tribal societies kept war captives and allowed for the enslavement of others, for example. Even more significantly, they argue that modern archaeological evidence suggests the city-states that emerged beginning thousands of years ago, first in Mesopotamia, did not necessarily follow a generalizable societal evolution from egalitarianism to monarchy.

First evidenced in recorded history in Mesopotamia and Egypt, beginning some 5,500 years ago, human settlements began to grow beyond the size of a village into modest city-states with populations of a few tens of thousands. While Graeber and Wengrow acknowledge that social stratification became a defining feature of the ancient cities that emerged over millennia, they also document cases in early cities where diverse and egalitarian systems of government took hold. Some early cities lacked structural features like temples, palaces, central storage facilities, or narrative glyphs and inscriptions that would have signaled social stratification. Even truly large city-states like Teotihuacan in Central Mexico (c 1-500 C.E), with a population that rose to estimates of 125,000 residents, seemed to have begun as a hierarchical settlement but reversed course to follow a more egalitarian trajectory "supplying high-quality apartments of nearly all the city's population, regardless of wealth or status."[323]

The pre-Columbian city of Tlaxcala, Mexico, a city still occupied at the time of European contact with Spanish conquistadors, was ruled by a senate of some 200 individuals who earned their position through service to the state—one among many examples of flexible chiefdoms or meritocratic democracies that existed in tribal societies worldwide before contact with Europeans. Importantly, Wengrow and Graeber suggest that questions about the evolution of political hierarchy should be turned around to ask how the qualities of resource flexibility and political creativity, which they posit were once more common in human society, became fixed on a narrow view of how societies develop. Governance in pre-modern tribal societies could be variously equal opportunity, warrior cult-oriented, meritocratic, ruled by a religious order, or bureaucratically variable depending on the size and needs of the populous.

Consensus and Greek Democracy

The Eastern Mediterranean and Middle East went into decline, a Dark Age from 1200 BCE to 800 BCE. But during that time, the seafaring people of the Mediterranean—the Phoenicians—perfected the first alphabet that the ancient Greeks adapted. Coming out of its dark age, Greece was not a unified country; rather, it was a land of one hundred or so small-scale city-states (*polis*). Trading in olive oil obtained from a hard-scrabble agricultural system rooted in dry, rocky lands, the ancient Greeks created an economy of exchange and trade across the Mediterranean. Athens arose from the Dark Ages to become the preeminent city of trade in the region. In the 6th century BCE, Athens was an oligopoly, ruled by a government of aristocrats with an *archon* or chief magistrate heading affairs of state with the help of a *boule*, a council of nobles appointed to run city affairs. One benevolent and far-sighted archon named Solon came to power in 594 BCE during a crisis thought to have been caused by the debt servitude of many of its citizens. As an archon, Solon forgave citizens with protracted debt and abolished debt servitude permanently. Solon's great political innovation lay in creating an *ecclesia*, a voting general assembly of male non-elite landing-owning citizens who would become responsible for declaring war, formulating military strategy, and electing other officials.

Though Solon set the stage for political transformation in ancient Greece, ancient Athens' break with oligopoly and its embrace of a radical, experimental form of democracy occurred almost overnight. In 510 BCE, two political leaders, Cleisthenes and Isagoras vied for the position of archon. Isagoras usurped power with the help of soldiers from Athens' rival city-state, Sparta. He dispossessed hundreds of Athenians from their homes and sent his rival Cleisthenes into exile. Isagoras had become a *túrannos*, a "tyrant," and he set upon dissolving Athens' *boule* to rule as a supreme leader. The *boule* resisted, however, and a popular revolt ensued. The citizens of Athens surrounded Isagoras and his Spartan soldiers atop the high point, the Acropolis in Athens, and besieged him for two days. On the third day, Isagoras fled the city with his contingent of soldiers, and the citizenry banished him and immediately recalled Cleisthenes from exile.

Cleisthenes set about radicalizing the Athenian constitution, enabling the *demos,* or ordinary landowning male citizenry, to assume roles in diverse governmental functions, including the judiciary of Athens. Each member of the *demos* was required to register and serve for a term in the governing assembly. Cleisthenes also broke up and remolded traditional aristocratic tribes, radically democratizing positions of power and membership in a new, larger, and more inclusive *ecclesia.* Enabling the abrupt transformation of Athenian democracy were substantial increases in the literacy rate of Athens since the Dark Ages facilitated by an easy-to-learn alphabet, a rise in the autonomy of a merchant class, and a valorization of independent thought.

What was radical about Athenian democracy was the recognition that the power of elites was deeply embedded and that the path to democracy required a complete structural overhaul of the rules and membership of governance. The tyranny of Isagoras created a societal *flashover event* where momentum for change and transformation carried Athens into uncharted territory for political governance, a full break from emplaced structures of power, remolding city governance toward a path of participatory and deliberative consensus. Civic republicanism was not only valorized, it became an essential practice in a political system that mandated civic duty. Athens required all male landowning citizens to hold office as representatives in the Greek assembly at some point as adults. Perhaps the greatest legacy of Ancient Athenian democracy remains largely unheralded: it was Athenians' ability to acknowledge failure and continually work to make their form of Democracy function more smoothly and inclusively with every milestone in its evolution.

At its best, democracy in ancient Athens created legendary solidarity and strong independent thinking, exemplifying the power of people taking ownership of their society. Athenian solidarity was exemplified in the Battle of Marathon (490 BCE). Athenians faced a much larger Persian army. The Greek army, with better technology and battle tactics, but more significantly with ownership of their fate as free individuals, lost 192 men (to 6,400 Persians) and secured an overwhelming defeat. Democratic assemblies, at their worst, were a populous mass assuaged by charismatic orators to undertake impulsive actions that lacked foresight or caution. In 415 BCE, Athenians were persuaded by a young Athenian (Alcibiades) from a powerful family to mount a military expedition to the island now known as Sicily during the Peloponnesian War with Sparta. The expedition was initially corrupted by exaggerations of the plunder that could be had in the city-state of Syracuse—their destination and opposition. Expectations of an easy victory were overplayed, and the decision to return home and cut losses came too late. Athens lost two hundred ships and thousands of soldiers, a sizeable portion of its total army, and most likely ensured defeat to Sparta in the Peloponnesian War.

The Athenian democratic assembly failed to consider the cautions of a senior general, Nicias, who unwittingly increased the scale of the disaster by stating in the Athenian Assembly that the expedition would require an enormous force, believing this would quash any arguments to send a military expedition at all. Regardless, the Greek assembly agreed to go forward with the plan and added numbers to it, ignoring caution and advice, obsessed with the potential material gains. The disaster of the Battle of Sicily demonstrated that a government run by an assembly is only as strong as the collective intelligence of its members, the integrity of the information it provided, and the willingness of its leadership to take a stand against irrational and material mob-ruled decision-making.

Cautions from Roman Republicanism

"Acrimonious Debate, Strategies of Obstructionism Grip the Senate" might resemble a recent headline in Washington D.C., but it also mirrors scenes from Ancient Rome during the Late Republic (c.130 BCE). Ancient Rome threw out the rule by tyrants at about the same time as Ancient Greece. In 509 BCE, the last of the kings of Rome (Tarquin "the Proud") was deposed by a just leader, Lucius Junius Brutus. Romans built a political system of annually elected bureaucrats and magistrates with two elected consuls (co-supreme rulers) and an advisory council (a Senate of oligarchs). Later, a system of voting for Roman citizens and people's representatives known as *tribuni* were introduced into Rome's shared governance. The tribunes were the voice but also the hammer of the common citizens. They were positions that presided over the people's assembly, could propose legislation, and veto actions and legislation supported by Roman consuls or the senate—thus protecting the interests of the ordinary citizens of Rome.

Despite the framework for shared governance that the Roman Republic became lauded for, Rome's voting system was heavily weighted toward wealthy elites. It offered commoners some ownership of state policy—though income was proportional to representative power. A century after the philosopher Aristotle (384–322 BCE) wrote his many treatises which defined whole fields of knowledge, a Greek philosopher Polybius (200-118 BCE) wrote about the Roman Republic. When the Romans invaded the city-states of ancient Greece, Polybius was enslaved for a time and brought to Rome.

Rome's rising power and influence, its seemingly indefatigable will to the conquest of the Mediterranean peoples, prompted Polybius to study how the once small city had grown so powerful. Polybius asserted that Rome's governance combined elements of a monarchy (consul), oligarchy (senate), and democracy (plebiscite) and, in so doing, had created a resilient system of governance, a *republic* with built-in checks and balances that restrained the excesses of power inherent in each political structure on its own—one of the reasons why ancient Rome was considered a model government framework by the writers of the United States Constitution.

The Roman Republic faced a crisis between 133 BCE to 122 BCE, which eventually would help lead to the dissolution of its Republican framework. During those years, the Gracchi Brothers tried to reform the Roman Republic to meet the emergent needs of the common people. Both Tiberius Sempronius Gracchus and his brother Gaius were part of the elite class of Romans, who, nonetheless, championed common citizens' rights. Each was elected tribune in non-sequential terms. They both vigorously sought to redress economic instabilities and social inequality, including the lack of pay for soldiers. The Gracchi aimed to reclaim lands from wealthy members of the senatorial class, grant property to soldiers in pay for their service, clothe the poorest Roman soldiers, restore land to displaced peasants usurped by elites, provide subsidized grain for the needy, and expand citizenship to include the people of the Latin (Italian) Peninsula—especially to those who served in the Roman military. Unlike the Ancient Greeks, however, Roman elites were less willing to share their wealth or compromise their status. Tiberius Gracchus was clubbed to death in the Roman senate for pursuing this reform legislation, and Gaius was later sentenced to death during his tenure as tribune.

Unwilling to provide necessary reforms to the Roman Republic as it expanded its influence and territories, the Roman Senate would ensure that governing consuls-turned-generals like Julius Caesar would pay Roman armies out of their own pockets and plunder. The control and loyalty of the military were essentially taken away from the state and put into the hands of military leaders who assured the future of soldiers' prosperity. Had they been enacted, the Gracchi Reforms may have preserved the system of power-sharing that brought Rome to dominance in the Mediterranean region and beyond. The balanced power-sharing system ended abruptly with Julius Caesar's dictatorship, leading to cyclical governing instability by erratic dictators of the Roman Empire. The rule by dictators that was ushered in during the Roman Empire ensured that transitions of power would be bloody affairs and that the needs of the people would be wholly subject to the whims of the emperor. The change from a Republic to an Empire has been cited as one of the causes of the eventual dissolution of Ancient Rome. Much of the blame for the abrupt end of the Roman Republic can be attributed to the lack of solidarity in the Roman Senate and to factionalization that created divided loyalties and imploded the space for strong and decisive consensus when it was needed most.

How did US national politics become so divisive?

The Founding Fathers of the United States were well-versed in Greek and Roman history and concerned about factionalization in America as a consequence. However, a two-party political system came to define American political membership beginning in President Washington's second term. Political ideologies divided Thomas Jefferson's Democratic-Republican party, which championed civic republicanism and agrarianism, and the Federalist Party of Alexander

Hamilton and John Adams. The Federalist Party espoused a national federal system of governance with centralized banking, emphasizing a trade-oriented industrialized America. The polarization and enmity of the two parties prompted George Washington to dedicate his farewell address in 1796 to his concerns over increasing factionalization.

Washington believed party-line ideologies would divide the electorate into competing groups who might use violence to advance their interests, disrupt the separation of powers, and threaten effective representation by tempting elected officials to represent only fellow party members and to leave opposition groups without a voice in government.[324] Significantly, Washington also warned that societal division brought by party politics might bolster the rise of a despot:

> The alternate domination of one faction over another, sharpened by the spirit of revenge, natural to party dissension...is itself a frightful despotism. But this leads at length to a more formal and permanent despotism. The disorders and miseries which result gradually incline the minds of men to seek security and repose in the absolute power of an individual: and sooner or later the chief of some prevailing faction, more able or more fortunate than his competitors, turns this disposition to the purposes of his own elevation, on the ruins of Public Liberty.[325]

The ideological division gulf represented by the two prominent American parties of today is part and parcel of the tribalism inherent in winning political primaries. Primaries have put enormous pressure on Republican politicians to focus on a narrow bandwidth of galvanizing conservative issues, which represents a small portion of the many centrist policies Republican politicians once espoused. Democratic candidates facing primaries face the risk of becoming mired in identity politics, destabilizing the loyalty of working people whose primary concerns are economic security. It should be understood, however, that the ideologies that most define Republicans as conservative/libertarian and Democrats as liberal/populists have shifted considerably through time. Traditional party-line ideologies in the Trump era have ruptured abruptly, and new alignments and coalitions will play a strategic role in campaigns of the future.

In his recent book *Why We Are Polarized*, journalist Ezra Klein draws his readers back to the time in recent US history when fixed ideologies among Democrats and Republicans were less important than the party's brand.[326] Klein points out that before the 1980s, Republican and Democratic politicians were ideologically diverse. Republican presidential candidate Barry Goldwater, for example, was a staunch Right-wing libertarian who nonetheless supported the NAACP and the US Civil Rights Acts of 1957 and 1960. His strongly ideological views often collided with liberal Republicans like Jay Rockefeller and Mitt Romney's father, George Romney, governor of Michigan from 1963 to 1969. In Barry Goldwater's anti-centrist, libertarian acceptance speech at the 1964 Republican Convention, he stated:

> Extremism in the defense of liberty is no vice. And let me remind you also that moderation in the pursuit of justice is no virtue![327]

To which George Romney later replied:

Dogmatic ideological parties tend to splinter the political and social fabric of a Nation, lead to governmental crises and deadlocks, and stymie the compromises so often necessary to preserve freedom and achieve progress.[328]

Not so long ago, Republic presidents espoused views that would even be considered progressive today. Gerald R. Ford helped establish special education, admitted thousands of immigrants fleeing South Vietnam, expanded anti-trust laws, imposed more restrictions on campaign finance, and supported the Equal Rights Amendment. Richard Nixon helped to desegregate public schools and pass consumer protection laws and environmental legislation. He also created the EPA and OSHA, ended the military draft, raised the minimum wage, and expanded Social Security. Republicans were much more broad-minded. Even Ronald Reagan created amnesty for illegal immigrants who had established residency. For their part, the Democratic party, which was once popular in the American South, espoused conservative views on social justice and race issues. Klein points out that voters in the 1960s and 1970s often split their ticket and voted Republican and Democrat depending on the candidate and the position.

Since the 1980s, two factors have greatly contributed to the polarization of political views in Congress and the inability of congressional members to find consensus. Following every decennial census since 1980, state legislatures redraw congressional districts that favor incumbent candidates or tend to favor one party by concentrating the numbers of projected party-aligned voters in state congressional districts through remapping. The manipulation of congressional redistricting, known as gerrymandering, may involve tactics by state lawmakers like *cracking* (diluting the voting power of the opposing party's supporters across many districts) or *packing* (concentrating the opposing party's voting power in one district to reduce their voting power in other districts).

Gerrymandering has meant that political candidates now campaign in ever more partisan districts, often of their party's invention. Candidates' views are more highly partisan, particularly in red districts, in ever more competitive races that favor political philosophies that are ideologically more extreme and narrowly focused. Winning a primary in a congressional district now encourages candidates to be further to the Left, or to the Right to win over a more partisan base. This has also meant that the political ideologies of the candidates themselves have transformed toward those who favor and espouse more radical views. Success in politics is ever more predicated on ideological extremism, though political primary results registered in 2024 may be signaling movement toward the center in Democratic primaries.

How is money influencing politics?

In a January poll taken at the beginning of election-year politics 2024, the top of the public's "to-do" list for national legislatures remained to strengthen the economy. Rising in importance, however, was a concern over money in politics. While there are wide partisan differences on most policy goals, 65 percent of Democrats and 60 percent of Republicans rate this as a top priority, a super-majority by bipartisan consensus.[329]

High-stakes spending in political lobbying ballooned to enormous portions directly after the landmark *Citizens United v. Federal Election Commission* decision by the US Supreme Court on January 21, 2010. In the decision, the majority held (5-4) that the free speech clause of the Constitution's First Amendment prohibits the

US government from restricting independent financing of political campaigns by corporations, non-profits, labor unions, and other associations. In practice, political donations can be unlimited and anonymous. The *Citizens United* ruling took the restrictions off contributions, enabling large PACs, or Super PACS, to collect unlimited contributions from individuals, corporations, labor unions, and other PACs as well.

PACs, or *political action committees*, have existed since the early 1940s. PACs pool campaign contributions from members and donate those funds to campaigns for or against candidates, ballot initiatives, or legislation. To make an unlimited anonymous donation, a corporation gives money to *dark money* groups, which are 501(c)(4) and c(6) non-profit organizations that can accept unlimited contributions as long as this is not considered their primary activity. Normally, political contributions and donors are reported to the Federal Election Commission. Dark money spending is still reported to the Federal Election Commission but is reported without disclosing donors. Super PACs can contribute to a political cause and pay for travel and expenses, but most monies are spent on advertising for a political cause, party, or candidate. Funds are not paid directly to a candidate—this is still against the law. Justice Stevens wrote the minority dissent in the *Citizens United*, arguing that the ruling:

> Threatens to undermine the integrity of elected institutions across the Nation. The path it has taken to reach its outcome will, I fear, do damage to this institution... A democracy cannot function effectively when its constituent members believe laws are being bought and sold.[330]

In his short article titled "The Scale of US Election Spending Explained in Five Graphs," political scientist William Horncastle points out that the total US election expenditure by independent sources, including Super PACs, rose from $200 million in 2010 to $1.4 billion by 2016, a seven-fold jump.[331] During this same time, the proportion of undisclosed large donations doubled from $2 billion to $4 billion. This money comes from less than 1 percent of the US population and accounts for 74 percent of total contributions. OpenSecrets, a non-profit, non-partisan organization that tracks money in US politics and its effect on elections and public policy, estimated the total cost of the 2022 US midterm election at $8.9 billion, almost double what it was in 2014.[332]

The *Citizens United* decision was a victory for capital and lobbyists' influence over politics, most notably at the time it helped promote conservative/libertarian Republican ideologies. Now, however, Super PACs from both parties equally vie for the enormous expenditures on political influence. Two huge Super PACs that pool money from small donors have emerged: ActBlue, an American nonprofit technology organization established in 2004 raised $2.3 billion in 2021 and 2022. Likewise, WinRed, a similarly designed fundraising platform created for Republican causes and candidates, raised $1.8 billion in 2021 and 2022 in small contributions.[333]

One way the windfall in issue-directed revenue of Super PACs has influenced politics is in the tone of advertising, which tends to distort and magnify the consequences of legislation. Political adverts also tend to create *straw man arguments* or blame-oriented narratives focusing on a contender's personality, distracting from a candidate's role in policy decisions, legislation, or consensus-building. The hundreds of millions of dollars added to campaigns have only amplified the fear and distrust in the political public sphere of the United States. Following Justice Stevens' prognostication, overall revenue for political action is now in the control of far fewer hands, and the public's concerns are being manipulated by manufactured crises, such as election integrity. The profusion of ideologically infused advertising sows confusion and division, transforming common-sense reality into questionable truths for the benefit of special interests. Editors for *The New York Times* coalesced examples of election misinformation provided by 4,000 readers and noted trends in the ways this information was distributed through social media outlets that included:

- **Hoax floods** after major news events, in which misinformation across multiple platforms is released all at once to cover a wide zone of media coverage to sow confusion and uncertainty.
- **Poorly labeled campaign ads** that juxtaposed candidates next to WWII Nazis.
- **Russian Reddit manipulation** in which Russian nationals posted ads directing readers back to a false US-sounding address that, in fact, originated in Russia.
- **Voter suppression attempts** of all feints and disguises, urging voters like Democrat men to stay home in support of women's voting rights, for example.
- **Deceptive claims of candidates**, a strategy as old as the two-party election in the US, doctored photos, misquoted text, or decontextualized statements. And
- **"Sketchy" text messages** that seem to have no source or come from innuendo posted on social media.[334]

The overriding effect of Super PACs and political lobbyist influence on politics is that they work to erode any consensus of the voting public. Legislative priorities become focused on the single-issue policies of wealthy donor corporations and individuals who lobby for less regulation or restriction on their industry under the guise of "liberty" or to stifle policies and legislation that are popular to the American electorate at large, like corporate tax increases, or anti-trust enforcement and legislation that might increase free-market competition in the US.

Why are the most divisive politicians wielding the most power in the US?

During the 118th US Congress startup in late January 2023, two congressmen from the Problem Solvers Caucus, Josh Gottheimer (D-NJ) and Brian Fitzpatrick (R-PA), were interviewed on CNN. The Problem Solvers Caucus is a bipartisan group in the US House of Representatives that includes members equally divided between Democrats and Republicans, who seek to foster bipartisan cooperation on key policy issues. The group was created in January 2017 as an outgrowth of meetings held by the political organization No Labels starting in 2014. The discord in the Republican Party leading up to the election of a House Speaker in January 2023—with 15 votes taken and backstage deals with the 20 members of the Freedom Caucus—points to a big problem in the two-party American political system: a few more radical voices from each party are capable of holding an entire legislative branch captive to meet the narrow demands of a small minority.

The attention of national news media, particularly television newscasts, is heavily focused on the headline-grabbing politicians whose working output in Congress is often minimal. Most of the bills they propose are dead on arrival in a pluralistic congress, and what is approved is relatively minor—like funding for public spaces or statues in their district. But what is significant about the Problem Solvers Caucus is that they seldom receive any press coverage for compromising, consensus-seeking, and pushing bills through—arguably the most important part of the job of politicians. As philosopher Max Weber stated in the late 1800s:

> Politics is a strong and slow boring of hard boards. It takes both passion and perspective. Certainly, all historical experience confirms the truth – that man would not have attained the possible unless time and again he had reached out for the impossible. But to do that a man must be a leader, and not only a leader but a hero as well, in a very sober sense of the word.[335]

In Weber's assertion, the measure of legislative and leadership effectiveness is the ability of a politician to represent their community and their collective interests inclusively, then to translate those interests through compromise and legislate to solve urgent issues, however difficult the process might be. That is their job. Increasingly, national political progress has been obstructed by a vocal minority in Congress empowered by the sole prospect of winning primaries in heavily gerrymandered districts—a *tyranny of the minority*, as Teddy Roosevelt noted, responding to John Stuart Mill.

Writing in the mid-1800s at a time when British colonialism was beginning to spread throughout the world, the British political philosopher John Stuart Mill believed a "tyranny of the majority" should be of most concern in politics, stating that:

The evils against which society requires to be on its guard... there needs protection also against the tyranny of the prevailing opinion and feeling; against the tendency of society to impose, by other means than civil penalties, its own ideas and practices as rules of conduct on those who dissent from them...There is a limit to the legitimate interference of collective opinion with individual independence: and to find that limit, and maintain it against encroachment, is as indispensable to a good condition of human affairs, as protection against political despotism.[336]

Fifty years after Mill's essay, Theodore Roosevelt, in a speech delivered on March 20, 1912, observed that the reality of a democratic system linked directly to capitalism meant the political world had shifted from Mill's time. The rise of the very wealthy meant there would always be a tendency toward a "tyranny of the minority," of those seeking profit and political influence at the expense of public welfare:

I have scant patience with this talk of the tyranny of the majority. Wherever there is tyranny of the majority, I shall protest against it with all my heart and soul. But we are today suffering from the tyranny of minorities. It is a small minority that is grabbing our coal-deposits, our water-powers, and our harbor fronts. A small minority is battening on the sale of adulterated foods and drugs. It is a small minority that lies behind monopolies and trusts. It is a small minority that stands behind the present law of master and servant, the sweat-shops, and the whole calendar of social and industrial injustice. It is a small minority that is today using our convention system to defeat the will of a majority of the people in the choice of delegates to the Chicago Convention.[337]

Certainly, US national politics have been stultified by majorities within the Houses of government. In the 1950s, the tyranny of the white majority in the South's legislature was deeply at odds with their Black and "invisible" constituencies, the Northern states, and the trajectory of the natios of the world as a whole. Lingering Jim Crow Laws codified by "separate but equal" euphemisms were, in fact, separate and very unequal. In the United States, the tyranny of the majority can be rebalanced by the power-sharing of the three branches, one of the key insights of the founding fathers. However, more often, it is the tyranny of the minority purporting to represent the majority in the US who take away from the fundamental liberties and legislative priorities of the larger consensus of Americans.

In the early 1950s, the hunt for communist infiltration in the US government by Senator Joe McCarthy began with grandiose declarations of the widespread scale of the infiltration, bringing even more anxiety to a nation living with the prospect of atomic Armageddon. The media coverage for McCarthy's senate hearings was sensational in their day and lifted McCarthy into national prominence as the chair of the Senate Permanent Subcommittee on Investigations. In the end, however, the national search for communist operatives yielded nothing and no one. Instead, the investigations worked to blackmail film producers and homosexual government workers into testifying against their cohorts. During the same time, the US was leading covert CIA operations that would undermine democratically elected governments in Guatemala, Iran, and Chile, setting the table for dictators and quashing legitimate political dissent for decades in many parts of the world. Historically, it is often a bombastic minority in US politics that has worked to distract the eyes of average Americans away from less visible threats to liberty and democracy in the nation and in the world.

Is the two-party divide as polarized as it seems to be?

There is a lot of variation in Democratic and Republican views. Political ideologies can be grouped or broken down in numerous ways, even atomized into basic units of one individual with one unique political outlook. The diversity of perspectives within the two large parties in the United States has increasingly made it harder to form consensus in one party, let alone in an entire legislative body. Pew Research suggests political polarization represents an overly simplistic understanding of shifting ideological groupings within the parties; ideological coalitions more clearly define voters within the parties now. Ideologies long associated with the GOP, an affinity for businesses and corporations (which includes support for low taxes), and opposition to abortion are being fractured by individual candidates strategizing for a longer road toward general elections. For Pew:

> Democrats [also] face substantial internal differences as well – some that are long-standing, such as on the importance of religion in society, others more recent. For example, while Democrats widely share the goal of combating racial inequality in the United States, they differ on whether systemic change is required to achieve that goal. These intraparty disagreements present multiple challenges for both parties: They complicate the already difficult task of governing in a divided nation. In addition, to succeed politically, the parties must maintain the loyalty of highly politically engaged, more ideological voters while also attracting support among less engaged voters—many of them younger—with weaker partisan ties. Democrat-leaning voters are ideologically divided between the *Progressive Left*, voters seeking substantial societal reorganization of power structures, and *Establishment Liberals*, who are less persuaded of the need for sweeping change.[338]

Pew also identifies *Democratic Mainstays* in the electorate at large, older party folks who are moderate on views, and *Outsider Lefts*, younger voters who are deeply frustrated with politics and politicians in general (see Figure 2).

According to Pew Research, Republican-leaning voters have coalesced into four groups: Faith and Flag Conservatives, voters who are intensely conservative voters on all social and economic issues; Committed Conservatives who have a "somewhat softer edge, particularly on issues of immigration and America's place in the world"; and the Populist Right, voters with less formal education than most other typology groups and are among the most likely to live in rural areas. Significantly, the Populist Right voters are highly critical of immigration but also of major US corporations and tax breaks for the rich, an Achilles heel now for Republican policies that have favored special interest groups and tax policies for the wealthy. New to Republican coalitions is an Ambivalent Right, according to Pew:

> The youngest and least conservative GOP-aligned group, which holds conservative views about the size of government, the economic system and issues of race and gender. But they are the only group on the political right in which majorities favor legal abortion and say marijuana should be legal for recreational and medical use.[339]

Significantly, the *Ambivalent Right* and the *Populist Right* also compose the most independent voters on the Right, presenting an interesting political dynamic for politicians staking our political territory in either party. The last coalition Pew identified is the *Stressed Sideliners*, "who comprise 15 percent of the public but constituted just 10 percent of voters in 2020."[340] With a mix of conservative and liberal views, they are "largely defined by their minimal interest in politics." Still, they may be an important factor in future elections if voter enthusiasm or revulsion for a candidate is mobilized.

More and more voters may be put into play across party lines as Republican candidates outline unpopular policies like outlawing abortion, promoting no-license gun carry laws, or tax breaks for the wealthy or corporations. Democrats face their challenges with how far progressives push identity politics in the heartland or focus on social issues that ignore the broader demographic of underclass Americans. Florida's governor, Ron DeSantis, greatly politicized education in Florida. Polls indicate, however, that the insertion of politics into education is unpopular nationally, and legislation that allows governments to intervene in mostly autonomous institutions is unpopular among the Ambivalent Right and libertarian conservatives, and a growing number of Democratic coalitions.

In California, the state assembly naively politicized higher education in 2021. California assembly members passed AB 928 in an attempt to streamline college general education. They ended up altering long-debated and coalesced college curriculums (foreign language curriculums were gutted), subverting consultation with higher educators, and throwing more adjunct faculty out of work in a time of decreasing enrollments. As a result of AB 928, college students can now receive a Bachelor of Arts degree in California State Universities without taking a single course focused on the world outside of the United States. While this may not seem a high priority for some Americans, national and state government intervention in institutions and individual liberties may galvanize new political coalitions to cross party lines in our political assemblies. There are many shared concerns between the *Populist Right* and *Democratic Mainstays* on labor concerns and economic inequality, for example, or between *Progressive Left* and *Populist Rights* on political structural changes. *Committed Conservatives* and *Democratic Mainstays* might find consensus on abortion and immigration issues easier to negotiate on the national stage. There may be a future ideological connection awaiting between *Libertarians, Stressed Sideliners,* and *Outsider Lefts* who want politics out of institutions that have thrived on autonomy and self-governance. Such coalitions may help bridge the impasse of Right and Left partisanship and smooth the process of consensus-building in Congress in the near future.

Are we concerned about the health of our democracy?

In a poll conducted in June of 2023 by Pew Research, just below "inflation" and "the affordability of health care," 63 percent of Republican-leaners and 62 percent of Democrat-leaners polled believed the inability of Dem-Reps to work together to be a very big problem in the US.[341] What do Americans believe is the cause of divisiveness in the nation? When asked what the answer of US voters ranged across various concerns and causes. A quarter of those polled believed divisions among Americans were tied to political polarization and tribalism. In 1994, only 21 percent of Republicans had a "very unfavorable" view of the Democratic Party, and of Democrats at that time, only 17 percent had a "very unfavorable" view of Republicans.[342] As political rhetoric and venom ratcheted up in the media, so did the antipathy. By 2022, 62 percent of Republicans had a "very unfavorable" view of the Democratic Party, and 54 percent of Democrats had a "very unfavorable" view of Republicans.[343]

More concerning than political polarization is what polarization has done to the social fabric of the United States. Americans' confidence in other Americans has declined precipitously in the last thirty years, with 71 percent of Americans believing interpersonal trust has declined in a Pew Research poll taken in 2019. When asked why, 11 percent of the respondents believed that Americans, on the whole, have become more lazy, greedy, and dishonest. Some 16 percent of respondents make a connection between what they think is poor government performance—especially gridlock in Washington—and the toll it has taken on their fellow citizens' hearts. About one-in-ten of these respondents say they blame the news media and its focus on divisive and sensational coverage.

Have we lost all trust in one another? Twenty-five percent of US adults describe a lack of interpersonal confidence as a big problem for the nation, and another 50 percent stated it was a moderately big problem—we are at least acknowledging our issues, the first step in resolving our differences.[344] How far does our mistrust extend? In a poll of 2019 Pew Research poll of 5000 adults of mixed politics, a fifth or 21 percent of those surveyed agreed with the statement that "personal trust is dropping even though people are as reliable as they have always been."[345] In another report initiated in 2021 by the Harvard School of Education, about two-thirds in their survey of US respondents stated that they still cared about other Americans regardless of their political news.[346] Certainly, when Americans see fellow citizens suffering due to weather extremes like floods or wildfires, we can still feel enormous compassion for another's loss and muster support in generous ways. Americans have the potential for compassion for people they don't know or are unfamiliar with. But barring natural catastrophes, citizens in the US mostly confine their empathy to people they know, family, and fellow Americans they understand well.

However, Americans, by and large, still mostly appreciate our diversity. Two-thirds of Americans polled believe—if given the option—they would rather live in a politically diverse neighborhood than a politically homogenous one. Americans are ambivalent about communicating with others with distinctly different political views.[347] And yet, the 61 percent of Americans polled would talk to someone whose views differ if assured they "would be listened to respectfully."[348] If our conversations could be mediated productively, we would be more willing to address our differences. It is the lack of good mediation environments more than our ability to converse with someone that divides us today. It is also still easier to understand one's "band" than to try to understand the abstraction of US society's many or to relate to a group generalized into one of many popularly used labels. Americans acknowledge societal divisions but they also signal they want to move beyond them.

For a time, it seemed the US democratic process itself began to be questioned directly before and after the national elections of 2020. A Pew Research poll in March of 2018 found that most Americans still expressed approval of the main tenets of the balance of governmental powers. Large majorities in both parties, for example (70 percent of Republicans and 83 percent of Democrats), opposed the idea of giving presidents more power.[349] Despite the frightening views of insurgents storming the US Capitol to wrest control away from Congress, most Americans still stated that politicians should heed the will of the majority even if their views differ:

> Three-quarters of Americans say that in a hypothetical scenario, a governor should sign a bill that has support from most people in their state, even if most of his or her supporters oppose it.[350]

Most Americans still fundamentally believe in the authorizing power of consensus.

How can Americans mobilize the full power of the consensus we have?

While watching one of the Black Lives Matter protests in Oakland, California, in the Summer of 2020, I was watching local television news when I saw a picture of a middle-aged African-American woman carrying a sign that read: "Black Lives Do Matter - Now Go Vote!" I had just spent the spring semester telling my students that if they wanted to engage in consequential and effective activism, they should help register people to vote. The overall voting rate in the US presidential elections in 1968 was 68 percent. With so much on the line in elections, including the Vietnam War national draft, young adult white voting participation was at a high of 53 percent, which has not been duplicated since.[351] By 1996, voting participation had shallowed out to 54 percent nationally and 32 percent for younger voters.[352] Voter participation climbed in 2020, reaching 61 percent for all ages nationally and 48 percent for younger voters, a marked increase from 2016 and an indication that overall political participation in the nation was growing once again across all ages—though not back to the all-time high for young African-American voter participation in 2008.[353]

Americans are becoming more engaged politically, following the high levels of community-level participation that have defined American democracy. A February 2018 Pew Research poll queried Americans' political activities in the five years leading up to that poll. Twenty-eight percent of Americans stated they participated in a political rally, 42 percent shared their political opinions with others through social media, 29 percent contributed money to political organizations or had attended a local government meeting, and 40 percent contacted an election official.[354] Overall, a large majority

(67 percent) reported having engaged in at least one politically motivated activity in the past five years.[355] Many Americans may not consider themselves politically active, but community/political participation is common among US citizens. The relatively high rates of community participation and the large numbers of community organizations in America correspond to the observations of a French intellectual named Alexis de Tocqueville (1805-1859), who toured the US beginning in 1831 and wrote up his observations in a book titled *Democracy in America* (1835 & 1840).

De Tocqueville looked at America as an experiment in democracy, a sample of how democratic nations would decrease inborn social privilege in the world overall as modern governments came of age. De Tocqueville also saw in America an absence of traditional community and history that was vital to the European social fabric. Without established organizations like guilds common in Europe, Americans created voluntary community organizations like the National Parent Teacher Association (founded in 1897) or church groups. De Tocqueville discussed possible threats to US democracy as well. These include his belief that our democracy may tend to degenerate into "soft despotism" caused by "a network of small complicated rules" degrading civic cohesiveness.[356] De Tocqueville pointed out possible paradoxes in the US in what came to be known as the *Tocqueville effect*, defined as an overall societal frustration that increases as social conditions improve. In effect, he was stating that democratic/economic success in and of itself breeds discontent, an *affluenza*, that a percentage of our electorate believes afflicts Americans today. He was cautious about the independent disposition of Americans, that our valorization of personal independence might contribute to social isolation and the conditions for community fragmentation.

As the first territory in modern history to partition from an immensely powerful colonial, the United Kingdom, the United States pioneered the very conception of a democratic revolution. But ironically, the US owes some of its successful partition to the anti-monarchial Whig Party which managed to defund the war and thwart King George III's desire to keep fighting on. The United Kingdom, for its part, pioneered the democratic processes we hold dear, including the successful transition of power which has been forged through centuries of bloodshed that led to a representative government in the United Kingdom. America owes part of its founding to its refusal to pay taxes without the vote of the governed, a grounded centuries-old English parliamentarian ethic, and to the vote in the parliament of the United Kingdom to discontinue the Revolutionary War. In essence, the key to our success is the vote. When asked what makes a good citizen in the 2018 Pew Research Poll, "voting" polled as the number one most significant way to be a "good citizen" in the US by 74 percent of those Americans polled, with an even higher percentage (90 percent) of Americans conceding it is at least somewhat important to being a good citizen.[357] If voting is a core value in American democracy, shouldn't we continue to make voting convenient for working men and women while ensuring accuracy and fidelity?

In their book *100 Percent Democracy: The Case for Universal Voting*, E. J. Dionne Jr. and Miles Rapoport suggest there are several ways voter participation in the US could be increased, which include (1) same-day registration, already in place in the 1970s in the states of Maine, Minnesota, and Wisconsin.[358] Twenty states and the District of Columbia have adopted (2) automatic voter registration policies, and California has enacted "safe harbor" provisions to protect against those few added my mistake. E. J. Dionne Jr. and Miles Rapoport also suggest (3) enfranchising Americans with felony convictions, (4) including all states in online voter registration (40 states now provide this), (5) allowing early voting (43 states now allow), and (6) vote by mail (29 states)—measures that facilitate no-excuse absentee voting.

Voter turnout in the 2020 US general election soared, fueled by the bitter campaign between Joe Biden and Donald Trump. Voter turnout was also facilitated by pandemic-related changes that eased the voting process in most states, verifying at least to some extent that making voting more convenient to working men and women increases turnout. This is one of the primary assertions in E.J. Dionne Jr. and Miles Rapoport's book. According to US Census data, 66.8 percent of the American voting-age population voted in 2020.[359] Leading up to the 2022 midterms, according to a Pew Research Center survey, 72 percent of registered voters stated they were "extremely" or "very" motivated to vote, and significantly, 65 percent stated that it really mattered to them which party wins control of Congress.[360] This signals that voters in all demographics may be reasserting their political agency once again, contrasting with periods following 1968 when low voter turnouts became the norm.

Americans are more conscious than ever that elections have consequences. A backlash against voter suppression tactics has hardened the resolve of voters on the Left, where 20 percent more progressives have indicated they are less willing to support candidates who compromise. Political consciousness has risen generally, particularly among younger adults. Non-partisan organizations like *Global Citizen* have emerged that have made civic republicanism "cool" again, making grassroots activism on urgent global issues accessible to motivated younger voters.[361] Other non-partisan organizations like The League of Women Voters (founded 1919), The Voting Rights Alliance, and HeadCount—which register people to vote at concerts and online—are reaching traditionally less-represented voting demographics, particularly younger voters, where they live and where they associate.

At some point in the near future, the American political duopoly may fragment into a number of different coalition parties. The Republican Party platform in many congressional districts has become so narrowed to the far-Right—to sustain primary challenges—that it doesn't seem likely the party will ever win a presidential election without a considerable partition of swing-state Republicans embracing centrist policies that win general elections. And almost half of all Republicans polled in January 2023 believed it was more important to compromise than to get all they want in national policies. Donald Trump is holding back the Republican Party, increasing the party's prospects of remaining a permanent minority. In May 2023, both frontrunners for the US Presidential race, Trump and Biden, were "strikingly unpopular—two-thirds of Americans don't want Trump to run for president again, and just 41 percent approve of Biden's job performance," according to a poll from NPR/PBS NewsHour/Marist.[362] However, "the [surprising] Democratic performance in the 2022 midterm elections and other recent polling suggests voters who don't like Biden might [have] cast a ballot for him anyway." There are more registered American independent voters now than there have been in the US. Staying out of the middle political ground in the US will increasingly factor into being (un) elected in subsequent elections. Divisive rhetoric may yet outlive its utility.

National non-partisan organizations that register voters have a history of unparalleled consequences on national politics: in 2008, they helped elect the first biracial president. Though voting turnout in the US was 68 percent in 2020—and the highest since 1968—how much would the political landscape in the United States change if we had the kind of voting percentages of other countries like Belgium (87.2 percent), Sweden (82.6 percent), Australia (79 percent), Italy (71 percent), or South Korea (78 percent)?[363] It was estimated that over 50 percent of young people, ages 18-29, voted in the 2020 presidential election, a remarkable 11 percent increase from 2016 (39 percent) and one of the highest rates of youth electoral participation since the voting age was lowered to 18 in 1972.[364]

However, if voting participation goes up to just 60 percent for those aged 18-29, politicians would have to address a slate of concerns that come closer to the true consensus of the US population. Do we have to make voting compulsory to get citizens to the polls in the US, as they do in Sweden, Australia, or Brazil? I think not. We have the motivation, we just need to make it less time-consuming and convenient to a working nation. Why not make election day a national holiday? This idea was part of the Federal Freedom to Vote Act, which was blocked by a US Republican Senate filibuster in 2021, but we need to revisit portions of the bill where consensus can be met. What a message of hope and confidence this would send to the world, to those still living under the repression of dictatorships—a simple act, a profound gesture, a US national holiday that honors democracy. Seventy-two percent of Americans polled in early 2024 favor an Election Day Holiday. Let's make it happen.[365]

Discussion – Is it Time to Recenter and Focus?

Are we going to be able to cure polarization or alleviate it? In his book *Why We're Polarized*, Ezra Klein confesses that the causes of US polarization are complex and multidimensional. Rather than alleviating it, he suggests we focus on managing it. Both the US Senate and US House of Representatives could change standing rules to unblock much of the political gridlock. "Bombproofing" the debt ceiling in the US House of Representatives would be a start. In May 2023, House Republicans provided the President and Democratic-controlled Senate with a list of programs to defund before they signed off on legislation already voted and approved. Refusing to sign off on the debt ceiling has become a backdoor political tactic by Republicans to block national expenditures in programs already legislated, subverting any consensus previously reached.

As the rules stand now, the US Senate Majority and House Majority Leaders schedule the daily legislative program. This rule gives enormous power to one person to obstruct voting or to hold politicians accountable for their vote on legislation. US Senate and House leaders can stall or even eliminate legislation moving forward without producing a vote of record for bills that have overwhelming support in the US electorate on a host of urgent issues outlined in this book. The degree to which the US Congress has enabled grid-lock by their own device is truly frustrating to Americans and one of the primary reasons why approval ratings of the US Government doing the "right thing most of the time" fell from 77 percent in 1964 to 20 percent by 2015.[366] The Congress of the United States, like the US populace in general, has become more polarized. This follows. But they have also promulgated rules that ensure political gridlock is here to stay, like filibuster rules in the US Senate or the fact that the leaders of the US Senate and House control when or if to vote on proposed legislation. The public should insist that on all legisla-tion every politician's vote be recorded, that their policy position be transparently acknowledged.

The radical transformation to full democracy in Ancient Greece occurred in a historical instant, but it was centuries in the making. The Ancient Greek epic of the *Iliad* portrayed a patriarchal society that could be polarized by strong independent voices in intense debates that nonetheless resolved into powerfully unified and decisive action. But democracy in Ancient Greece was only one noteworthy template for a society ruled by shared governance. For tens of thousands of years, democracies of the small scales thrived in all parts of the world. The challenge to creating democratic societies was creating culturally appropriate models that could function sustainably, adding bureaucratic orders as populations grew, and scaling down or reforming republics when power became too concentrated. For the Ancient Greek writer Polybius, a system of balanced power created by ancient Romans melded the strengths of monarchy (consuls), oligarchy (senate), and democracy (plebs) into a functional and flexible system that adapted to empower those from below.

The Roman Republic was not demolished overnight. A series of elected consuls (chief magistrates) expanded the power of their position by paying their armies and enacting popular policies for the masses that the Roman Senate could not obsessed with preserving their elitism. Julius Caesar crossed the Rubicon River and brought his legion to Rome with a template for a dictatorship that would follow to this day: using populist rhetoric and support, installing supporters in governing legislatures, and mobilizing a personal army. Rome never came back to its Republican political structure that enabled its rise from a small city-state. At the Rubicon River, Julius Caesar read over a Roman Senate declaration that stated he was to disband his legion and walk into Rome, where he would face judicial scrutiny for his actions against the state. It is at this moment when democracies are most vulnerable, when popular leaders are faced with conceding their power or to "go all in" on the dice they have rolled and assert authoritarian control.

How much of our political polarization in the US is real, and how much of it is due to what politicians would like us to believe, motivating us to vote for party-as-tribe? True political/ideological differences in the US can be broken down not by which side of a political issue one stands on. Rather, an individual's total political outlook is where, on an ideological continuum, they stand on a whole set of sociopolitical and socioeconomic issues in the aggregate. But this leaves an immense amount of nuance along this continuum for individual choice, sorting where one stands on hundreds of policies, ideologies, and transition points. If you, as a US voter, feel people should be able to own guns without restriction, then you must inherently be less concerned that people need restrictions on gun ownership; your concerns, therefore, might be considered libertarian on the freedom of gun ownership. Suppose you feel that gun ownership should be restricted or even banned. In that case, you are inherently Hobbesian or conservative on gun ownership, wary that human beings seem less capable of controlling their baser instincts and require more gun restraint. Voting to lower taxes on billionaires—which inflates the national debt—isn't a conservative gesture, it is a liberal one. We need to understand that the meaning of terms like "conservative" or "liberal" have mostly lost their meaning. Comparing candidates' policies one by one with our own is more important than ever.

In July 2022, Andrew Yang, one of the independent voices in the 2020 presidential elections, announced the founding of a new centrist Forward Party. Forming coalition parties based on new groupings of political ideologies offers the chance to break the political two-party dichotomy in the US. If such parties are accompanied by ranked-choice voting (RCV), which is now used statewide in Maine and Alaska and in local jurisdictions in some Blue States, there is a chance that third-party candidates may win office and force Republican and Democratic politicians to compromise and form voting coalitions in the congressional chambers. In RCV, voters prioritize (rank) their choice of candidates among many, potentially allowing small support of an outside candidate to balloon up with successive voting. Yang promises not to be a "spoiler" party. This could be accomplished by campaigning but dropping out if a critical mass of voters hasn't been reached a few weeks before mail-in ballots go out. In this way, third-party candidates may be able to break up the duopoly in the US in the near future. More importantly, in leveraging coalition capital, third-party politicians may help provide more representative political groupings of today's population demographics.

Sixty-five percent of the people polled in the US, including half of Republican voters, would accept a rational compromise to alleviate some of America's toughest problems. So where, then, is the center in the United States? And why has it seemed to have moved to the Right? The short answer is the American political center hasn't moved to the Right, but Republican members of the US national legislatures have. This has dramatically altered our view of the extent of polarization in the US, but also where the true political center of the country lies. The General Social Survey (GSS) has tracked national lawmakers' roll call votes and placed them ideologically through time from the 92nd Congress in 1971-72 to the 117th Congress of 2021-22, comparatively. According to NYU researchers using GSS data, representatives of both "parties have moved further away from the ideological center since the early 1970s. Democrats, on average, have become somewhat more liberal, while Republicans, on average, have become much more conservative."[367]

As polarization has increased, both parties over time have grown more ideologically cohesive. There are now only about two dozen moderate Democrats and Republicans left on Capitol Hill, versus more than 160 counted in 1971-72.[368] At the same time, Americans' attitudes and behaviors have actually become more liberal overall in the past 50 years on matters of gender, sexuality, race, and personal liberty than they were in the 1970s.[369] Though the center has remained static on a few hot-button issues such as gun ownership, abortion, taxes, and law enforcement, all of which have remained polarized over the last half-century, there is abundant middle ground for solutions on these hot-button issues now as there was then. The political will to make change will ultimately have to come from below—the vote.

Gerrymandering has ensured that most of our national politicians are ideologically very partisan, particularly on the Right. This has contributed to the false perception that there has been a Right tilt in the center of national politics when, in fact, the tilt of the center over the last forty years has been to the Left. This warps our views of national consensus and where rational center-based compromise might exist. The Lugar Center, established by Republican Senator Richard Lugar, has published a Bipartisan Index, "an objective measurement of the frequency with which a Member co-sponsors a bill introduced by the opposite party and the frequency with which a Member's bills attract co-sponsors from the opposite party."[370] As a US senator, Joe Biden ranked "very good" on the Lugar score, demonstrating his willingness to work with Republicans, exemplifying a comparatively centrist legislative record.

Biden's presidential and legislative successes were still comparatively populist and centrist, emphasizing infrastructure, education, healthcare, and green technology with economic repercussions in mind. Realistically, whoever owns the middle ground in the US can galvanize independents and will win the national election for the foreseeable future—so long as they can communicate effectively and define their own and their opposition's ideology clearly, with governing policy in focus. To win, both parties will have to broaden their appeal to independents and the populist center. For Republicans, that seems like a much heavier lift, or may at least force them to run through their primary on the hard Right and pivot to the middle in the general election, hoping most independents simply forget all of their statements and legislation that has gone before. While polarization rules primaries for the moment, the growing chorus of independent voters will rule the general election.

To make clear where US consensus exists in the US, I propose a new index following the purpose of the Lugar Center's Bipartisan Index. This nonpartisan index would measure the degree to which individual US Senators and Representatives work across party lines on legislation. We need to tie that index to polling data, to see where the US populace stands on proposed legislation nationally, and apply a corresponding score to measure how closely national candidates follow the national consensus. We need a clear and concise way to measure a candidate's ability to get work done and to hold them accountable to the many and not a few. We should have an index that equates factors like the ability to negotiate and engage diplomatically as fitness and not just the ability to attract attention, manufacture outrage, or raise money.

Majoritarian democracy creates robust citizen buy-in. To get beyond polarization, the US needs more nationally televised town halls and citizen panels; mediated conversations that enable understanding of the concerns of the other side to know where concerns are coming from. It is not enough to hear politicians spin the concerns of ordinary Americans, it is important to hear them for ourselves. This was exemplified at the local level in Croydon, New Hampshire. The structure was in place to exercise meaningful public sphere discussions in Croydon, but complacency had set in. It was thought that funding education would be agreed upon, "business as usual." There was a feeling, like there was once in the US, that the democratic process could function well without the need for active participation. "Showing up. That's the big lesson…And not just showing up, but also knowing what's going on," reflected Croydon resident Chris Prost."[371] The cure for political gridlock, for producing legislation that mirrors the majority's will, lies in the vote. Increasing voter turnout across a diversity of demographics sends an unequivocal message to candidates. Nothing opens up the mind of a political candidate more than needing a broader public to win their election.

Growing shares of both Republicans and Democrats say members of the other party are more immoral, dishonest, closed-minded than other Americans

% who say members of the *other* party are a lot/somewhat more ___ compared to other Americans

⚬ Republicans say Democrats are more …
⚬ Democrats say Republicans are more …

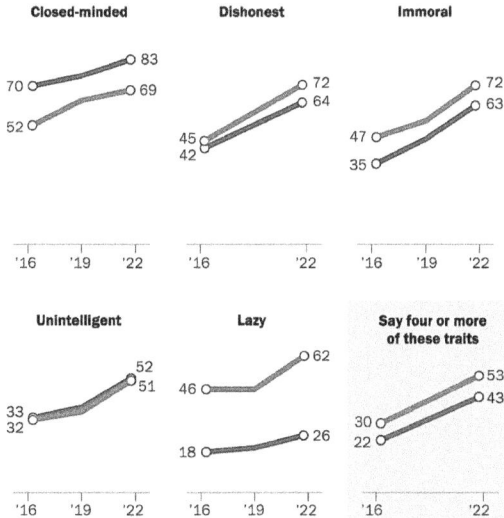

Closed-minded

70
52
83
69

'16   '19   '22

Dishonest

45
42
72
64

'16   '22

Immoral

47
35
72
63

'16   '19   '22

Unintelligent

33
32
52
51

'16   '19   '22

Lazy

46
18
62
26

'16   '19   '22

Say four or more of these traits

30
22
53
43

'16   '22

Note: Partisans do not include those who lean to each party.
Source: Survey of U.S. adults conducted June 27-July 4, 2022.

PEW RESEARCH CENTER

Figure 1 - Partisan generalizations of the opposite party members

The 2021 political typology

% of ____ who are ...

	General public	Rep/Lean Rep	Dem/Lean Dem
Faith and Flag Conservatives	10	23	6
Committed Conservatives	7		13
Populist Right	11	15	16
Ambivalent Right	12		
Stressed Sideliners	15	23	28
Outsider Left	10	18	23
Democratic Mainstays	16		
Establishment Liberals	13	15	12
Progressive Left	6		

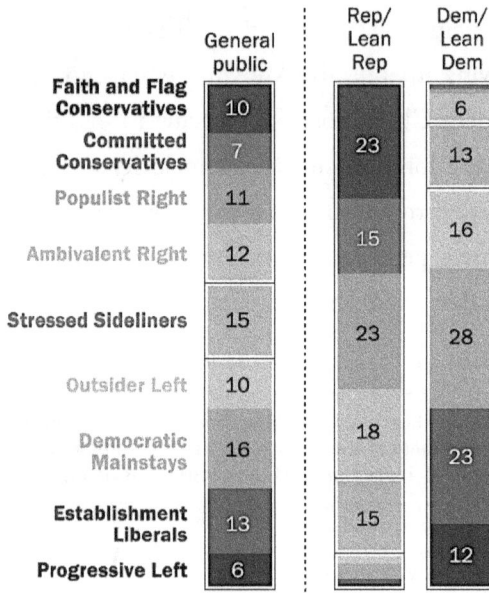

Source: Survey of U.S. adults conducted July 8-18, 2021.

PEW RESEARCH CENTER

Figure 2 - 2021 Pew Research political typology groupings

Chapter 6

Consensus and the US Public Sphere

Are tweet-storms or extra-terrestrials dividing us?

With a cursory examination of mainstream television news, it is not difficult to imagine the US Electorate is deeply and hopelessly divided on critical issues in economics, the environment, diversity, and gun rights. On the evening of June 28, 2022, if you were watching the evening news, you would have seen Jake Tapper on CNN covering the January 6th Committee's Sixth Congressional Hearing when former White House Chief of Staff Mark Meadows aid Cassidy Hutchinson provided evidence for the committee. Political insiders like Gloria Borger provided analysis, trying to get inside Trump's mind on that day and adding commentary like: "…the fact that he didn't think the picture was going to look really good…So, he didn't care about the magnetometers. He didn't care."[372]

Bob Woodward and Carl Bernstein spoke at length about how the events of January 6, 2021, compared with Watergate. Woodward recalled his interview with Trump: "He was a determined person that all of these people couldn't stop…all the administrators who are not calling him out!" On Fox News, at that exact moment, Tucker Carlson was reporting from Brazil all week long. His report focused on UFOs spotted along the Brazilian coasts, with his guest insisting that "the first step is to bring one of these things down and get some answers…" Carlson's broadcast, filled with diatribes against Liberals who "are angry, bitter, [and have] higher rates of mental illness… and there is a lot of data to back this up in *Liberal Misery*."[373] At the exact moment of the day on June 28, 2022, very different views of current events in the world were being represented in a news mediascape representing an enormous range in tone from modulated to bombastic and covering topics from national politics to deep-state extra-terrestrial conspiracies.

Public perceptions of journalism as an industry have changed much since the heyday of US political news coverage: Woodward and Bernstein's investigative reportage of the Watergate scandal in the early 1970s Washington D.C. The public's trust and confidence in journalism in the US hit its highest point in 1976 when 72 percent of Americans expressed at least a fair amount of trust in journalism.[374] Since then, trust in mass media, which includes print journalism, radio, and national television news in a Gallup polling sample, has become far more polarized and politicized. In 2016, in the runup to national elections, trust in mass media hit its low point, with only 32 percent of Americans in a Gallup poll stating they trusted mass media at least a fair amount. By 2022, perceptions of mass media had risen for Democrats, with a majority (70 percent) stating they trusted mass media at least a fair amount "to report the news fairly and accurately," with only 14 percent of Republicans believing the same.[375] More significant is the loss in trust registered by Independents, declining from 74 percent in 1976 to 27 percent in 2022—an increase of distrust registered among politically centrist Americans.

In a US mediascape full of hyperbole and polarization, it is a challenging time for both news reporters and the news public who are increasingly finding information in the US public sphere less credible, and for good reasons. Journalists have had to adjust their reporting methodologies, just as news audiences have had to adapt their information filters to contend with baseless claims posted on social media and the volume of fallacious tweets and declarations posted. A new cohort of politicians have politicized information and factuality itself, and social media companies are not filtering content to most Americans' satisfaction. A poll conducted by the Pearson Institute/AP-NORC in September of 2021 found that 82 percent of Americans surveyed believed the spread of misinformation was a major problem. Of those surveyed, significantly, 72 percent believed social media companies were responsible "a great deal" for the spread of misinformation, and fully 77 percent also stated social media users were culpable as well.[376] In a poll conducted one year later, 40 percent of those polled were concerned they had been exposed to misinformation, and 43 percent were at least "somewhat concerned" that they may have spread it.[377] While blame for the spread of misinformation has been primarily attributed to social mediascape, trust for news media among Republicans has declined considerably since the late 1980s in part due to conservative media and talk radio hosts like Rush Limbaugh, who sounded the first trumpet calls against liberal bias in mainstream news reportage.

And yet polling data also suggest an evolution in the American news audience who are asking deeper questions about the American public sphere. We are expressing concerns about the amount of political bias in news media and the confusion sowed by competing claims. We're concerned about the volume of misinformation rampant on the internet and the future impact of artificial intelligence on the news. The American news public is also skeptical about the overall credibility of information in the public sphere—a rational response to an upsurge in disinformation in a world dependent on source transparency for informed decision-making.

This chapter reviews the history of the US public sphere, asking: What societal functions does journalism serve? Does it still fulfill the role of "watchdog" for the public, to keep the power of the rich, famous, and political in check, to keep their influence measured and their messaging honest? Why have a majority of American Independents and Conservatives lost trust in mass media? Are there ways to maintain a resilient, open, and transparent public sphere that works to inform and illuminate the ordinary American?

How do Americans feel about the health of our public sphere communications?

In 2017, during the early part of the Trump Administration, nine in ten Democrats agreed with the statement "media criticism of political leaders keeps them from doing things they shouldn't"— referencing news media's "watchdog role" in society. Only four in ten Republicans believed the same.[378] According to Pew Research, this gap stands in sharp contrast to a similar January-February 2016 poll when Americans were asked the same question. Then, amid the presidential primary season, nearly the same majority of Democrats (74 percent) and Republicans (77 percent) believed the press' role as watchdog was effective.[379] However, the role of the gatekeeper in journalism was widely acknowledged by both Republicans and

Democrats in the mid-1970s and remained in place up until 2016. In one year the perception of this effectiveness changed substantially as reportage of Trump's presidency polarized views between conservative-leaning and left-leaning media audiences.

Other national polling numbers on the state of news media suggest a perceptual disjuncture between how journalists rate their connection to readers versus how the public views their own relationship to news media. In March 2022, for example, 46 percent of journalists polled believed new outlets did at least a somewhat good job of "giving voice to the unrepresented," while only a quarter of US adults believed they did.[380] It wasn't so long ago that journalists and newspaper publishers vied to be the voice of the people; low polling numbers suggest an absence of community connection that used to be highly prized by large newspapers and news media. Two-thirds of Journalists polled believed news organizations both reported the news accurately and did a good job at covering the most important stories of the day. Only one-third of the news public believed news media reported the news accurately, and only 41 percent believed they did a good job at covering the most important stories of the day. And, while journalists were equally divided on whether their industry did at least a somewhat good job correcting misinformation, only a quarter of the news public believed the same (see Figure 1).[381] These differences in assessments of news media generally speak to a diminishment in trust and performance in news media registered by the American electorate.

Americans are also more broadly concerned with the truth and transparency in the American public sphere, including social media. A poll conducted by the Pearson Institute/AP-NORC in September of 2021 found that 85 percent of over 1000 Americans surveyed believed the spread of misinformation is a major problem. Of those surveyed, most blamed social media companies, social media users, and US politicians for its spread. Almost 80 percent of respondents in the same poll believed the Russian and Chinese governments were at least moderately responsible for misinformation in the US public sphere. What the Pearson Institute/AP-NORC exposes is a deeper concern with the purposeful and intentional proliferation of disinformation—in a world where wars and political offices are won through public relations. The transition from a web awash in misinformation to one infiltrated by disinformation signals a new era, a cyber cold war with *dezinformatsiya* (disinformation)—as it was known in the former USS.R.—posing the real potential for harm.

Some of our concerns about the public sphere are as old as human communication and the societal need for reliable information. Other concerns raise new challenges and new questions the global public and national legislatures are coming to terms with: How are we going refine and redefine what constitutes free speech or establish use guidelines for internet content? Who pays for news?—concerns over the monetization in journalism and the corporate influence on news media. We are also concerned that polarized news and social media have created a *silo effect* on human interaction and communication in a media market that selects narrow viewer demographics. The birth of the World Wide Web radically transformed the global public sphere of news and information, forcing us now—in its current evolution—to reconsider what we value in news and information in a media era increasingly defined by pseudo-journalism, infotainment, and hyperreality.

What is the story of the modern public sphere?

The German philosopher Jürgen Habermas (b. 1929) first defined the *public sphere* simply and broadly as a gathering of private people who come together "as a public...articulating the needs of society with the state."[382] In his book, *The Structural Transformation of the Public Sphere* (1962), Habermas looks closely at the history of the modern public sphere, which emerged in 18th European coffee houses and literary societies by a growing merchants class who needed public spaces to consult each other for accurate information about distant markets. With the rise of a new social class, public spaces in coffee houses and literary societies opened up discussions on philosophical issues, including individual liberty and popular sovereignty. The public sphere became a space between private individuals and the governing states where people could meet and have critical debates. They served as critical spaces for questioning political authority and circulating new ideas on creating a perfect society. Significant in Habermas' claim is that through the development of the public sphere, public opinion also became more important in society, a force for societal change and transformation, and a vital component to the maintenance of democratic governance.

Another remarkable book published in 1962 provided more context to the value and transformation in the modern mass media public sphere, looking at the medium of communications themselves and how they transformed society. *The Gutenberg Galaxy: The Making of Typographic Man*, written by Canadian mass media scholar Marshall McLuhan, begins by dividing the public spheres of communication into four epochs: the first one defined as a pre-literate "oral tribe culture" where individuals of a social group come together to discuss and identify societal problems, relate stories and make collective decisions. The next phase in the public sphere is a manuscript epoch, where literature and shared knowledge are hand-written. McLuhan then analyzes the social and cultural transformation brought on by the invention of the printing press by Johannes Gutenberg in Mainz,

Germany, c. 1450 CE, an epoch that ushered in the "Gutenberg Galaxy," that accelerated, intensified and ultimately enabled cultural and cognitive changes.[383] McLuhan argues that media technologies are not simply inventions with which people communicate; the technologies themselves alter human behavior. In democratizing the availability of media, the printing press also helped to democratize societies.

Certainly, the tone of the message and the content/context contained within media are quintessentially important. Still, McLuhan argues that the medium itself by which messages are conveyed is also culturally important and power-laden. Examining news and information, for example, the medium of print journalism differs from television journalism substantially. Though they both may cover the same story, the format for televised news and podcasts can be highly charged and directly emotive, owing to the speed of visual/oral inputs into the human psyche. Reading news allows added space for the writer to provide context, getting deeper into the "why?" or "how?" of news stories, for example, supplying additional nuance in stories written and additional time for reflection by the reader. Television news and podcasts, like their direct precursors, the photographic newsmagazine, can elicit strong reactions that can extend through a whole slate of reactions from abhorrence or sympathy. Visual/oral mediums also favor narrative conviction: with less time for an audience member to take in relevant information, they are more dependent on the conviction of the speaker. In television media, conviction perceptually equals truth.

Print journalism, like McLuhan's description of the new world Guttenberg's printing press ushered in, is a medium that favors objectivity. If one reads a summary print conclusion by a news reporter that seems biased but full of conviction, as in an op-ed, a reader is apt to take a side and be more wary of any arguments that follow. In visual/oral mediums like radio, television, and podcasts, the human ear and visual cortex are hyper-receptive to innuendo and emotive cues; a broadcast on one electronic medium can convey different messages depending on where the listener is in place and time, traveling to work or relaxing at home, information and arguments can be perceived differently. During the televised Nixon/ Kennedy presidential candidate debate in 1960, for example, more of the television news audience believed Kennedy won the debate because he represented himself visually with more confidence and conviction. Simulcast on the radio, more listeners over the airwaves believed Nixon won the debate because his points of argument sounded measured and assured—each candidate was able to express their points convincingly but in two different mediums.

One of McLuhan's other contributions to media studies is to explain how the printing press, as a new medium for communication, was able to revolutionize the systems by which information was created and disseminated in Europe coming out of the Middle Ages. Gutenberg's printing press with its moveable alphabetic type, made information replication and dissemination far easier. Though he tried to keep his invention under wraps, his technology did not stay secret for long. Within two generations, print shops began opening for business all over Europe. By 1502 CE, print shops had opened in the town of Wittenberg, a university town located in present-day Germany.

There, Martin Luther posted his *95 Thesis* to a church door, a research assignment for his seminary students that questioned the selling of indulgences and other religious practices of the Catholic Church in his time. After printers got ahold of the sensational document, in just a few days, copies of this revolutionary query made it across Europe at a gallop to Spain. The publication of the *95 Thesis* has been cited as the match that struck the fire of religious wars in Europe for the next century. Though the Christian bible was the best seller in its day, Luther's *95 Thesis* was perhaps the first broadcast piece of short media. Whereas before the print revolution, Luther's critique may have been quietly discussed in the upper echelons of the Catholic Church, and his voice subdued, mass dissemination made this impossible. It also gave a new *gravitas* to best sellers, the power to transform society rapidly, and to grant a writer instant notoriety.

From the Gutenberg Galaxy into McLuhan's fourth stage of the public sphere, the "electronic age," a new global media ecosystem would turn the world into a global village of shared communications with all the pitfalls and potentials inherent in an enormous village with instant communication. Pitfalls would include increasing alienation of people measuring themselves against each other, increasing distraction and less reflection in a world of instant gratification, and the spread of misinformation in a village game of telephone where second-hand news spreads like wildfire. Though McLuhan didn't address the positive potentials so much of a new interconnected world, the visualization of people who have inherently remained invisible is one such positive: the ability to share information and the experience of others globally—and thereby the increased potential for cross-cultural understanding one another. The electronic public sphere ushered in an era where societal attitudes could transform overnight, speeding the circulation of popular trends and cultural transformation with its enticements of market capitalism and democracy.

Freedom of Speech to the US Bill of Rights

The translation of the Old and New Testaments into common languages during the Protestant Revolution in Europe brought with it a plethora of new interpretations of the scripture of the bible. The importance of being able to speak to one's religious conscience led scholars like English poet John Milton (1608-1674) to write the first defense of the freedom of speech in 1644.[384] During Milton's time, the English Parliament controlled publication through licensing and, in so doing, preserved the power to censor material they found objectionable or politically dangerous. In Milton's *Areopagitica; A speech of Mr. John Milton for the Liberty of Unlicensed Printing, to the Parlament of England,* he made a libertarian argument that banning a book, even before its publication, was censorship beyond the pale—even in ancient Rome or Greece—arguing free speech promotes truth. Countering conformity and ignorance, free speech was among the greatest assets to building a strong, intelligent, understanding society.

Areopagitica was written in direct response to The Licensing Order of 1643 issued by the English Parliament. The Order created government controls over publishers and writers that included pre-publication licensing and publication approval, the destruction of any books offensive to the government, and imprisonment for any offensive writers, printers, and publishers. A few years later, England's Parliament presented to the new King William of Orange a Bill of Rights (1689), which asserted that "debate or proceedings in Parliament…not…be impeached or questioned in any court or place out of Parliament." The freedom to publish without censorship in England was not achieved until 1695 when the English Parliament chose not to renew the Licensing Order. Freedom of speech and publication coincided with the growth of England as a dominant world power in the 1700s.

The first law explicitly granting press freedoms was introduced in Sweden in 1766. Its chief supporter, parliamentarian and Ostrobothnian priest Anders Chydenius, provided an eloquent defense for the (Swedish) Freedom of the Press Act:

> No evidence should be needed that a certain freedom of writing and printing is one of the strongest bulwarks of a free organization of the state, as, without it, the estates would not have sufficient information for the drafting of good laws, and those dispensing justice would not be monitored, nor would the subjects know the requirements of the law, the limits of the rights of government, and their responsibilities. Education and ethical conduct would be crushed; coarseness in thought, speech, and manners would prevail, and dimness would darken the entire sky of our freedom in a few years.

Passed on December 2, 1766, the adoption of the act prohibited censorship and introduced the principle of public access to official records in Sweden. Significantly excluded were defamation of the king's majesty and the Swedish Church. From the beginning, modern freedom of expression laws came with some caveats, among them rules that prohibited sedition by members of the government. Still, the Freedom of Press Act constituted a monumental step toward opening society so that decisions at the highest levels would be more transparent to all.

Explicitly granting press and speech freedoms was more of an enlightened afterthought than the highest priority for the writers of the US Constitution. In 1776, during the second year of the

American Revolutionary War, the Virginia colonial legislature passed a Declaration of Rights drafted by George Mason that included the sentence, "The freedom of the press is one of the greatest bulwarks of liberty, and can never be restrained but by despotic Governments." The First Amendment of the US Constitution is actually six key rights suffused in one brief amendment and contained in the larger body of amendments in the US Constitution's Bill of Rights. Virginia became the 10th of 14 states to approve the first ten amendments that James Madison provided to the United States Constitution, and the amendments were adopted on December 15, 1791.

Ironically, Madison and other framers at first believed that adding amendments to the Constitution may be misconstrued and perhaps redundant; they "believed the structure of the new Constitution by itself placed limits on government, so they were concerned that by listing some rights, the government might think it had the power to do anything it was not explicitly forbidden from doing," according to historian Corey Brettschneider.[385] The Amendment and the specific Rights it covers are:

- Congress shall make no law respecting an establishment of religion, or
- prohibiting the free exercise thereof, or
- abridging the freedom of speech,
- or of the press; or
- the right of the people peaceably to assemble, and
- to petition the Government for a redress of grievances.

Madison was assuaged by Thomas Jefferson to include a Bill of Rights because it would serve to mollify the anti-Federalists in state assemblies who were wary of federal powers, helping to convince them to ratify the US Constitution. The United States Bill of Rights, as it is now known, helped to ensure minority rights are protected in a country of majority rule, rights that are equally necessary for self-government, Brettschneider points out.[386] Significantly, the drafting of the First Amendment came at the end of a European century of revolution in both philosophy and politics, and new press freedoms in England, Sweden, and France played a significant role in fundamentally reshaping Western society.

News Print up to the Hearst Era

Even though paper printing is a Chinese invention dating back almost two thousand years, the modern newspaper is a European invention. The first newspapers began as news sheets, information marketed to merchants and the bourgeoisie in large European cities. Johann Carolus in Strasbourg, near the German border with France, published the German-language *Relation aller Fürnemmen und gedenckwürdigen Historien* (Account of all Distinguished and Commemorable Stories) beginning in 1605. Other newspapers followed in Amsterdam (1618), Paris (1631), London (1702), and Boston in 1704 with the publication of *The Boston News-Letter*, a weekly that became the first continuously published newspaper in the colonies. The first newspapers provided news and information on wars, politics, current prices, and political and economic news. The British government subsidized *The Boston News-Letter,* and all copies were subject to the approval of the Royal governor before circulation.[387]

In an era of Aristocratic authority, the early newspapers were typically censored by the government, where the daily or weekly was published. After the Licensing Order of 1643 expired in England in 1695, English-language newspapers started flourishing in Great Britain. They were modest enterprises, a sideline for printers. The

First Party System in the US (1792-1824) pitted Federalist Party members, including Alexander Hamilton, against rival Jefferson Democratic-Republican Party members, and during this time in American history, the number of American newspapers grew rapidly. Both parties sponsored newspapers for their loyal supporters, politically one-sided deferential renderings of politics and events— some of this history is recounted in the American musical *Hamilton* (2015). *Penny press* newspapers began to be produced by the 1830s. They were cheap, mass-produced tabloid-style newspapers produced *en masse* following the shift from hand-pressed to steam-powered printing. Low prices made news reading accessible to the middle and lower classes in the US for the first time.

By 1900, almost every urban area of the United States with a population of over 5000 had a town newspaper. The number of dailies grew in the United States from 971 in year 1880, to 2226 by 1900. Newspaper publication became a major growth industry, and New York City became an epicenter for fierce competition in viewership. The famous news publisher William Randolph Hearst started with *The San Francisco Examiner* given to him by his wealthy father in 1887. He then acquired the *New York Evening Journal* and the *New York* (morning) *Journal* in 1896 and entered into a circulation war with Joseph Pulitzer, who ran the *New York World*. Both publishers competed for the same market share, a blue-collar reader base. Hearst began to run sensationalist and alluring front-page stories of murder and crime and had his reporters *muckrake* to increase circulation—that is, dig up the "muck" on politicians in a time of endemic city office-holder corruption. Pulitzer followed suit to compete for circulation. By late 1898, in New York City, circulation reached 1 million copies a day for both Pulitzer's *World* and Hearst's *Journal*. While smaller papers relied on loyal Republican or Democratic readers who appreciated the intense partisanship of the editorials, the big-city papers of Hearst and Pulitzer realized they would lose half their potential audience by excessive partisanship, so they took a more ambiguous political position except at election time.[388]

In New York, Hearst "helped to usher in the multi-perspective approach we identify with the modern op-ed page," where different voices and views of journalists balanced out bias to some extent.[389] This isn't to say that Hearst's papers always took a balanced approach in the views. Much of the coverage in his papers leading up to the Spanish-American War (1898) beginning with the outbreak of the Cuban Revolution in 1895, was squarely biased against Spain. Hearst created several schemes to spark US intervention in the war. The most well-known involved the imprisonment and release of Cuban prisoner Evangeline Cisneros, daughter of a Cuban nationalist Augustin Cosio. Hearst reported that she was jailed after turning down the advances of a Spanish Colonel—one of many *partial truths* that would come to define bias in journalism. He had a hand in her dramatic escape and successfully used publicity to rally US interest in the Cuban struggle for independence from Spain.

The Cuban Revolution of 1895 came at a perfect time for Hearst and his New York Journal. With the eyes of a businessman and a politician, Hearst saw the events in Cuba as a way to place himself and his paper on center stage. Journalism in the late 1890s became tainted by what is now known as "yellow journalism" because Heart's sensationalist articles were generally written on the same pages that carried a popular yellow cartoon character, the Yellow Kid, and included narrative marketing techniques of exaggerating news events, circulating scandal-mongering, and including sensational stories of crime, sex or violence.[390]

The penny press, which emerged in the 1830s in NE America

and evolved into tabloid journalism, also relied on over-the-top sensationalist, but tabloid presses also fabricated news. Falsification, however, was never allowed by large daily papers with reputations to preserve, though increasingly editors looked for muckraking stories that sold copy: exposing political corruption, corporate crime, child labor, conditions in slums and prisons, unsanitary conditions in food processing plants (such as meat), fraudulent claims by manufacturers of patent medicines, labor racketeering, and similar topics. Woodward and Bernstein's muckraking coverage of the Watergate Scandal in the early 1970s cemented journalism's reputation as gatekeeper to the most powerful state media systems in modern society, and the popularity and prestige of America's free press were at an all-time high. Woodward and Bernstein also made muckraking substantive and even glamourous for a new generation of would-be journalists entering college.

Political investiture in America's public sphere

A history of biased and provincial newsprint in America, and a television media landscape of commercially sponsored content inspired calls to provide objective and educational television content in the early-1960s. Subsequent public discussions became part of the 1964 Democratic Party Platform.[391] The Public Broadcasting Act of 1967 issued the congressional corporate charter for the Corporation for Public Broadcasting (CPB), a private nonprofit corporation funded by taxpayers to disburse grants to public broadcasters in the United States, which helped to establish the Public Broadcasting Service (PBS, 1969) and National Public Radio (NPR, 1970). The act charged the CPB with encouraging and facilitating program diversity and expanding and developing non-commercial broadcasting. The CPB would have the funds to help local stations create innovative programs, thereby increasing the service of broadcasting in the public interest throughout the country. The creation of PBS would also ensure that the US public sphere would have at least some broadcast media that would remain objective, non-commercial, and community-based in a rapidly evolving global mediascape.[392] One of the first charges of PBS was to broadcast the United States Senate Watergate Committee proceedings beginning on May 17, 1973, with Robert MacNeil and Jim Lehrer as commentators. Nightly gavel-to-gavel broadcasts drew great public interest and raised the profile of the fledgling PBS network.[393]

In 1949, the US Federal Communication Commission (FCC) introduced the fairness doctrine, which was a policy that required the holders of broadcast licenses to present controversial issues of public importance and to do so in a manner that fairly reflected differing viewpoints. The basis for the fairness doctrine came into being with problems of political editorializing on the radio just before WWII. Witnessing the Fascist takeover of national media in Germany and Italy, the FCC was understandably concerned that radio could be used for political propagandizing. In 1941, the commission made a ruling that came to be known as the Mayflower Decision, which declared that radio stations, due to their public interest obligations, must remain neutral in matters of news and politics. They were not allowed to give editorial support to any particular political position or candidate.

In 1949, the Mayflower Decision was repealed by the FCC, which replaced it with the fairness doctrine, which had two basic elements: It required broadcasters to devote some of their airtime to discussing controversial matters of public interest, and to air contrasting views regarding those matters. Stations were given wide latitude as to how to provide contrasting views: it could be done through news segments, public affairs shows, or editorials. The doctrine did not require equal time for opposing views but required that contrasting viewpoints be presented. It should be understood that for more than thirty years, national television was the purview of three networks (CBS, NBC, and ABC), and national viewership was much more concentrated on these few stations.

In 1987, the FCC during the Reagan Administration abolished the fairness doctrine, even though in *Red Lion Broadcasting Co. v. FCC* (1969), the US Supreme Court upheld (by a vote of 8–0) the constitutionality of the fairness doctrine, in response to challenges that the doctrine violated the First Amendment to the US Constitution. In 1985, under FCC Chairman Mark S. Fowler, a communications attorney who had served on Ronald Reagan's presidential campaign staff in 1976 and 1980, the FCC released its report on *General Fairness Doctrine Obligations,* stating that the doctrine hurt the public interest and violated free speech rights guaranteed by the First Amendment. The commission could not, however, come to a determination as to whether the doctrine had been enacted by Congress through its 1959 Amendment to Section 315 of the Communications Act. The FCC opened an inquiry inviting public comment on alternative means for administrating and enforcing the fairness doctrine.[394]

Then, in its 1987 report, the alternatives—including abandoning a case-by-case enforcement approach, replacing the doctrine with open access time for all members of the public, doing away with the personal attach rule, and eliminating certain other aspects of the doctrine—were rejected by the FCC for varying reasons.[395] The FCC vote was opposed by Democratic members of Congress who said the FCC had tried to "flout the will of Congress" and the decision was "wrongheaded, misguided and illogical."[396] In June 1987, Congress attempted to preempt the FCC decision and codify the fairness doctrine, but the legislation was vetoed by President Reagan. Another attempt to revive the doctrine in 1991 was stopped when President George H.W. Bush threatened another veto.

One of the most persuasive arguments for ending the fairness doctrine in 1987 came from the FCC Commission's counsel, Diane Killory who noted the major growth of broadcast media outlets. There were more than 1,300 television stations and more than 10,000 radio stations in the United States at that time, and 95 percent of viewers received five or more television signals. Radio listeners in the biggest 25 markets received an average of 59 radio stations. "Numerical scarcity simply cannot justify different First Amendment treatment," Killory pointed out, nor what she called "allocational scarcity"—the idea that more broadcasting licenses were needed than available.[397]

It has been widely circulated that the 1987 repeal of the fairness doctrine enabled the rise of talk radio and conservative *shock jocks* like Rush Limbaugh, who, according to *The Washington Post*: "From his earliest days on the air...trafficked in conspiracy theories, divisiveness, even viciousness" (e.g., "feminazis").[398] It was nearly impossible to listen to Limbaugh without having a strong emotive reaction, whether you were on the Right or Left, and this was the marketing plan borrowed from other shock jocks of the day. Limbaugh exploited the role of Right-wing provocateur in a media stream that had hitherto been generally politically modulated—though American radio had had its share of provocateurs from the Left in the 1960s and 70s. Nicole Hemmer points out in her book *Messengers of the Right: Conservative Media and the Transformation of American Politics* (2016), however, that before 1987, people using much less controversial verbiage had been taken off the air for obvious violations of the fairness doctrine from both sides of the political spectrum.[399]

The short story of propaganda

In the year 1095 CE, Pope Urban II held a mixed synod (assembly to help decide policy) of ecclesiastics and laypeople of the Catholic Church in Clermont, France. The synod focused on implementing the monastic reforms, enacting decrees, and settling local and regional issues, including an attempt to reduce feuding among Frankish nobles. However, the meeting became primarily known for Pope Urban II's speech on the last day, a call to arms against "infidels" that would lead to the First Crusade (1096–1099) and the temporary conquest of Jerusalem by Christian forces. Several accounts of the speech survive. One was by a Catholic priest named Fulcher of Chartres, who later accompanied the crusaders to Constantinople and the Holy Land. According to Fulcher, Pope Urban II gave an offer to the defenders of the Christian faith that would be hard to refuse:

> All who die by the way, whether by land or by sea or in battle against the pagans, shall have immediate remission of sins. This I grant them through the power of God with which I am invested. O what a disgrace if such a despised and base race, which worships demons, should conquer a people which has the faith of omnipotent God…Let those who have been accustomed unjustly to wage private warfare against the faithful now go against the infidels and end with victory this war which should have begun long ago.[400]

Properly defined, *propaganda* is communication that is primarily used to influence or persuade an audience to further an agenda, which may selectively present facts or invent reality to produce an emotional rather than a rational response to information being presented.[401] Propaganda derives from the plural gerund form of the Latin word *propagare*, meaning to spread or to propagate a message, and originally the word wasn't considered as pejoratively as it is today—if you were Catholic. The word derives from a papal congregation created to propagate Counter-Reformation messaging by the Catholic Church in non-Catholic countries, the Congregatio de Propaganda Fide.

Shaping communication narratives to persuade audiences or to further an agenda is an ancient practice. The very oldest inscription of an oral language dates to around 3100 BCE in Egypt and tells a pictographic tale of the exploits of the Pharoah Narmer and his conquest and unification of Upper and Lower Egypt with pictures meant to invoke domination and intimidation. The exploits of Kings, Queens, and colonizers have been recorded on diverse mediums ever since to assuage their subjects to accept the events, histories, and realities as the powerful present them. The term propaganda began taking a pejorative or negative connotation in the mid-19th century when it began to be used more extensively in the political sphere.

The first large-scale use of propaganda by modern states was occasioned by the outbreak of the First World War in 1914, and it was utilized by all combatants. The United States, under President Wilson, was neutral in the War. Still, after the sinking of the RMS cruise liner *Lusitania*, and the declaration of war, Wilson's administration quickly pivoted from being neutral to "all in" for the war effort. Wilson appointed his campaign manager, George Edward Creel—who had been an investigative journalist—to serve as the head of a new governmental organization during WWI, the United States Committee on Public Information, which was ostensibly a propaganda organization. Historian John Mitchell Hamilton goes so far as to say this committee helped to establish pervasive, systematic propaganda as an instrument of the state.[402]

After the defeat of the Central Powers in WWI, German military officials like General Erich Ludendorf suggested that British propaganda used during the war was instrumental in Germany's defeat. Adolf Hitler came to echo this view that propaganda had been a primary cause of the collapse of morale and revolts on the German home front. According to British historian Robert Ensor, Hitler's book *Mein Kampf* (1925) expounded upon his theory of propaganda, which provided a powerful base for his rise to power in 1933. According to Ensor, Hitler put "no limit on what can be done by propaganda; people will believe anything, provided they are told it often enough and emphatically enough, and that contradicters are either silenced or smothered in calumny."[403] Significant in the purpose of propaganda is the manufacture of the consent of the masses, outlined by political theorist Antonio Gramsci, who witnessed the rise of Mussolini and later the dominance of fascism from his jail cell. For Gramsci, political propaganda became necessary for usurping political power because, in the 20th Century, people in democratic states would not surrender their own agency in a representative forms of government voluntarily, the public had to be manipulated. Dictators had to gain the consent of the governed through control and domination of information streams.

Following theorists like Antonio Gramsci, research scientists like Noam Chomsky and Edward S. Herman, in their book *Manufacturing Consent: The Political Economy of the Mass Media* (1988), demonstrate how news media, perceived as "obstinate…in their search for truth and defense of justice," often in practice work to defend "the economic, social, and political agendas of the privileged groups that dominate domestic society, the state, and the global order."[404] For Herman and Chomsky, mainstream media's behavior, performance, and income derive from the system they are touted to critique; as such, they are complicit rather than critical of corporate wealth, for example. Significant to Chomsky and Herman's research is an increasing concern among the American electorate on the corporate influence over news media. Most local news dailies around the US have been bought up by large corporations, and only six megamedia corporations now control an estimated 75 and 95 percent of the media in the United States. In a February 2020 Pew Research survey, 72 percent of those Americans polled believed US news organizations did not do a good job of telling their audience where their money comes from. [405] The lack of financial transparency is one the greatest impediments to the public trust of news media in the United States, speaking to basic issues raised by the American news audience who, along with Chomsky and Herman, are asking of media, "Who are you speaking for?" Since 1987, independent news media in the US has nearly all been swallowed up in media consolidations, diminishing public sphere news diversity and independence in the United States.

The dissolution of the basic tenets of a fairness doctrine has stripped away the obligation to present counter-perspectives where multiple sides to any one argument could be presented, allowing patently false assertions to go unchallenged on biased news media. Most news organizations still adhere to the spirit of balanced reporting, presenting multiple sides to a story. However, from 2008 on, television news—like print journalism—has become increasingly subscriber-focused and more narrowly tailored to a specific audience's taste, age, and political outlook. Emblematic of this change was Fox News' change in their slogan from "fair and balanced" to "most watched, most trusted" in 2017, signaling a change from the multiperspectival reporting that William Randolph Hearst fostered to the embrace of political one-sidedness in broadcasting.[406]

Rescinding the tenets of a fairness doctrine opened the door to raw, unfiltered, and often unhinged voices from the far Right in broadcast media. However, some have argued that cable television and satellite radio were never defined in the scope of the doctrine, which specifically targeted the very limited broadcast media selection of the mid-20th Century television and radio. With the wide selection of channels and stations available in subscription-based media or satellite radio service providers, there are abundant opportunities to represent all sides of political speech. "Therefore, it's unlikely that the Fairness Doctrine would have impacted Fox News, even if it were in effect in 1996, when Roger Ailes launched the channel," as journalist Camille Caldera from *USA Today* points out.[407] It was the explosion of new cable television channels and satellite radio beginning in the 1980s in a free-speech nation with few media restrictions that opened the door to political divisiveness in broadcasted media because more stations began to narrow their market to a specific demographic niche that might have profiled white working-class men between 45 and 70 who are "fed-up" with the liberal media.

Where is the American consensus now on a divisive mediascape?

The debate around *bothsideism* or giving equal weight to two opposing views is far from over, certainly not in polling data. It remains one of the big issues Americans have concerning the health of our public sphere: Where is the other side of the argument, the checks and balances of truth claims? How do we define journalism today? With so much infotainment, paid advertising (in the guise of news,) corporate cross-marketing, and AI-generated internet content, should we make it clearer and more transparent to the news audience what is and isn't journalism, or which corporation is driving content criteria and why? If the Left or Right-leaning press willingly defends the fallacies spoken by a political candidate, haven't they abrogated their duty as a watchdog for democracy and become a *spokes organization*, a propaganda arm for a political candidate or party?

Journalists and the media-consuming public view the new paradigm of news coverage that caters to a targeted audience very differently. US journalists are more likely than the public to say all sides don't always deserve equal coverage, for example. When asked, "Should journalists always strive to give every side equal coverage," 44 percent believed this should be the case, with 55 percent answering not every side deserves equal coverage. Responding to the same questions, 76 percent of US adults surveyed believed journalists should always strive to give every side equal coverage.[408] Journalists and the US public value "bothsideism" very differently, as researchers for Pew Research conclude. Missing here is the public desire for journalists to interrogate truth claims directly, but also the desire in the news public for journalists to hash out political differences in civil and mediated spaces so that the news audience doesn't have to. Polling numbers indicate there is still a strong reluctance in most Americans to speak to others with different views in confrontational arenas.

Looking at views from the other side of the reporter/reader journalist spectrum, in March 2022, a Pew Research poll asked journalists if it is a problem when people get their news from only one news organization. Of the American journalists who were queried, fully 94 percent of journalists thought the public relying on one source for news was at least a minor problem, with 75 percent of journalists stating it was a major problem (see Figure 2).[409] Of the American public surveyed, 75 percent believed one-source news was at least a minor problem, and 23 percent not a problem.[410] In essence, most journalists and news consumers are concerned to some extent that many Americans have narrowed the lens through which they watch news to one dominant site, podcast, or television program. In so doing, they rely upon situated narratives and political views that are narrowly defined, with news analysis that may instill fear and uncertainty with sensational soundbites, provided without counter-point or holistic analysis, and embedded with summary conclusions largely based on conjecture and uncertain generalizations.

The debate around giving equal weight to two oppositional views took on a new level of intensity during the disinformation campaigns waged against the science of immunization. A small minority of alternative medicine practitioners, for example, were given equal weight to the research knowledge and medical proto-cols of the vast majority of medical doctors. Giving equal weight to untested and sensational medical claims—where retraction or fact-checking comes late or not at all—can be dangerous. It proved fatal to many vulnerable Americans who believed immunization was ineffective for everyone in the first outbreak of COVID-19. Increas-ingly, finding both sides of an argument has been left to the news audiences to find another source. The problem with bothsideism, expressed by journalists in today's media market, is that simplistic dualisms, or that every issue has two equally equivalent sides is itself a fallacy because bothsideism doesn't take into consideration:

1. **Consensus, which matters,** particularly in life and death matters like war and health. If an overwhelming majority

of medical professionals, scientists, or civic leaders support an established claim, the weight of their consensus should also be acknowledged or represented.

2. **False equivalency:** Providing two sides of an issue comes back to a problem of political one-sidedness overall; in framing two sides of an issue, it is implied that each of the two sides has equivalent weight or, more significantly, that each represents two sides of a complex issue that is simply not reduceable to two sides.

3. **Strategic distraction:** Combating disinformation or refuting false information is time-consuming and continues to focus attention on false claims rather than legitimate solutions. One of the primary goals of disinformation is confusion and distraction, making consensus and accord more difficult—ultimately eroding strength through solidarity.

However, a majority of the US public still believes it is valuable to present both sides of an issue, and up until recently, this was a common practice and helpful to an American public in search of an independent space to synthesize their views. One of the tragic lessons learned from the COVID-19 crisis is that in an era where fallacious claims gain immediate traction, it has also now become the responsibility of institutional professionals to patiently dispute false claims, even if it takes refuting them meticulously one at a time. Not addressing fallacious information has also become dangerous. The role of institutional professionals will have to expand to include debunking (or at least acknowledging) counter-claims and distortions of evidence that they may not have even imagined.

The net effect of the opening up of broadcasted media and a new social mediascape has Americans concerned. An April 2022 Pew Research poll indicated that "US adults under 30 are now almost as likely to trust information on social media sites as information from national news outlets."[411] More significantly, however, in that poll, trust in the integrity of information from social media remained fairly constant from 2016 to 2022. Still, trust in national news organizations went down considerably during that time, especially among Americans over 30 years of age.[412] Accordingly, by June 2023, Pew Research found that most Americans wanted the US Government and technology companies to take steps to restrict false information, pitting the risk of receiving false facts and content against the unrestricted freedom to post. The percentage of US adults who stated the US government should take steps to restrict false information—even if it limits freedom of information—rose from 38 percent in 2018 to 55 percent in 2023, and support for tech companies to take steps to restrict false information from tech companies rose from 56 percent to 65 percent during the same time.[413]

There was a marked change in partisan attitudes on freedom of information between 2019 and 2021. For Republicans, the percentage of those believing the government intervention of content was necessary went down from 37 percent to 28 percent by 2021, reflecting a time of increased partisanship over election results and the D.C. riot. Support among Democrats, on the other hand, went from 40 percent to 65 percent during that same time, reflecting a major liberal shift in attitudes around the unrestricted freedom of speech and expression. There was a time in the last century when liberalism in the US connoted fewer restraints on expression and speech. What has changed is the normalization of hate speech, long condemned by liberals. But by June 2023, more Republicans began to favor content restriction, with approval ratings bouncing up again to 39 percent and Democrat approval climbing yet further to 70 percent, reflecting an overall consensus that online content should be moderated either by the government or the tech companies themselves. About seven in ten Americans (71 percent) believed that tech companies should also restrict violent content online, and 60 percent of those polled said that the government should do so.[414]

Findings from a 2023 Gallup Poll place Americans' overall trust in media at a 50-year low, with only 32 percent of those polled registering a great deal/fair amount of trust in mainstream news reportage.[415] Despite these figures, as of 2020, nearly three out of four US adults queried (73 percent) stated that, in general, it's important for journalists to function as watchdogs over elected officials.[416] And though trust in mainstream journalism has declined, Americans are much more inclined to blame the structure or the industry of news rather than the individual broadcaster or journalist. Of those Americans who say news coverage favors one side, 83 percent of those surveyed believed it was mostly because of the news organization, with only 16 percent believing it was mostly due to the journalist.[417] Sixty percent of the public polled also believed journalists could put aside their views when reporting.[418] Trust in the individual newscaster is not as high as it once was, but it remains substantial. Trust in the individual messenger extends to the audiences who gather news from podcasters. Of the listeners who get their news from podcasts, 87 percent believe the news they receive to be mostly accurate.[419]

Significant is the way views on free speech have transformed generationally in 60 years is recorded in polling data on media and teens. In a March 2022 Pew Poll, a majority of teens ages 13 to 17 (62 percent) stated a welcoming, safe online environment is more important than people being able to speak their minds freely online.[420] However, in the next age group, 18-29, the majority of those young adults (57 percent) stated being able to express their minds freely was more important than safe online environments, marking a transition into adulthood and a greater desire for independent expression. The overall adult population in the US is split on whether it is more important to speak one's mind freely online (47 percent) versus those who believe a safe environment online is more important (50 percent).[421] Finding consensus on the regulation of free speech and media necessitates a national conversation about what constitutes free speech.

Does news gathering and journalism still hold value in the view of the American public? When asked to look beyond the "current political environment" in a Pew Research poll conducted in October 2019, about six in ten Republicans and independents who lean toward the Republican Party (61 percent) stated it is important for journalists to function as watchdogs—compared with about eight in ten Democrats and Democratic-leaning independents.[422] In November 2022, CNN's chairman for much of 2022, Chris Licht, during an appearance on the podcast *On with Kara Swisher*, stated, "We have fact-checkers ready to go. We will put things in perspective. We will not let everything [Trump] does consume the news cycle, right?... There are other things that are important."[423] Licht said CNN would not cover former President Trump as much as it did during his first run for president in 2016 and his four years in the White House. With all of the indictments lobbied against Trump beginning in 2023, it is nearly impossible for major networks not to cover the former president ad nauseum.

For a great majority of Americans, mainstream news has been overly focused on the drama and performance of politics rather than on substantive issues. Even before national political coverage in the run-up to the 2024 national election, almost four-fifths of Americans in a July 2023 Pew Research poll believed too little attention was being focused on important issues facing the county.[424] Sixty-one percent of Americans believed news media intentionally ignores important stories in a December 2018 Pew Research poll.[425] Two-thirds of Americans polled in July 2023 stated they often feel exhausted thinking about politics. Political coverage focused on drama and performance has left a majority of Americans psychologically fatigued and emotionally frustrated that the everyday issues that consume their lives are being largely ignored.

Can we improve our news and information system while assuring the right to speak freely?

Many unlikely pathways to improving the health of our information stream are already in place, others may have to be innovated, and some are suggested by research critiques of the public sphere. Certainly, the COVID crisis, where good information made the difference in a life-or-death health outcome, brought to light the urgency for good, timely, and accurate information. With the professionalization of newsprint beginning in the late 1800s, the journalist was born, a muckraker sniffing out rampant corruption in the local urban political scene. Journalists took on great responsibilities in support of ordinary citizens. However, an editorial staff also emerged, committed to preserving the public's trust and receptive to its criticism. A tension still resides in credible newspapers and online journals of our day between the reporter and their editorial content checkers, a system of checks and balances that has made the work of journalists generally reliable for more than a century. This healthy tension between narrative independence and editorial objectivity is necessary to maintain America's news media tradition.

Certainly, news stories are written that emphasize the political points of view from the Left or the Right, raising questions and writing copy that can be politically framed, but this has always been part of the newsprint. The major newspapers differentiate fact-based objective reporting from commentary, opinion, editorial, and advertising. Television news programming is often followed by news analysis that engages in both news reportage and conjectural opinion. The problem with this format is that there is no clear delineation between opinion-oriented programming and factual news reporting. This issue came up in court. In 2018, Tucker Carlson on the Fox Channel was accused of on-air slander and a misrepresentation of facts by Stormy Daniels, characterizing her actions as "extortion" against Trump. In a court case of libel that Daniels lost, the Trump-appointed judge, following from Fox Lawyers' defense, stated in her ruling: "Fox persuasively argues that given Mr. Carlson's reputation, any reasonable viewer 'arrive[s] with an appropriate amount of skepticism' about the statement he makes."[426] It took a court ruling to make clear that Carlson wasn't a journalist, though his role on *Fox News* was never so clear.

The problem is that loyal viewers trust in the factuality of television anchors who present news and information all too often. US television news networks need to be more transparent about what constitutes news and what constitutes opinion. More broadly, the public sphere—which includes the internet—needs to have clearer guidelines that delineate news from opinion, advertising content from objective news, or human-written content from AI-generated. Most importantly, US citizens, by and large, believe anything that purports to be news should have a higher standard of factuality and align to stricter guidelines that include correcting mistakes in reporting and not avoiding simple but sometimes unpleasant facts. The US Congress, together with the FCC, news networks, and large social media sites, can firm up guidelines including further labeling content, using on-screen watermarks to delineate: AI content from human-produced, opinion from fact-based exposition, and age-ratings for teens and children—a population who desire further protections as noted in polling numbers.

All too often, when truly harmful information is uploaded onto the internet, individuals and corporations have the choice to file a defamation of character or libel lawsuit for information that may harm another. Defamation of character has been recognized as a wrongful act going back to antiquity, in Ancient Rome for example. In a recent infamous case, a tort was filed against Fox News Network by Dominion Voting Machines Inc. for repeating conspiracy theories for months that Dominion's voting machines were being rigged to produce votes for Democrats. The $787.5 million settlement was the largest in history. More significantly, law courts are the one place in US society where there are real consequences for deception and disinformation. People and organizations can deceive the public up to a point, but we still have the means to confront persistent and harmful deception in the US through civil lawsuits. Free speech has always had limits, and those limits are bound all over the world to cultural mores and laws restricting harmful consequences. Libel laws protect Americans from truly harmful and persistent abuses of otherwise free speech; we need only enforce provisions in those laws and protect those who are most vulnerable with free or low-cost legal aid should they need it.

Though there are structural limitations in short-form telecasts, limited by time and content, when television news is infused with diverse perspectives and panels of ordinary citizens, television news comes closer to a televised community town hall, closer to a more democratic, transparent, and engaging use of news broadcasts. CNN and other networks like Vice and PBS, with its *FRONTLINE* series, produce investigative documentaries that come closer to answering the "why" and "how," demystifying generalizations and politically dualistic framings of societal issues in the minds of Americans. On one memorable episode from *This Is Life with Lisa Ling* titled "Sex Work: Past, Present & Future" which aired October 24, 2021, Ling tackled the then-current debate to decriminalize sex work. In an issue fraught with value judgments, this docu-television segment presented multiple sides for and against legalizing sex work and left viewers open to the humanity of those represented. There have been some furtive attempts to diversify the voices found on broadcasts of television news media. The fact that 65 percent of Americans feel exhausted thinking about politics is an opportunity for candidates and media to speak to policy, enable civil discussion, and prioritize consensus and solutions in primetime, even on issues that are con-textually complex and represent particularly vulnerable populations.

Hearsay on the internet today is much like hearsay from a medieval village of a thousand years ago. Was rumor or hearsay ever trustworthy? Regarding vital information, haven't we always needed to find trust through verification? When pollsters ask the question, "Do you trust social media?" it should be understood that social media itself showcases many different forms of media, from people ranting, to recirculated posts and credible news segments, to documentary films with journalistic investigative techniques on important but out-of-the-mainstream topics. Social media comprises an incredibly varied media universe. We do have an information stream where we can compare sources to see if there are disjunctures in the versions of truth we may have been given. As an anthropologist, I give first-person accounts a lot of weight and validity—acknowledging there are limitations in one person's perspective. For the most part, I also trust the information I receive from articles written in peer-reviewed journals by researchers who have invested much time and discovery in their analysis and whose work is also reviewed by the academy to which they belong. With a society rich and media and news sources, we have in our hands in the US the opportunity to form our independent views of events and issues, and to conduct our research, so long we come out of our media viewing silos to view the broader mediascape.

Though television news broadcasters on the Left may implicitly paint conservatives as those who sip too much of the Right propagandist's tea, a large majority of Americans are aware of media bias. Two-thirds of US adults polled in 2020 said they've seen their news sources report facts meant to favor one side.[427] Most Americans are aware of media bias and see skepticism of news media as healthy. When asked what makes a news story trustworthy, a March 2021 Pew Research poll summarized insightful news audience responses:

> Broad majorities of US adults say it is at least *somewhat* important to consider each of five surveyed factors when determining whether a news story is trustworthy or not: the news organization that publishes it (88%); the sources cited in it (86%); their gut instinct about it (77%); the person, if any, who shared it with them (68%); and the specific journalist who reported it (66%). Just 24% of adults say it's at least somewhat important to consider

a sixth factor included in the survey: whether the story has a lot of shares, comments or likes on social media.[428]

One of the solutions for polarization and protections against disinformation discussed in the US public sphere has been to create more information and media literacy in the US. Polling suggests that Americans may be over-trusting the people sharing information with them and perhaps over-reliant on their "gut instinct" or intuition in reviewing credibility. However, critically reviewing the organization providing news and the sources they use and cite would be an essential part of any Information Literacy 101 course, and most Americans are already doing this. In 2018, Pew Research found that the ability to classify statements as factual or opinion increases with "political awareness, digital savviness, and trust in news media."[429] Engagement rather than disengagement with media is essential in creating a more informed media populace.

An abiding concern of Marshall McLuhan and many other media theorists, including Noam Chomsky and the entire Frankfurt School of cultural researchers, is the corruptive force of money in media. Craigslist decimated the classified ad revenue stream that newspapers were dependent upon with estimated revenue losses between 2000 and 2007 at around $5 billion for the newsprint industry in the US.[430] News departments on local television stations from the 1980s on became increasingly dependent on audience ratings, and along with newspapers, on ad and subscription revenue. The old model of providing news and information for public service on television stations, when television news was broadcast as a budget deficit from the 1950s through to the 1980s, was abandoned. Most of the US newspapers that survived the revenue shortfall after 2000 were bought up by massive media publishers like Gannett, fulfilling one of the predictions of Marshall McLuhan that information would become increasingly uniform, the same news stories replicated in a thousand local newspapers.

The reliance on ad revenue and/or being part of a larger media conglomerate has put pressure on news production to change to friendlier, less troublesome stories that gloss over class politics and any deeper discussions: infotainment has increasingly been built into the news format. The other day, I watched an early morning news segment that seemed to be dedicated to a famous singer/songwriter's newly designed $1 million Louis Vuitton handbag. *Schadenfreude*, or making ordinary people feel better by shaming the wealthy and powerful, is a staple of reality television. Still, it seems out of place in a newscast where people are looking for answers to real problems in their local economies. Matt Taibbi in *Hate, Inc.* documented what he and other media researchers perceive as changes in the political economy of the newsroom. News writing in America up until the 1970s had a workforce deriving from diverse socioeconomic backgrounds, and many of the muckrakers up until that time came from the working class. They were writing stories that came from below and documented the lives and concerns of lower-income groups in America from an emic place. Journalism after Woodward and Bernstein's Watergate expose became a destination career with curriculums in college and the potential for prestige and visibility.

The new journalism workforce of college education professionals understood race and gender justice. Still, the intersectional edge of class and income has been lost from the journalism of the 20th Century when it was a top concern. This it has led many news readers and consumers to think of journalism as the purview of elites. Advertising dependence, together with corporate ownership, has also created subtly conflicted spaces. As big corporations are increasingly called out for price controls in an evermore monopolistic market-place, news and journalism are increasingly dependent on corporate ad revenue for their very existence, at times cross-marketing media or corporate interests within their broadcasts. Advertising and corporate marketing increasingly "colonize our consciousness," as social theorist Hannah Arendt wrote in the 1950s. It has become increasingly harder to distinguish between sponsored information and critical reportage, and the lines may continue to blur.

The New York Times weathered the media sensationalism wars brought on by William Randolph Hearst at the end of the 19th Century as the "grey old lady of journalism," with the ethical content mandate of "all the news that's fit to print." In 2017, Art Cullen, the editor for the 3,000 circulation *Storm Lake Times* out of Iowa won a Pulitzer prize for his editorials that followed the money on how too much nitrogen was being seeped into the drinking water of NW Iowa communities.[431] Cullen's story was reported in another independent newspaper out of the UK, *The Guardian*. In the space of large corporate-owned media companies, a new wave of not-for-profit news organizations have emerged, like *The Texas Tribune, ProPublica*, and the *Center for Investigative Reporting* out of Emeryville, California, with investigations that continue to follow the corrupting influence of money and influence. Independent news sources remain the surest antidote to disinformation and propaganda and for euphemistic advert-style news stories that avoid hard questions—*issue-washing* in its various guises. Receiving the lion's share of the operating income from the media-consuming public, PBS also remains a space dedicated to the concerns of the public they serve. For many Americans, trustworthy news still emanates from stations and sources that cultivate a neutral and objective tone like *Forbes Magazine*, the BBC, *USA Today*, and PBS.[432]

Discussion – Looking beyond the media distortion field

Even though the mediascape in America has expanded exponentially in a few short years, I believe there is still room in the US media landscape for more inclusive and participatory news and information on curated social media sites and within the field of citizen journalism. We've seen some of the uglier conceptions of how the global village might be realized with scandal sheets and sensationalist stories. Still, we are also bearing witness to the vastness of human diversity uploaded onto social media platforms. Though social media has been transformed into a space of revenue and influencers, I don't think we have even come close to realizing the full potential for a bigger role of social media, communication across societies, and new visibility of people and concerns that have remained in the shadows.

Blogs and podcasts have already opened up a space for first-person storytelling, aiding cross-perspective understandings. With mainstream news hyper-focused on national politics, independent journals on good muckraking reportage, and blogs dedicated to surfacing issues in law and order and counter-intuitive insights, an opening presents itself for a view of the world from a wider lens. A view that could utilize the insights of embedded researchers all over the globe able to focus on documenting newsworthy issues, but also solutions to some of the world's most urgent problems. In a March 2020 Pew Research report, three-quarters of those surveyed stated it is possible to improve the level of confidence Americans have in the new media.[433] The news audience hasn't lost faith in news media; they have just become more aware of its limitations, and they want better and more transparent news.

In the absence of substantive discussions for fixing the urgent problems of today, some media sites on the political fringe are committed to a "forever polarization" format to sustain audience shares.

By maintaining Right-wing anger and Left-wing indignation, news media imitates reality television programming, pitting people against other people in a hyperreality where escapism and melodrama mask real-world problems and dialogue. Until the whole of the US audience has grown exhausted from polarized news coverage—as the majority already have—the same old strategy of divide-and-anger will be the bread-and-butter for those seeking power and influence, with no clear imperative for why they need those super powers.

College campuses are now debating the boundaries of free expression as antisemitism becomes more of a threat to Jewish students of inner-city colleges. Some of the debate has swirled around allowing right-wing commentators to speak on campus or concern with left-wing agitators during the Israeli military campaign into the heart of Gaza. The response toward free speech by administrators on some college campuses has been a bit mischaracterized. Administrators believe in free speech, but they are also wary of violence; at times, student safety-first policies have been overly paternal. This, in turn, has also prompted some college administrators like the University of Chicago's Dean of Students, John Ellison, back in 2016 to post a welcome letter to first-year college students stating that the school would not support "safe spaces" or "trigger warnings" in classes on sensitive material. It should also be understood that colleges draw radicalized non-students to campus, that college geographies function as epicenters for free speech. Violence and vandalism are not what universities stand for.

Professors in our higher education system—generally rational, measured, and objective communicators—are not immune to a new media world replete with excess hyperbole. A February 5, 2024, review essay written by senior editor Len Gutkin of *The Chronicle of Higher Education* addressed a new and "hyperbolic style in American academe" emphasized in news releases and tweets that exaggerate imminent threats of violence, and for evidence tend to rely on "distant historical analogies meant to heighten…urgency."[434] It is a rhetorical style that is alarmist, exigent ("something needs to happen, and it needs to happen now"), and meant to persuade, but does so in a way that is replete with catastrophism and arguments that can be "breathless, declaratory, at once aggressive and aggrieved."[435] The amplitude and rhetoric of divisiveness and melodrama have spiraled up in a media economy driven by attention, affecting civil and rational disagreements across the public sphere in the US. Nonetheless, substantive research in academia goes on, and truthful, relevant information is still disseminated on the world wide web—following the intention of its founder.

In November 2022, Right-wing commentator Ann Coulter went to Cornell to speak. She was disrupted by "attendees playing loud music and sound effects, and shouting profanities," according to the Vice President of University Relations, Joel Malina.[436] Given a perfect venue to use their education, hone debate skills, and take on the assertions of a well-known right-wing policy defender, some would rather shout down than listen. A media culture of biased opposition is always in danger of falling into stereotypes and malicious generalizations, blaming all Jews for Netanyahu's disproportional response to Hamas' terrorist incursion in October 2023, or all Palestinians for the actions of Hamas' version of apocalyptic nationalism. News media must continue to avoid simplistic dualistic pitfalls that generalize one side in opposition to another. Listen to comments by the protestors on both sides, and you'll hear the consensus: violence itself is the enemy.

Stepping away from US national media, the non-profit group Reporters Without Borders (RWB) has compiled a World Press

Freedom Index, which evaluates the political and social environments for journalism in 180 countries and territories from around the world every year in May.[437] The index measures press freedom in countries and provides a score from 0 to 100, with one hundred as the highest score. RWR tallies abuses against news media with survey data from journalists, human rights workers, academics, and researchers. North Korea registers at 21.72, the low, and Norway at 95.18, the high. The Nordic countries are among five of the top six countries most highly rated. Ireland has risen to #2, Lithuania (#7) and Estonia (#8) round up the top eight. The United States ranks 45th with a score of 71.22. According to RWB:

> The country's slight decline in the 2023 index was due to the continuing economic difficulties of the media, the murders of two journalists (Jeff German in 2022 and Dylan Lyons in 2023), and the end of efforts to support freedom of the press at the legislative level (the PRESS Act), as well as former President Donald Trump's continued attacks on the media.[438]

The European Union, as an aggregate of countries, has improved its score because, according to RWB, EU legislatures are discussing:

> unprecedented legislation that would establish common press freedom standards. Moreover, the rise in the Index by most of the EU's eastern members goes hand in hand with the realization that independent reporting can serve as a bulwark against Kremlin propaganda.[439]

It is no coincidence that one of the countries with the highest purchasing power of any citizen is Ireland, or that Norway has some of the lowest income inequality and highest social mobility of any country. Creating a population of freer and wealthier citizens normally parallels the development of a free press or the means for a citizenry to meet and discuss issues freely in the public sphere.

Pew Research compiled a similar index in 2015, a Free Expression Index, and they found Americans much more tolerant of offensive speech than people in other nations.[440] Writing for Pew Research, Richard Wike concluded:

> For instance, 77 percent of the US support the right of others to make statements that are offensive to their own religious beliefs, the highest percentage among the nations in the study. Fully 67 percent think people should be allowed to make public statements that are offensive to minority groups, again the highest percentage in the poll. The US was one of only three nations where at least half endorsed the right to sexually explicit speech. Americans don't necessarily like offensive speech more than others, but they are much less inclined to outlaw it.[441]

According to Pew's Index, a larger percentage of citizens in the United States, 71 percent in 2015, believed that people should "be able to say what they want." Latin Americans followed the US in their valorization of speech tolerance. In 2015, US citizens and Latin Americans by large majorities also believed that media should be able to report the news without any state censorship.[442] "

However, American attitudes have changed. The percentage of US adults who believe the US government and/or Tech companies should take steps to restrict false information online, even if it limits freedom of information, grew from 39 percent in 2018 to a majority

55 percent by 2023. Americans have grown wary of our information stream; it is no longer open season for producing disinformation.

As we have been debating the role of the media and information here at home, press freedoms around the world more generally have eroded. Free speech, as a global right charted in the United Nations, may be under threat internationally. According to Reporters Without Borders, in 2013, 29 percent of 180 countries around the world had at least a "satisfactory situation" with press rights and press freedom.[443] By 2023, in many of those 180 counties, press freedoms slipped from "good" to merely "satisfactory," the number whose press freedoms registered in a "difficult situation" increased, and the number with "very serious situations" ballooned up substantially. Overall, "poor" sociopolitical environments for journalism exist in seven out of ten countries in the world and are "satisfactory" in only three out of ten countries worldwide. As we have been debating the role of the media and information here at home, press freedoms around the world have eroded. We must remind ourselves that press freedom is intrinsic to the sustenance of democracies around the world. A healthy press is also an allied partner in the emancipation of people worldwide.

Should we agree that the first job of journalists should be to present factual information, even if it flies in the face of their own personal convictions? At the end of the book *Hate, Inc.*, Matt Taibbi interviews Noam Chomsky about his book *Manufacturing Consent*. During the interview, Chomsky, at one point, opines that some of the readers of his book took away the feeling that they could not trust the media. "But that's not exactly what [the book] said. If you want to get information, sure, read *The New York Times*, but read it with your eyes wide open. With a critical mind."[52] The days of Eric

Sevareid covering the Apollo 11 rocket launch and trying to provide both sides of a story—the technological miracle of the launch and the aims of a civil rights demonstration at the launch—may have diminished, but they are not gone. Many journalists and newscasters earn their audience loyalty by simply being fair; it is also a good, safe marketing strategy.

Has bothsideism run its course with television debate formats like the one in the show *Crossfire*, which pitted someone on the Left debating with someone on the Right? Ironically, Americans' tolerance of offensive speech is matched by the number of Americans who say we are too easily offended by things we say to others. Sixty-five percent of Americans polled in July 2021 believed that it was a "major problem" in America that too many of us were easily offended by things we say to each other. [444] Yet, 91 percent of Americans state that saying things that are very offensive to others is at least a minor problem in the country today. [445] Americans want the freedom to speak offensively if they like, but they also believe there is too much offensive speech. Do many of us want it both ways in the United States, or are we signaling through this poll that we're ready to dialogue with each other in a civil but frank manner?

As Jon Stewart of *The Daily Show* often points out, dualistic television talk formats that pit two people of opposite political stances seem endlessly confrontational and sometimes meritless. The days of right-wing pundits using sharp analytical tools and warmly inviting debate with left-wing journalists over policy on national television became much rarer after William F Buckley Jr. left the show Firing Line, in 1999. Discussion panels during television news coverage engage now in *multisideism*, providing some nuance of perspectives between journalists, attorneys, and political commentators. A great potential remains for panel discussions on mainstream news to be more inclusive of other voices or to host more town hall formats where ordinary Americans can be given a voice in the public sphere of news. Those who watch or read the news in the US have trust in one or more journalists, and some journalists embrace other perspectives. Bret Baier from *Fox News* regularly hosts guests from both the Right and Left on his program and does something even more laudable: he listens intently to his guests.

If you had been watching the news in the early summer of 2023 and tuned into *CNN Tonight* with Alisyn Camerota, you would have seen a good example of inclusive media in progress. At the time, CNN was composing guest panels of four guests with diverse voices from both the Left and Right. They occasionally videotaped and broadcast panel discussions of ordinary Americans moderated by Camerota professionally and respectfully. Americans need more, not less, space for civil interaction; many are ready to listen to other perspectives. It is clear to me, listening to ordinary Americans, that political beliefs can be imagined as degrees of difference rather than as a political faultline. Listening is key to transforming our information stream and finding consensus therein.

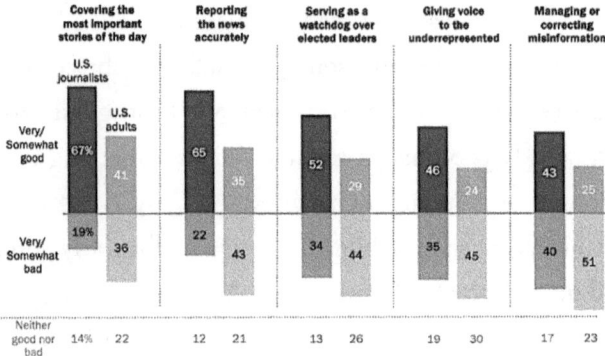

Journalists and the American public stand far apart on how well they think news outlets do in many of their core functions

% who say news organizations do a good or bad job at ...

	Covering the most important stories of the day	Reporting the news accurately	Serving as a watchdog over elected leaders	Giving voice to the underrepresented	Managing or correcting misinformation
Very/Somewhat good (U.S. journalists)	67%	65	52	46	43
Very/Somewhat good (U.S. adults)	41	35	29	24	25
Very/Somewhat bad (U.S. journalists)	19%	22	34	35	40
Very/Somewhat bad (U.S. adults)	36	43	44	45	51
Neither good nor bad (journalists)	14%	12	13	19	17
Neither good nor bad (adults)	22	21	26	30	23

Note: Respondents who did not answer not shown.
Source: Survey of U.S. journalists conducted Feb. 16-March 17, 2022. Survey of U.S. adults conducted Feb. 7-13, 2022.
"Journalists Sense Turmoil in Their Industry Amid Continued Passion for Their Work"

PEW RESEARCH CENTER

Figure 1 - Journalists and the US news public differ on journalism effectiveness

Journalists are far more concerned than the public about politically like-minded people clustering around the same news outlets

% who say it's a ___ when people with the same political views get their news from the same news organizations

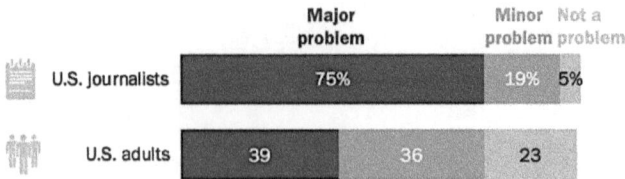

	Major problem	Minor problem	Not a problem
U.S. journalists	75%	19%	5%
U.S. adults	39	36	23

Note: Respondents who did not answer not shown.
Source: Survey of U.S. journalists conducted Feb. 16-March 17, 2022. Survey of U.S. adults conducted March 7-13, 2022.
"Journalists Sense Turmoil in Their Industry Amid Continued Passion for Their Work"

PEW RESEARCH CENTER

Figure 2 - Journalists are concerned about tunnel vision in the US

On These Issues, We Agree
A Synopsis

Economic Issues

I began this book with a suggestion that Americans believed themselves to be polarized and that there was an abiding perception between Republicans and Democrats that they could not even agree on the facts. Two-thousand twenty-three was a year of intense partisanship, the most dysfunctional year in the House of Representatives in 50 years, according to former Congressman Ken Buck (R) of Colorado, and this wasn't lost on the American electorate.[446] In the lead-up to a contentious and polarized 2020 US Presidential Election, 63 percent of Democrat voters still believed it was important for a Democratic candidate to focus on finding common ground with Republicans if elected. In a Pew Research December 2023 poll, half of Republican-leaning voters also believed it was important to find common ground, even if it meant "giving up some things Republicans want."[447] Though polarizing soundbites fill our news, most Americans want national politicians to focus on the issues that concern them most and find consensus for the benefit of all Americans.

In the winter of 2024, the national economy remained a top concern for 75 percent of Americans polled. Deep party differences have traditionally polarized Republicans and Democrats over finding the solutions to improving economic conditions for the average American. Democrats have favored a progressive tax system, more government regulation of financial markets, and priority spending on social programs. Republicans have favored lower taxes, smaller government, and less financial market regulation—*laissez-faire* free market policies that drew their original inspiration from Adam Smith's ideas of an invisible hand of market competition that would lift everyone.

A Harris poll in August 2022 found that 60 percent of Americans polled wanted to be a billionaire one day, and 44 percent believed they had the "available tools to become a billionaire."[448] According to *Forbes Magazine,* only 1 in 500,000 Americans are billionaires, and about 6.5 percent of the population are millionaires in terms of wealth assets, but the American aspiration for wealth goes on undiminished.[449] A new attention economy where internet influencers accrue wealth with little effort has contributed to expectations in younger Americans that boundless wealth is only right around the corner. The seduction of free-market capitalism has threaded its way through all generations, as Canadian historian Ronald Wright describes:

> It lures us onward like the mechanical hare before the greyhounds, insisting that the economy is infinite and sharing therefore

irrelevant. Just enough greyhounds catch a real hare now and then to keep the others running till they drop. In the past it was only the poor who lost this game; now it is the planet.[450]

Globally, the US is a wealthy nation by any standard, and we live lives of abundance compared to our American ancestors. During the industrial era and into WWI, most Americans nearly worked themselves to death with long hours and short-lived lives. Questioning whether they had enough "work/life balance" would have been an alien idea: as they strove to improve the lives of the next generation, they sacrificed much of their own. But now, many Americans question whether the next generations will be as fortunate as theirs. Many middle-income Americans suffered an economic reversal in the 2008 global financial meltdown, and inflation kickstarted by the supply chain crises during COVID has pushed many Americans past the affordability point. Many Americans simply cannot afford the basic expenses to live without adding another job, working still more hours, coming out of retirement, or forestalling middle-class aspirations like sending children away to college or saving money for a home. From 2019 to the start of 2024, inflationary costs of goods rose 22 percent on average.

That means some commodities and services did not rise in price, while others rose dramatically during that time. For the nation to match the rise in costs, all Americans would have had to receive a pay raise of 22 percent during that same time. Who of us can say that? The presidents of California State University did indeed receive large pay raises during those four years, so-called "equity adjustments," just as adjunct professors in the CSU system lost jobs in great numbers with declining student enrollments. Executive income, as an aggregate, has risen proportionally over inflation costs over the last forty years. Had you been the 1 out of 20 Americans in the executive class, lawyers, medical doctors, entrepreneurs, college presidents, or those working in the upper echelons of government, inflation would be something that affects everyone else. There is a dissonance that exists between elites in news media and politics who use economic indexes to demonstrate how healthy the US economy is and how high 401ks have risen in value in a nation where half of its citizens have no money in stocks or investments, and whose purchasing power remains critically low.

The world is now entirely linked to a global economy, a gig economy, in which the US has become dependent on cheap overseas labor and resources. On the one hand, global poverty rates have been lowered overall, but this has come at a cost. America is now at the crossroads. All citizens of the world are now more dependent on the economic policy choices of our representative government, and for forty years those policy choices have increased economic inequality. Our national economic policies have hollowed out the middle classes, leaving many to simply work to pay bills, and this hurts the American economy as a whole. Economists like Joseph Stiglitz and Thomas Piketty point out that much of the American economic system runs on the expenditures of middle and lower-income Americans. When given a choice, 90 percent of Americans surveyed wanted a fairer wealth and income distribution than we have currently in the US. The question is, how do we get there? Governmental policies can't fix all of our economic woes, but as Joseph Stiglitz states, economic inequality is, first and foremost, a national economic policy choice.

So much of our national economic policy is driven by myth and platitudes, that it is difficult to get facts in order and to understand the consequences of any policy because the prime directive for politicians is to get reelected, and before the current hyperreal era of national politics, that was based primarily on outcomes for the American people. However, in the last forty years, other nations have increased social mobility, decreased economic inequality, and created happier citizens largely as a result of economic policies built from the middle up.[451]

Affordable healthcare and education are key to the success of any nation's economy because—in economic terms—they are also investments in our national human capital. Education provides the tools for the next generation workforce, and healthcare provides for the maintenance and physical welfare of that workforce. An investment in human capital is an investment in national capital in the long term. For that reason, Americans need to continue to have a vibrant public discussion over how much we want these institutions privatized and capitalized. Certainly, administration bloat has been part of the rising cost of healthcare and higher education, and this needs to be addressed with a critical review of programs and staffing costs. Boards of trustees and directors responsible for executive salary inflation—while doing nothing to increase the wages of most workers—should be replaced; they are part of the problem and not the solution.

Making a good living is such an essential part of America's identity and of Americans' aspirations. Not being able to afford the cost of living drives tensions between couples, families, and even between ethnic groups in the US. All Americans, particularly people whose families may not have had the chance to establish intergenerational wealth and who have no assets or nest egg to fall back on, are deeply affected by a decline in purchasing power. In the past, the blame for poverty (a lack of money and assets) was directed at lower to middle-income Americans because it was thought they did not work enough or that they simply weren't driven. Building wealth in the

US takes generations, and the income and opportunities for African Americans for generations were affected deeply by segregationist policies. Many 1st, 2nd, and even 3rd generation Americans started from a place of zero wealth in America, and their diligence may just now be paying off. Every American who has had a generation of economic reversal has had to start again, and the economy of the US now allows for less social mobility than it has perhaps since the Great Depression. Effort and diligence alone may not be enough to rise above the economic structures in place: a low national minimum wage, low-salary gig work where the most vulnerable are first to be let go in an economic downturn, and tax policies that have ensured the wealthiest Americans pay lower tax rates than middle-income Americans.

Human beings in every corner of the world live in a globally interconnected economy with consequences that Americans are becoming fully aware of: (1) it is difficult to live outside the global economic system, and therefore, our dependency upon it requires a careful calibration toward economic fairness with an acceptable consensus-based level of economic inequality, an economy that is not an oligopoly but a demopoly. (2) Our importation dependency on resources like fossil fuel is a national security issue; we don't want to embolden totalitarian states or negotiate with dictators, and this requires America to have a more holistic system, a self-contained system with vital industrial output, and a future that makes us less import-dependent while preserving trading relationships with our key democratic allies. (3) Americans on the Right and Left don't want monopolization, and in a world dependent on fewer but larger mega-conglomerates, we must foster free market competition in our American economy. (4) We can take steps as consumers and small producers to combat supply-chain dependency by using our property or community land more efficiently, growing food sustainably as we once did, and consuming with awareness.

Abortion

In general terms, Americans tend to favor policies and laws that allow for broad individual liberties in so far as those liberties do not influence the quality of life of others. Locating a balance of fairness within the scope of social justice issues in the US, with policies that ameliorate racism, provide for equal opportunity, or grant legal protections to control the autonomy of one's own body, is part of a sometimes contentious, ever-evolving discussion held in the US public sphere. One of the policies that were floated by the Republican Party in the run-up to the 2024 election is that abortion should be severely restricted and outlawed before the first trimester. Allowing states to restrict abortion to less than three months has already proven deeply problematic for the healthcare sector and, when put to the vote, has been voted down the six times amendments or laws with such restrictions were put to the vote in red states.

As of January 2024, Abortion was nearly or completely banned in 14 states of the union.[452] However, political consensus nationally on this complicated issue favors personal choice over pro-life restrictions. One-third of US adults polled in March 2022, for example, believed life began at conception *but* also believed the decision to have an abortion belongs solely to the woman.[453] Only 11 percent of those polled believed that an abortion should be illegal if the woman's life is at risk. Support for legal abortion jumped after the *Dobbs* Decision in June 2022, but it has been growing steadily overall since the *Roe v. Wade* US Supreme Court decision in 1973. With voters aged 18-29, support for legalized abortion is more than ten percentage points above the national average, and with older Americans

(65+) at least 5 points below the national average—time is on the side of the pro-choice position in states that are more conservative on the issue now.

The patchwork of laws regarding abortion is also affecting in vitro fertilization procedures: women have found it harder to get pregnant and couples to start families. In one of the most conservative states on abortion, Alabama, a state supreme court ruling that classifies frozen embryos as people pushed the rights of the unborn to the cellular stage and ignited discussion and anxiety for those struggling with fertility who have aspirations for a family.[454] Legalizing abortion nationally to the first trimester, or for any reason that a medical doctor deems for the health and life of the pregnant woman (including the use of embryos for IVF), meets the consensus we have on a difficult and highly personal topic, about the two-thirds of the American public. It also gives medical doctors the legal and ethical autonomy they require to practice medicine, and their patients the ability to put aside one of the many concerns they face on the way to becoming pregnant or finding out they cannot carry a child to term.

As state laws now dictate abortion, we have injected legislatures between a woman and her doctor into a private sphere where long-standing Western cultural precedents before the Victorian era held that these were personal and not political issues. Polling evidence also suggests about 65 percent of Americans want abortion restricted after the first trimester, to some degree. We will not solve the moral ambiguities surrounding the issue, nor will we resolve what rights the unborn are due or even when human life begins. Still, those rights have become part of our national conversation even as a substantial majority of Americans have evolved to favor the freedoms and restrictions in the original *Roe v. Wade* ruling more than fifty years ago. A large majority of Americans want that decision legislated into national law.[455]

Racism and Diversity

In a July 2021 Pew Research poll, most Republicans (71 percent) believed "a lot of progress" had been made on racism in America over the last fifty years.[456] Only 29 percent of Democrat-leaning voters in the sample acknowledged that "a lot had been done" to ensure equal rights in the last fifty years, and 61 percent acceded that a little had been done. Three-quarters of Democrat-leaning voters believed that a lot more needed to be done, with only 22 percent of Republicans believing the same. On the issue of racism in America, it is not the lack of acknowledgment that racism still exists that divides the parties, it is the consensus on how far the nation has progressed toward eliminating racism that is the issue, versus how much further we have to go.

One of the most revealing comparative data points in racial and economic equality is the difference in the median wealth between Black and White citizens in America. What the data show is that "US households headed by people who are White have significantly higher levels of wealth than those headed by people who are Black or Hispanic."[457] The racial wealth gap between White and Black households peaked in 2007, before the Great Recession. Still, the average household wealth represented by Black Americans in 2019 was $24.1k (stagnant since 1998) compared to the average White household income at $189.1k, a $165k differential that has grown since the 1980s. It is close to the ethnic wealth gap represented between Hispanic and White Americans as well.[458] Following this disparity is an embedded cynicism registered in Black America. In an October 2021 poll, only 13 percent of Black adults say achieving equality for Black people in the US is extremely or very likely.[459] Most Black Americans (65 percent) polled after the Black Lives Movement in 2019 and 2020 believed that the movement had not led to any changes that would improve the lives of Black Americans.[460]

A majority of adult Black Americans (79 percent), conservative to liberal, polled in October 2021 believed they had personally experienced racism in our laws (85 percent) and by other individuals (77 percent).[461] A majority of Americans polled in March 2021 also believed Black (79 percent), Asian (71 percent), and Hispanic (76 percent) Americans faced some discrimination in US society.[462] Most Republicans believe the causes of racial inequality derive from family instability, lack of good role models, and lack of personal motivation to work hard, while Democrats tend to believe structural discrimination is better explanated by racial inequalities: less access to good schools and high paying jobs are a two of the primary factors noted.[463] Lower marriage rates in the US overall—but particularly among Black Americans—may account for some of the disparity in household wealth among Americans. However, the consensus in the US is that non-white Americans still face some discrimination in the US.

In just three generations removed from segregationist policies in the US that exacerbated the racial wealth gap in the US, the most extreme poverty has substantially declined for all Americans, particularly for Black Americans. Still, 1 in 5 Black Americans in 2020 lived below the poverty line, and in the US economic system, it has been estimated that it takes six generations for a family to level the playing field of economic equality, and we are only three generations removed from segregationist policies that structurally ensured the disenfranchisement of Black Americans. The majority of

Americans agree we have made progress on racial inequality, but we are not where we could be either. The larger question then remains: how can we solve issues of racism with the consensus that we have in America?

Individual racism is caused by ignorance and fear of another and can be bolstered by the scapegoating of others, especially during times of national economic insecurity. Racism measures phobia and insecurity, not patriotism or pride. The solution for individual racism derives from the education of the history of race discrimination in the US and a consciousness and recognition of our default, ethnocentric impulses. The structural solution to racial inequality suggested by polling consensus lies in structuring economic policies that ameliorate economic inequality and ensure *equal opportunity aspiration* for all to combat the structural hopelessness embedded in racial inequality.

Equal opportunity aspiration means that the US should endeavor from a child's earliest years to provide them with the tools to imagine a life that fosters talent and rewards effort and hard work, no matter one's ethnicity or race. Funding universal Pre-K and good public education sufficient to the demands of teaching loads is a good start and a popular solution acknowledged through polling. Though equal opportunity programs in higher education and direct monetary remittances have lower popular traction in America, the amount of diversity in college faculty today demonstrates the success of equal opportunity programs. Institutional leadership in key sectors of our national economy has also been diversified—the executives responsible for hiring inclusion. Many families of all ethnicities have been affected by the ravages of opiate addiction; even in America's heartland, there is popular support for lifting Americans from the bottom up, for programs that give a hand up rather than a handout, to ensure the pathways for social mobility are available to all Americans.

Environmentalism and a Green Economy

Enthusiasm for ecological wellness and the prioritization of environmental problems is tempered in the United States with the financial cost of going green in the US. However, as a society, the US has evolved, and what were once progressive ecological concerns supported mainly by the young and the few in the 1960s have become mainstream concerns and discussions in families today. At least 80 percent of Americans are at least concerned "a fair amount" about water pollution in drinking water, rivers, lakes, and reservoirs. Very few Americans, 8 percent, are "not at all" concerned about air pollution, and less than 1 in 10 Americans are not concerned at all with the extinction of plant and animal species, water pollution, or the loss of tropical rainforests.[464]

In the United States, environmental policies have historically been driven by public concerns that have been reactive rather than proactive to ecological events and industrial consequences. It is harder to galvanize a critical mass of people for future environmental devastation than the ecological crises of the now. But most older Americans who lived or at least passed through Los Angeles or New York City in summertime remember days when leaded smog was thick like fog, pollution was seen and breathed. Some may even remember when the Cayahoga River, choked with pollution and an oil slick, caught fire on June 22, 1969, just southeast of downtown Cleveland, Ohio. In the US, we have come a long way in cleaning up our rivers and our air. Global climate change, the loss of rainforests, species extinctions, these abstract consequences of environmental loss are less tangible and lesser still as many Americans struggle to catch up to the cost of living.

However, the interconnectedness of ecological systems is so much better understood since the birth of the environmental movement in the late 1960s. We know far more about the impact of tropical forest deforestation on greenhouse gas absorption, what causes species loss and endangerment in shrinking habitats, and how extinction can be measured. We know more about the extent of plastic pollution worldwide, and the near failure of US recycling programs to limit it. Corporations, non-governmental organizations, individuals, and governmental agencies like the Environmental Protection Agency (EPA), however, are applying solutions to environmental problems with substantial results. Many of the solutions, like wind technology and solar projects, need only be scaled up and better integrated into our electrical grid to balance the cost of implementation with the rewards of transitioning our energy production to green and domestic sources.

Crafting policies that ensure that the transition to green technologies is conducted with economic ramifications in mind is broadly popular, and would allay the fear (especially on the Right) that green technologies necessarily come with economic sacrifices. Providing tax credits to businesses for developing carbon capture/ storage is broadly supported by 70 percent of Republican and 88 percent of Democrat-leaners. A surprising number of Republicans also support requiring power companies to use more energy from renewable sources (49 percent), taxing corporations based on carbon emissions (46 percent), and providing incentives to increase the use of electric vehicles (46 percent), all policies with overwhelming support from Democrats polled.[465]

Still, a significant portion of Americans remain ambivalent

about the transition to green energy, that it would have a more negative than positive impact on consumer prices. In the long term, this may be a dangerous misconception. The US already produces enough gasoline for its consumption domestically. We don't need to import more oil, we need to update our refining technology. Ultimately, economic sustainability in the US is dependent on environmental sustainability. We need only look at the collapse of local economies driven by the demise of the whaling industry and the collapse of the Atlantic northwest cod fishery in North America to acknowledge this fact. Putin's invasion of Ukraine reminded us that reliance on imported resources can embolden and solidify the profit of dictators in authoritarian states, a dangerous trade dependency. In the future, the US economy and security will depend upon energy that is profitable, green, and domestically produced.

Pollution and loss of species and forests are the biggest concerns of Americans on environmental issues. Global warming, with a more abstract meaning with multiple consequences, is less concerning. However, one of the direct consequences of global warming is the warming of the world's oceans diminishing the number of tiny phytoplankton in the world's oceans—which produce as much oxygen as the remainder of the world's greenery. We are inured to the word "crises" from hearing it often in television news or as headlines in print media. Still, the greening of the planet is an issue deserving more urgency than the amount of prioritization registered through polling numbers. Environmental maintenance and restoration help us breathe abundant oxygen, drink clean and healthy water, and allows us to consume sustainably without fear that the systems that produce our food and the resources we depend on will simply run out and leave us scrambling to prevent societal devastation—as so many have prophesized.

Violence, Crime, and Gun Laws

While the incidences of property theft have leveled off or declined in most categories, and retail theft and car theft incidences have risen only slightly within cities overall, the material value of theft in the US has increased substantially, indicating a serialization of robbery, of organized theft rings making targets of higher value. While violent crime and property theft have not nearly increased to the proportions seen in the early 1990s, the cost of theft and the rise in mass shootings have elevated the perception of violence in America. Mainstream media coverage focused on violent crime contributes to a perception that violent crime is ever worsening in the US. As John Gramich, an associate director for the Pew Research Center, has pointed out:

> The public often tends to believe that crime is up, even when the data shows it is down. In 22 of 26 Gallup surveys conducted since 1993, at least six-in-ten US adults said there was more crime nationally than there was the year before, despite the general downward trend in the national violent crime rate during most of that period.[466]

During the national midterm elections of 2022, Republican voters were much more likely than Democratic voters to see violent crime as a key voting issue. Like many political talking points, the perception of crime and violence have become politicized topics. As Steven Pinker and other academic researchers have pointed out, when societal conditions improve—like lower crime rates or lowered incidents of violence—such progress seldom makes headlines.

Though genetic studies on criminal behavior have revealed specific genes associated with regulating neurotransmitter levels that may be tied to the small group of antisocial repeat offenders, the biggest predictor of violent criminal behavior statistically arises from living in areas of the country where residents "experience multiple forms of disadvantage, from poverty to disease to segregation to joblessness."[467] Poor and historically disadvantaged communities bore the brunt of the surge in violence in 2020, but the structural conditions for violence have been in place in disadvantaged communities for decades. Combining impoverishment and a lack of education or vocational training with the psyche of worthlessness that this cultivates is a potent cocktail for violent behavior. Inner-city programs like Baltimore's Safe Steet program, established in 2007, have successfully brought down the level of inner-city violence, and such non-profit intervention programs have helped bring down violence and violent crime overall in the United States. Community-based programs like the Safe Street Program—out of Baltimore—offer an outreach by social workers and former gang members who mediate disputes that could lead to violence. They intervene to offer social services, mentorship, and other support to individuals to lower the risks of violent actions—particularly in youth culture.[468]

In February 2022, the National Institute of Justice published some of the results of a database compiled over 53 years of people who had committed public mass shootings over the last half-century. People who have committed public mass shootings in the US over the last half-century were commonly troubled by personal trauma before their shooting incidents, nearly always in a state of crisis at the time, and in most cases, engaged in leaking their plans before opening fire. Most were insiders of a targeted institution, such as an employee or student. Except for young school shooters who stole guns from family members, most used legally obtained handguns shootings.[469] The most successful way to limit firearm casualties is to initiate sensible gun policies that follow the consensus of community members themselves, including input from law enforcement and surgeons—those who see the consequences of gun violence firsthand.

Gun safety courses could be mandated for anyone 21 and under who wants to purchase a gun, or for anyone, period. Community ordinances could mandate citizens buy and store weapons in gun safes with households with children, and citizens follow public safety protocols in public arenas. Red Flag gun hotline phone services with real enforcement and psychological screening are coming into place. More than any other action, intervening with someone with possession in possession of a firearm who is going through a personal crisis or in a period of elevated hostility is the best preventative measure for preventing gun violence. Concern for another citizen is not a violation of someone's rights, it is a throwback to a time when Americans cared for the welfare of each other—and such compassion is needed in a time of increasing social isolation in America and significant rates of suicide among our youth.

It is no coincidence that the US is seeing a spike in asylum registrations from immigrants from Venezuela, El Salvador, Mexico, and Honduras, some of the countries with the greatest homicide rates internationally. Human beings do not thrive in social geographies of violence, and as such, asylum requests claiming intense fear of the violent geographies refugees leave behind are generally quite legitimate. Other countries like Japan, which have very strict gun control laws record very few gun-related deaths, where only one person in every 300 owns a gun. However, there are other countries like Switzerland, Norway, Portugal, and Canada where gun ownership is common. Still, gun-related homicides are low because gun safety training and gun safety restrictions are set into law and approved in social mores. It is not incompatible to have a society awash in guns, with high gun ownership, but with low gun homicide.

We forget that the ability to have "life and liberty" is not only expressed as an aspiration in the US Declaration of Independence, but it is also a fundamental right written into the 14th Amendment of the US Constitution. A majority of Americans believe communities have the fundamental right to see that the life of their residents is not deprived in a landscape of under-regulated firearms, acknowledging that attitudes about gun rights differ in rural communities as they do within inner cities. For almost two centuries in the US, the right to set gun use ordinances and laws was given to small communities, and they negotiated issues of safety with the consent of their citizenry following the original 2nd Amendment language of a "well-regulated militia."

Immigration

In a February 2024 Gallup poll, immigration surged to the top of the most important problems "list" confronting the nation.[470] A Pew Research poll in January 2024 had "defending against terrorism" and "dealing with immigration" rising as issues demanding priority for national politicians, two issues driven by conservative media broadcasts.[471] As Pew reports:

> Over the course of Biden's presidency, the share of Americans citing immigration as a top priority has increased 18 percentage points – from 39% to 57% – with the change coming almost entirely among Republicans and Republican-leaning independents. Republicans have also grown more concerned over terrorism, especially in the past year.[472]

Democrats and Republicans differ on the causes of the influx of immigration, with more Democrats believing a "major reason" for the emigration out of their home countries is due to violence (79 percent). More Republicans believed a "major reason" for emigration is that US immigration policies make it easy to stay in the US once they arrive. Democrats and Republicans also describe the problem of immigration differently, with more Republicans seeing the US/Mexico border in full crisis, with an influx of international terrorists arriving with immigrants, and Democrats seeing the border issues as a lower priority for national politicians to tackle in 2024.[473] Most Republicans (72 percent) also believe expanding the border wall along the US border would make the situation at the border better, with only 30 percent of Democrats expressing this view.[474]

Though the perception of our US immigration problem differs along party lines, eighty percent of Americans polled believed the US government was doing a bad job handling the immigration influx. The immigrant surge has become a great bipartisan concern overall. Democrats and Republicans have a consensus on causes and solutions as well. Majorities in both parties believe a large number of immigrants seek to enter the US at the Southern Border for better economic opportunities here in the US and bad economic conditions in their home countries. Half of Republicans and three-quarters of Democrats believe boosting resources for more border guards, updated technology, and more judicial magistrates making quicker decisions on immigrants at the border would improve the situation.

On February 4, 2024, the text of a $118 billion immigration bill written in the US Senate was unveiled, a bipartisan agreement between Senators James Lankford, R-Okla., Chris Murphy, D-Conn., and Kyrsten Sinema, I-Ariz. Though a bipartisan working group created the Senate Bill, many of the amendments to immigration that

Democrats have long sought, like provisions that naturalize "Dreamers," providing amnesty to undocumented Americans who came to the US as children or to those who have served in the US Military, these provisions were left out. However, the Senate Bill provided bipartisan albeit Republican-leaning solutions to the border crises, including (1) a new and greatly expedited system for processing asylum requests that would move the process into the Department of Homeland Securit (2) A new standard asylum seekers in which they would have to establish "clear and convincing" proof that they have a credible fear of persecution if they stay in their country (3) earlier rejections from asylum if the person has a disqualifying criminal history, or if they were living safely in a third country before seeking asylum, or if they could safely relocate in their original home country (4) and a new emergency authorization for the DHS to shut down the border if the if average migrant crossing numbers reach 4,000 per day, over seven days.[475] The bill also expanded the allocation of work visas. It provided more money to the US Immigration and Customs Enforcement and Customs and Border Patrol to make new hires, which would help to bring more manpower to the border in remote areas of crossings.

The rise of governments ruled by totalitarian cartels and presidents-for-life has and will continue to destabilize the world and send countless thousands of refugees from violence, corruption, and structural despair to countries with functioning legal systems and governments. Though opinion polls consistently report that Americans believe foreign aid is about 25 percent of the federal budget, it is actually less than one percent. In the long term, what is needed to stem the flood of refugees is political and economic stability internationally, foreign governments that hold and sustain well-functioning democratic governance helped by a strong and empowered United

Nations and NATO membership, and a resurgence of diplomacy that will allow wealthy countries to broker regional stability and help put problematic totalitarian regimes on a course toward representative governments and stable economies.

Amnesty International suggests in its "Eight Ways to Solve the World Refugee Crises" that every wealthy country like the US needs their legislatures to sit down and fix their immigration system in a bipartisan manner as soon as possible and to stop blaming immigrants for the structural conditions and political decolonizing histories in which ordinary people have died in the millions to try and change.[476] The primary way to fix the immigration and refugee crises is to leverage our power and diplomacy in the US to try and keep it from being a crisis in the first place and for Congress to find consensus on a lasting bipartisan immigration policy to do their job setting immigration policy as dictated in the US Constitution.

Politics, Beyond Division, Empowering Consensus

In a poll conducted in June of 2023, 63 percent of Republicans and 62 percent of Democrats polled believed the "[in]ability of Dem-Reps to work together" to be a very big problem in the US.[477] A quarter of those polled believed divisions among Americans were tied to political polarization and tribalism. In 1994, only 21 percent of Republicans had a "very unfavorable" view of the Democratic Party, and only 17 percent of Democrats at that time had a "very unfavorable" view of Republicans.[478] Anti-liberal rhetoric was ratcheted up in conservative media beginning in the late 1980s, and liberal reactions have followed. By 2022, 62 percent of Republicans had a "very unfavorable" view of the Democratic Party, and 54 percent of Democrats had a "very unfavorable" view of Republicans.[479] We aren't seeing individual Americans so much in the political public sphere anymore, their concerns; we're not registering their aspirations nor their experiences. We see fellow Americans much more as agendas and ideologies.

Despite polling numbers and media perceptions that paint America as a hopelessly divided nation, two-thirds of Americans polled stated they would rather live in a politically diverse neighborhood than a politically homogenous one. Even though Americans are ambivalent when it comes to communicating with others with distinctly different political views, the number of us who would talk to someone whose views differ jumps to 61 percent if we were assured we "would be listened to respectfully."[480] Americans anticipate the awkwardness and discomfort of speaking to someone with opposing views. If our conversations could be mediated productively, we would be more willing to address our differences. It is still easier to understand one's tribe than to try to understand the abstraction of the many or to see past popular generalizations or political labels. Americans acknowledge societal divisions but also signal that they want to move beyond them.

For a time, it seemed the US democratic process itself began to be questioned directly before and after the national elections of 2020. A Pew Research poll in March of 2018 found that most Americans still expressed approval of the main tenets of the balance of governmental powers. Large majorities in both parties, for example (70 percent of Republicans and 83 percent of Democrats), opposed the idea of giving presidents more power.[481] Despite the frightening views of insurgents storming the US Capitol to wrest control away from Congress, most Americans still stated that politicians should heed the will of the majority even if their views differ. According to Pew:

Three-quarters of Americans say that in a hypothetical scenario, a governor should sign a bill that has support from most people in their state, even if most of his or her supporters oppose it.[482]

Reviewing the nation's top concerns discussed in this book, how many political candidates and incumbents are expressing any solutions or outlining the details of policies they would undertake to fix the most urgent problems in America? Why go through all of the trouble to win a position in US national representation if you're not going to negotiate with others or propose solutions to get any worthwhile legislation passed? Perceptually, what seems to be the overriding goal in national politics—attention and fund-raising—distracts away from the fact that millions of people and organizations are working on the most urgent problems in the US right now. Americans are highly attuned and sensitive to fairness. As politics have become more national and less local, we have become much more sensitive to fairness in the national political theater. The equilibrium point between the Right and the Left in the American populace is now further to the Left than the representative body politic of the US Congress. The Right has won the information war politically since the 1980s, partly because the Left did not want to believe war was being waged in the first place.

But with the *Dobbs* Decision, the Left is now much more solidified; they have woken up to political gamesmanship because elections have had serious consequences for empowering minority policies in the US—as books like *Tyranny of the Minority: Why American Democracy Reached the Breaking Point* (2023) have pointed out. Former US Attorney General Eric Holder, speaking on *Real Time with Bill Maher* (3/15/2024) on gerrymandering in the United States—the subject of his 2023 book on the subject—stated that

"Republicans have made peace with the notion they're going to be a minority party, in terms of populous support, but they want majority power." Rather than depend upon voter suppression tactics or subterfuge in protecting numbers in a shrinking electorate with a shrinking slate of policies, politicians should work to earn the votes of their constituents by providing policies that solve real-world problems and do the hard work of finding bipartisan consensus with their constituents in mind. If they want to expand their electoral base they should do so the old-fashioned way, by earning votes, but also by being responsible leaders who can even-handedly gauge the destiny of our nation.[483]

In the ancient Greek Assembly in Athens, issues were solved quickly and decisively. Endless bickering was useless in a society where action was required and life short. Following Aristotle's framing of the *polis*, Americans need to be more politically engaged but far less polarized. In being more political in the public sphere, I mean to say that political engagement is good for America; acting on our civil republicanism is the cure for nihilism and apathy, and it starts with voting rates and civil dialogue that empowers deliberation, progress, and transformation. We need to ask policy questions of our candidates, and when they dodge these questions, continue and repeat those questions until we have answers. Like Deep Throat in the movie *All the President's Men*, polling data suggest we want our press to continue to scrutinize power and influence, to follow the money in politics—which has now risen to be a new top concern of Americans—and follow the legislation of our elected officials to see if it matches what we believed those candidates said they would do, and how effective they've been in office.

We must get beyond polarization in America because, simply put, polarization is isolation. The political strategy that seeks to divide, distract, and distort the truth in the hope that the ends of holding onto power justify the means of using fake outrage and critique without solutions only fosters eternal division and political nihilism. Polarization is a psychosocial impulse, and it is an unfortunate expedience or shortcut in our cognitive mapping; it is the simplest story, the easiest and lowest common denominator for gaming others; it is an implicit or explicit strategy that provokes inebriated short-sightedness: the "dust off our hands moment" when a cursory thought solves the complexity of our world; it is a policy by jingoism and tweet. Reince Priebus, who served as chairman of the Republican National Committee from 2011 to 2017, directed the Republican Party through a very successful midterm election (2014) and helped get Donald Trump elected president, stated candidly on *This Week with George Stephanopoulos* (3/24/2024), speaking about polarization in the US House of Representatives, "Division is pure profit, unity is a looser, and clicks and money, it all works together." We can defeat this strategy of nihilism.

New Media and the US Public Sphere

Can we fix the dysfunction in our information stream, label disinformation, and help shape the internet in the way that it was intended? Misinformation has Americans concerned and confused, though a majority of Americans acknowledge there is political bias in media. News media and information in the US have become more polarized primarily because political bias, explicitly and implicitly expressed, follows marketing to a Left or Right demographic. The shift in media marketing began on the Far Right with conservative pundits like Rush Limbaugh, a conservative talk radio personality who presented himself as a "tribune of the blue-collar America" who nonetheless lived in a 24,000 square-foot home in Palm Beach, Florida, and made $85 million a year at the height of this popularity.[484] Polarizing media paid well, it turns out, and polarizing comments garner the most attention in a US mediascape in an economy where getting attention in and of itself brings capital. *The New York Times* found that Donald Trump earned close to $2 billion worth of free media attention during his 2016 presidential campaign, eclipsing the total value of media attention given to all of his Republican competitors combined, more than six times as much free coverage as his closest competitor, Ted Cruz, and more than two-and-a-half times as much free coverage as Hillary Clinton on the Democratic side. Interjecting problematic comments into the US public sphere is what garners attention in the American mediascape, not conciliatory, announcements of bipartisan consensus. [485]

Despite growing polarization in new media, many news organizations are centrist by design, as many newspapers in major metropolitan areas used to be. According to *AllSides.com*, a non-profit organization dedicated to "freeing news readers and viewers from 'the filter bubble,'" news organizations like *Reuters, BBC News, The Hill,* and *The Wall Street Journal* (news) are among the most politically neutral.[486] According to YouGov, *The Weather Channel* and news coverage disseminated from The BBC, PBS, and *The Wall Street Journal* are rated more "trustworthy" than "not trustworthy" by the news public YouGov polled, indicating that their news stories' content and context are rated more neutrally or objectively voiced. Newscasters like Anderson Cooper (CNN) and Bret Baier (Fox News) are also viewed as more trustworthy because they maintain objective dispositions once common in US news broadcasts of the 1960s and 1970s. Americans equate objectivity with trust, and maintaining public trust in news media has proven a sustainable marketing formula over the long term.[487]

The tone of media historically has tended to be less politically biased during times when the drama in the world was real and imminent. The television and radio journalists who earlier covered WWII in print and the Vietnam War on television, like Walter Cronkite and Edward R. Murrow, resisted political framing. For them, in a world torn by chaos, objectivity and documentary were civic responsibilities. Polling indicates a majority of Americans still believe the press' watchdog role is important for democracy, and this reveals a central tenet of journalism: that it is supposed to speak truth to power, even when that truth is unpopular. When Edward R. Murrow took on McCarthyism in the communist-phobic US of the 1950s, it was highly risky to Murrow's livelihood and reputation, but he took those responsibilities on. When a journalist props up or advocates uncritically for a politician, we recognize this as propaganda, a system of mass communications that keeps tyrants in office, regimes in place, and ordinary citizens oppressed. The fact that some media and politicians have to resort to manufacturing drama is indicative that the US is not facing the kinds of crises that we faced in the middle and late 20th Century—a silver lining that most crises presented in mass media today are only shadows of the existential threats posed in yesteryears.

Polling indicates most Americans know their chosen news media can be biased, and we can, therefore, choose to expand our horizons and see the other side of the story if we choose to. One of the most American queries is to ask, "Why?" Whether we hear about newsworthy events, our friends and family express political views we don't understand, or we are briefed on legislation brought to the US House of Representatives—Americans aren't satisfied until they know the "why?" Often, our fast-paced, tweet/soundbite-oriented news and information stream creates more questions than answers because answering the "why" takes time, context, and adequate content space to pull together the disparate threads of a story. Polling suggests that a majority of Americans have become suspicious of declarations without substance, of the strategy that hides the truth, tweets, and pronouncements that mystify the public rather than clarify details—information in the service of outrage that purposefully keeps the American news viewer off-balance and embedded within a reality distortion field.[488]

A healthy US public sphere is driven by a querying, skeptical public that isn't satisfied with superficial claims. Within the internet and at our fingertips, we still have in-depth reportage in journalism and social science research dedicated to truth and transparency published in academic journals. We have rich sources of information that are under-utilized and libel laws that punish harmful deception and disinformation directed toward us or our institutions. At no time in recent public memory was this exemplified in such a demonstrative way when Fox News agreed to pay a $787.5 million settlement in the historic defamation case brought by Dominion Voting Systems in April 2023.[489] It was a blockbuster of a libel settlement, reminding Americans that in US law courts, generally, the truth comes out. Persistent deception and mendacity still have consequences.

Journalism was never so trusted in America as it was after Republican Bob Woodward and Democrat Carl Bernstein exposed then President Nixon's culpability in illegally spying on the Democratic Party headquarters. Today, social scientists and journalists are still working to reveal uncomfortable but necessary truths and get to the bottom of those "why" questions and "how." In 2017, Art Cullen, the editor for the 3,000 circulation newspaper *Storm Lake Times* out of Iowa, won a Pulitzer prize for his editorials that followed the money on how nitrogen-based chemicals had been seeping into the drinking water of NW Iowa communities.[490] All around the world, small independent newspapers still advocate for the public, for the ordinary citizen. The independent American daily newspaper, though a rarer find, holds on.

In March 2024, the inventor of the World Wide Web, Tim Berners-Lee, published an open letter to the public on the state of the Web.[491] In it, he expressed his original intentions for an open information society that would increase "collaboration, foster compassion, and generate creativity." But now Berner-Lee sees the several problematic issues that have emerged in the once open social structure of the web that include the:

> extent of power concentration, which contradicts the decen-
> tralised spirit I originally envisioned [which has] segmented
> the web, with a fight to keep users hooked on one platform to
> optimize profit through the passive observation of content. This
> exploitative business model is particularly grave in this year of
> elections that could unravel political turmoil. Compounding this
> issue is the second, the personal data market that has exploited
> people's time and data with the creation of deep profiles that
> allow for targeted advertising and ultimately control over the
> information people are fed.[492]

For Berner-Lee, the future of the internet:

> hinges on our ability to both reform the current system and create
> a new one that genuinely serves the best interests of humanity. To
> achieve this, we must break down data silos to encourage collab-
> oration, create market conditions in which a diversity of options
> thrive to fuel creativity, and shift away from polarizing content to

an environment shaped by a diversity of voices and perspectives that nurture empathy and understanding.

Despite its shortcomings, social media is mostly seen as a force for democracy across the nations of the world because it has brought public awareness to political and social issues and created more transparency of information in countries where information is more tightly controlled.[493] Like Tim Berner-Lee, I, too, see a bright future for the internet. Though we have problems to contend with, like AI and fake content uploads, we are only at the beginning of the potential for curated media sites that get deeper into questions of "why?," "where?," and "how so?;" that make use of the enormous potential of crowd-sourced consensus knowledge.

Though the US is the most deeply pessimistic nation right now about social media's impact on democracy, I believe we must empower media producers on the World Wide Web toward fostering consensus in the US as a force for democracy worldwide. Reporters Without Borders (RWB) has been tracking press freedom in nations for the last twenty years and has noted a startling phenomenon: since 2013, press freedoms have declined in countries around the world. More nations are under the control of authoritarian regimes, and press and internet freedoms are being actively curtailed. In 2013, 26 out of 180 countries had "good press freedoms," according to RWB. By 2023, this had declined to 8 countries.[494] The number of countries worldwide with very serious press freedom issues went up from 20 to 31 countries, and the overall percentage of countries in a free press "problematic zone" has grown in 10 years. A healthy press corps works to promote good checks and balances on power, to promote a healthy democracy. Press freedom also correlates with social mobility and greater equality in countries.

Let's Agree to Agree

Wherever in the world there is an ethnic conflict, where ethnic groups in a nation seem at odds over religious or political ideology, if one looks deeper at the conflict, more often than not, the conflict is rooted in the control of money and resources. The citizens who rebelled in the Peasants' Revolt of England in 1381 CE, for example, desired an end to serfdom that indentured them to a lord. Still, they also sought fair wage growth and a reduction in unfair and uneven taxation. Modern nation-states with higher economic inequality are at risk from the threat of social revolution, and populist dictators wait on the sidelines to ignite the flames. Financial discontent registered on a national level was used with great effectiveness in the early 20th Century to create centralized authority totalitarian states on the Far-Right (fascism) and on the Far-Left (communism). An economy driven by just, rational, and fair economic policies driven by the consensus of its citizenry is the basic ingredient for a strong and sustainable democracy.

As a nation, politics comes naturally to Americans, part of our heritage as independently-minded people of all stripes. In a 2021 Global Attitudes Survey, most of the citizens surveyed from 16 countries believed the United States used to be a good model for democracy but has not been in recent years.[495] Most Americans (68 percent) rationally acknowledge the decline in the perception of our global standing.[496] Most Americans (58 percent) are also unsatisfied with the way democracy is working in the US—among the few wealthy nations unsatisfied with the state of their democracy. Despite these dour polling outlooks, overall, Americans remain optimistic about our country's future. Three-quarters of Democrats and 62 percent of Republicans, majorities in both political parties, in a Spring 2022 survey stated that they had some or quite a lot of confidence in the future of the United States.[497]

At the heart of this optimism is the acknowledgment that democracy, when functioning and adjusting where it should, has historically been the most powerful form of government because public deliberation and consultation provide each a personal stake in the nation's outcome. We need more direct democracy and dialogue in the United States, more understanding of each other directly—a weekly national public square where our concerns can be hashed out and where Americans can understand each other from a deeper and more direct level. Polarization is a strategy, implicit or explicit, in a world of media and politics where social outrage can be manipulated for views and exploited in an attention economy that bestows capital on those who cultivate notoriety and division. But we can change polarization in Washington by electing politicians who seek consensus, supporting them at the polls, trusting but verifying their actions, and following their legislation to see if their voting truly represents the majority of their constituents' views. We can agree to disagree, but we can also agree to agree—to pressure our national legislatures to craft policies that allow America to thrive now and in the future, to harness the mandate provided by our consensus as it evolves, and to take communicative action together from it.

About the Author

Carlos D. Torres, Ph.D. is an anthropologist of societal communication and transformation, an interdisciplinary field that intersects with public sphere theory, and the comparatively new field of social informatics. Much of his research has been dedicated to documenting the ways Maya and other Native American groups have adapted media technologies to tell their own history from collective colonial memories, living in a modern globalized world, and the deep well of the cosmology of America's first people. His research has also included the documentation of an emergent mediascape, new visibilities that have come with internet media, and the quest for democratic autonomy by the insurgent group known as the Zapatistas—a group responsible for what has been defined as the first *netwar*.

Carlos' life-long quest is to try to understand the big story of human communication, and this has led him through the fields of comparative literature, history, media studies, and across the breadth of anthropology to try to distill this amazing story. He has also opened up new research arenas in Europe in this quest, looking at linguistic activism in Catalonia, examining paleolithic art in Southern France/ Northern Spain, and the process of personal transformation embedded in restorative rituals like walking labyrinths and the pilgrimage along the Camino Santiago.

Professor Torres' diverse occupational experience as a filmmaker, realtor, and restauranteur remains an asset in his work as a writer, media producer, and as an engaged academic who has worked across multiple departments at Sonoma State University and UC Berkeley. He continues to work with student cohorts from freshmen to retired folks, students of all ages. He has articles published in the American Anthropologist, the flagship academic journal of anthropologists worldwide, has written blogs and media reviews, and has posted his documentary media work online at https://carlosdtorres.com).

Endnotes

1   "First Debate with Stephen A. Douglas at Ottawa, Illinois (August 21, 1858)," *Collected Works*, 3:27 (Rudgers University Press, 1953).

Introduction – Why Consensus Matters

2   Aaron Blake, "Kellyanne Conway says Donald Trump's team has 'alternative facts.' Which pretty much says it all," *The Washington Post*, January 22, 2017.

3   Ibid.

4   Elisa Shearer, "Two-thirds of U.S. adults say they've seen their own news sources report facts meant to favor one side of an issue or published information that hasn't been fully verified." Pew Research Center, Washington D.C. November 2, 2020, https://www.pewresearch.org/short-reads/2020/11/02/two-thirds-of-u-s-adults-say-theyve-seen-their-own-news-sources-report-facts-meant-to-favor-one-side/

5   Arlie Hochschild, "Think Republicans are disconnecting from reality? It's even worse among liberals." *The Guardian,* July 21, 2019.

6   "Inflation, Health Costs, Partisan Cooperation Among the Top Nation's Problem." Pew Research Center, Washington D.C. June 21, 2023, https://www.pewresearch.org/politics/wp-content/uploads/sites/4/2023/06/PP_2023.06.21_national-problems_REPORT.pdf.

7   Founding Fathers on the Declaration of Independence. "Benjamin Rush to John Adams, 20 July 1811" (excerpt from first paragraph)," published online by the National Park Service, accessed July 8, 2023.

8   Wendy Wall, *Inventing the "American Way," The Politics of the Consensus from the New Deal to the Civil Rights Movement* (Oxford University Press, 2008), 9.

9   Becky Little, "The Native American Government That Helped Inspire the US Constitution." published online at History (Channel), updated July 12, 2023.

10   Lucas Bessire, from "Behold the Black Cayman," in *Cultural Anthropology: a Reader for a Global Age*, Kenneth A. Guest, ed. (W.W. Norton & Company, 2018)

11   Gregory Bateson, *Naven, a Survey of the Problems Suggested by a Composite Picture of the Culture of a New Guinea Tribe Drawn from Three Points of View.* 2d ed. (Stanford, CA: Stanford University Press, 1958)

12   Anthony Giddens, *The Consequences of Modernity 1st Edition.* Stanford University Press: Palo Alto, CA.

13   Azi Paybarah and Mariana Alfaro. "White House, lawmakers criticize university leaders' answers on antisemitism," *The Washington Post,* December 6, 2023.

14   Lee C. McIntyre, *Post-Truth.* (Cambridge, MA: The MIT Press, 2018)

15   Jurgen Habermas, *Between Naturalism and Religion*, translated by Ciaran Cronin (Cambridge, UK: Polity Press, 2008), 13.

16   Craig J. Calhoun et al., eds. *Contemporary Sociological Theory* (Wiley-Blackwell, 2002), 352.

17   Ibid.

Chapter 1 – The Cost of Living, Economic Equality

18   "Greenspan Admits 'Flaw' to Congress, Predicts More Economic Problems," *PBS NewsHour*, transcript of broadcast, October 28, 2008.

19   *The March 2023 AP-NORC Center Poll*. The Associated Press-NORC Center for Public Affairs Research with funding from The Associated Press and NORC at the University of Chicago. Interviews March 16-20, 2023.

20   "Inflation, Health Costs, Partisan Cooperation Among the Nation's Top Problems." Pew Research Center, Washington D.C. June 21, 2023, https://www.pewresearch.org/politics/2023/06/21/inflation-health-costs-partisan-cooperation-among-the-nations-top-problems/

21   "Views of the economy, economic concerns and inflation," Biden's Job Rating Slumps as Public's View of Economy Turns More Negative." Pew Research Center, Washington D.C. July 13, 2022.

22   Ibid.

23   Alexandra Hutzler, "How US national debt grew to its $31.4 trillion high," *ABC News*, May 19, 2023.

24   Ibid.

25   "Public concern over job situation has changed little in recent years but is much lower than in 2021; concern over budget deficit has risen since then," Americans' Top Policy Priority for 2024: Strengthening the Economy. Pew Research Center, Washington D.C. February 29, 2024, . https://www.pewresearch.org/politics/2024/02/29/americans-top-policy-priority-for-2024-strengthening-the-economy/

26   Ashley Kirzinger, Audrey Kearney, Mellisha Stokes, Liz Hamel, and Mollyann Brodie. "Economic Concerns and Health Policy, The ACA, and Views of Long-term Care Facilities" KFF Health Tracking Poll, March 31, 2022, https://www.kff.org/health-costs/poll-finding/kff-health-tracking-poll-march-2022/

27 Juliana Menasce Horowitz, Ruth Igielnik and Rakesh Kochhar, "Views of economic inequality." Most Americans Say There Is Too Much Economic Inequality in the US, but Fewer Than Half Call It a Top Priority. Pew Research Center, Washington D.C. January 9, 2020, https://www.pewresearch.org/social-trends/2020/01/09/views-of-economic-inequality/

28 Juliana Menasce Horowitz, Ruth Igielnik and Rakesh Kochhar, "What Americans see as contributors to economic inequality," Most Americans Say There Is Too Much Economic Inequality In The US, But Fewer Than Half Call It a Top Priority. Pew Research Center, Washington D.C. January 9, 2020, https://www.pewresearch.org/social-trends/2020/01/09/what-americans-see-as-contributors-to-economic-inequality/

29 Ibid.

30 WSJ/NORC Poll March 2023, NORC at the University of Chicago with funding by the *Wall Street Journal.* Interviews March 1-13, 2022, https://s.wsj.net/public/resources/documents/WSJ_NORC_ToplineMarc_2023.pdf

31 Thomas Piketty, *A Brief History of Equality,* translated by Steven Rendall (Belknap Press: An Imprint of Harvard University Press, 2024), 16

32 Dave Roos, "How the East India Company Became the World's Most Powerful Monopoly," published online on History (Channel), updated June 29, 2023.

33 *Adam Smith, An Inquiry into the Nature and Causes of the Wealth of Nations. Vol. II (1st ed.) (London: W. Strahan & T. Cadell, 1776), 35.*

34 Glenn J. Ames, *The Globe Encompassed: The Age of European Discovery, 1500–1700* (Pearson, 2008), 102–103.

35 Friedrich Engels, *The Condition of the Working Class in England in 1844* (London: Swan Sonnenschein & Co., 1892), 45, 48–53.

36 Ibid., 45.

37 Jacob A. Riis, *How the Other Half Lives: Studies Among the Tenements of New York* (Martino Fine Books, 2015)

38 Jeff Desjardins, "Chart: The Evolution of Standard Oil," published online on the *Visual Capitalist,* November 24, 2017.

39 Upton Sinclair, *The Jungle* (CreateSpace Independent Publishing Platform, 2019)

40 Thomas Piketty, *A Brief History of Equality* (Belknap Press, 2022)

41 Ibid.

42 Anna Kaufman, "Abolishing the IRS? A 30% national sales tax? Here's what the FairTax Act of 2023 would do." *USA Today*, updated December 6, 2023.

43 Charlie Giattino, Esteban Ortiz-Ospina and Max Roser (2020), "Working Hours," published online at *OurWorldInData.org.*

44 Ibid.

45   Drew Desilver, "For most US workers, real wages have barely budged in de-
      cades." Pew Research Report, Washington D.C. August 7, 2018, https://www.
      pewresearch.org/short-reads/2018/08/07/for-most-us-workers-real-wages-
      have-barely-budged-for-decades/

46   "Real Wage Trends, 1979 to 2019," published online at the Congressional
      Research Service., updated December 28, 2020.

47   Rakesh Kochhar and Stella Sechopoulos. "How the American middle class has
      changed in the past five decades," published online, *Pew Trust Magazine,* Sep-
      tember 20, 2022.

48   Michael D. Tanner, "Five Myths about Economic Inequality in America," pub-
      lished online at the Cato Institute, Policy Analysis No. 797, September 7, 2016.

49   Joseph E Stiglitz, *The Great Divide: Unequal Societies and What We Can do
      About Them* (W. W. Norton & Company, 2016)

50   Deborah Hart Strober and Gerald S. Strober, *Reagan: The Man and His Presi-
      dency* (Houghton Mifflin, First Edition, 1998)

51   Nick Rouley, "Consumer Cost of Inflation, by type of Good or Service (2000-
      2022)," published online at *VisualCapitalist.com* February 22, 2023.

52   Jonathan Ponciano and Will Yakowicz, "A Decade of Billionaires, 2010 – 2020,"
      Forbes Magazine, special ed. 2020.

53   Fang Block, "The World Added 412 Billionaires in 2020, Bringing the Total to
      3,288," *Barron's Magazine,* March 2, 2021.

54   Emmanuel Saez and Gabriel Zucman, *The Triumph of Injustice How the Rich
      Dodge Taxes and How to Make Them Pay* (W. W. Norton & Company, 2020)

55   Natasha Sarin (Deputy Assistant Secretary for Economic Policy), "The Case for
      a Robust Attack on the Tax Gap," published online for the U.S. Department of
      Treasury, September 7, 2021.

56   Ashley Kirzinger, Audrey Kearney, Mellisha Stokes, Liz Hamel, and Mollyann
      Brodie, "KFF Health Tracking Poll – March 2022: Economic Concerns and
      Health Policy, The ACA, and Views of Long-term Care Facilities," March 31,
      2022, https://www.kff.org/report-section/kff-health-tracking-poll-march-2022-
      economic-concerns-and-health-policy-the-aca-and-views-of-long-term-care-
      facilities-methodology/

57   Ibid.

58   OECD (2023), *Health at a Glance 2023: OECD Indicators*, published online by
      the Organisation for Economic Cooperation and Development: Paris, France.

59   Ibid.

60   Ryan Nunn, Jana Parsons, and Jay Shambaugh, "A dozen facts about the
      economics of the US health-care system," pubished online by the Brookings
      Institute, March 10, 2020.

61   Ibid.

62   Ibid.

63   OECD (2023), *Education at a Glance 2023: OECD Indicators*, published online by the Organisation for Economic Cooperation and Development: Paris, France.

64   Katherine Schaeffer "A growing share of Americans say affordable housing is a major problem where they live," Pew Research Center, Washington D.C. January 18, 2022, https://www.pewresearch.org/short-reads/2022/01/18/a-growing-share-of-americans-say-affordable-housing-is-a-major-problem-where-they-live/

65   Carlos Water, "Wall Street has purchased hundreds of thousands of single-family homes since the Great Recession. Here's what that means for rental prices," CNBC online. February 21, 2023.

66   Ibid.

67   "How this chart explains Americans' wealth across income levels," published online by *USAFacts.org*, updated March 28, 2023.

68   Michael I. Norton and Dan Ariely, "Building a Better America—One Wealth Quintile at a Time," *Perspectives on Pyschological Science*; Volume 6, Issue 1, February 3, 2011.

69   Ibid.

70   History.com Editors, "National Debt," published online at History (Channel), updated April 3, 2020.

71   J. Baxter Oliphant, "Top tax frustrations for Americans: The feeling that some corporations, wealthy people don't pay fair share." Pew Research Center, Washington D.C. April 7, 2023.

72   Ibid.

73   Isadora Milanez and Mark Strauss, "Americans are closely divided over value of medical treatments, but most agree costs are a big problem." Pew Research Center, Washington D.C. July 18, 2018

74   Bradley Jones, "Increasing share of Americans favor a single government program to provide health care coverage." Pew Research Center, Washington D.C. September 29, 2020.

75   Bradley Jones, "Most continue to say ensuring health care coverage is government's responsibility." Pew Research Center, Washington D.C. October 3, 2018.

76   "List of countries by income equality," (April 29, 2024), published online on *Wikipedia.com*.

77   *The Global Social Mobility Report 2020 Equality, Opportunity and a New Economic Imperative*, published online by the World Economic Forum, January 2020.

78   George Lakey, *Viking Economics: How the Scandinavians Got it Right* (Melville House, 2017), 76.

79   Ibid.

80   Kate Taylor, "These 10 companies control everything you buy," *Business Insider*, September 28, 2016.

81   Justin McCarthy, "US Approval of Labor Unions at Highest Point Since 1965," Gallup, uploaded August 30, 2022, https://news.gallup.com/poll/398303/approval-labor-unions-highest-point-1965.aspx

82   Amina Dunn, "Most Americans support a $15 federal minimum wage." Pew Research Center, Washington D.C. April 22, 2021, https://www.pewresearch.org/short-reads/2021/04/22/most-americans-support-a-15-federal-minimum-wage/

83   "Little Public Support for Reductions in Federal Spending," Pew Research Center Report, Washington D.C. Released April 11, 2019, https://www.pewresearch.org/politics/wp-content/uploads/sites/4/2019/04/PP_2019.04.11_federal-spending_FINAL.pdf

84   Hannah Hartig, "Democrats overwhelmingly favor free college tuition, while Republicans are divided by age, education." Pew Research Center, Washington D.C. August 11, 2021, https://www.pewresearch.org/short-reads/2021/08/11/democrats-overwhelmingly-favor-free-college-tuition-while-republicans-are-divided-by-age-education/

85   Hannah Wiley, "In groundbreaking plan, California allows affordable housing on some commercial properties," *Los Angeles Times,* updated September 28, 2022.

86   Ashley Kirzinger, Audrey Kearney, Mellisha Stokes, Liz Hamel, and Mollyann Brodie, "KFF Health Tracking Poll – March 2022: Economic Concerns and Health Policy, The ACA, and Views of Long-term Care Facilities," published online by the Kaiser Family Foundation, Mar 31, 2022, https://www.kff.org/health-costs/poll-finding/kff-health-tracking-poll-march-2022/

87   "CAF World Giving Index 2019," published online by the Charities Aid Foundation.

88   Charlie Giattino, Esteban Ortiz-Ospina and Max Roser (202), "Working Hours" published online at *OurWorldInData.org*.

Chapter 2 – Social Justice, Balancing Two Issues

89   Rodney King and Lawrence J. Spagnola, *The Riot Within: My Journey from Rebellion to Redemption* (HarperOne, 2012)

90   Chistopher Warren, *Report of the Independent Commission on the Los Angeles Police Department* (Los Angeles: The Commission, 1991)

91   Leah Asmelash, "The video camera that recorded Rodney King's 1991 beating by Los Angeles police is up for auction," *CNN,* July, 28, 2020.

92   Felicia Lowenstein, *The Abortion Battle: Looking at Both Sides* (Springfield, New Jersey: Enslow Publishers, Inc., 1996), 60.

93   Ibid., 65.

94   Ibid., 65.

95   Lee M. Miringoff, PhD, and Barbara L. Carvalho, PhD, "Americans' Opinion on Abortion," Marist Poll report, sponsored by the Knights of Columbus, uploaded January 2018, https://www.kofc.org/en/resources/communications/abortion-limits-favored.pdf

96   Ibid.

97   "One-in-three adults say both that human life begins at conception and that the decision to have an abortion belongs solely to the women," America's Abortion Quandary. Pew Research Center, Washington D.C. May 6, 2022, https://www.pewresearch.org/religion/2022/05/06/americas-abortion-quandary/

98   Ibid.

99   Andrew Dorn, "Data: How views on abortion have changed over the years," published online by *NewsNation*, updated May 10, 2022.

100 Daniel K. Williams, "The Partisan Trajectory of the American Pro-Life Movement: How a Liberal Catholic Campaign Became a Conservative Evangelical Cause," *Religions*, 6 (2) (June 2015), 451–475.

101 Andrew Dorn, "Data: How views on abortion have changed over the years," published online by NewsNation, updated May 10, 2022.

102 "Views on abortion by age, 2022," Public Opinion on Abortion. Pew Research Center, Washington D.C. May 17, 2022, https://www.pewresearch.org/religion/fact-sheet/public-opinion-on-abortion/

103 Jeff Diamant and Besheer Mohamed, "Most US abortions in 2020 were for women who had previously given birth," What the data says about abortion in the US. Pew Research Report, Washington D.C. January 11, 2023, https://www.pewresearch.org/short-reads/2023/01/11/what-the-data-says-about-abortion-in-the-u-s-2/

104 Juliana Menasce Horowitz, Kiley Hurst and Dana Braga, "Views on the Black Lives Matter movement." Support for the Black Lives Matter Movement Has Dropped Considerably From Its Peak in 2020. Pew Research Report, Washington D.C. June 14, 2023, https://www.pewresearch.org/social-trends/2023/06/14/support-for-the-black-lives-matter-movement-has-dropped-considerably-from-its-peak-in-2020/

105 *Deep Divisions in Americans' Views of Nation's Racial History – and How To Address It.* Report: Pew Research Center, Washington D.C. August 12, 2021, https://www.pewresearch.org/politics/2021/08/12/deep-divisions-in-americans-views-of-nations-racial-history-and-how-to-address-it/

106 Ibid.

107 Ibid.

108 "The Democratic coalition," Beyond Red vs. Blue: The Political Typology. Pew Research Center, Washington D.C. November 9, 2021, https://www.pewresearch.org/politics/2021/11/09/the-democratic-coalition/

109 "Deep Divisions in Americans' Views of Nation's Racial History – and How To Address It. Report," Pew Research Center, Washington D.C. August 12, 2021, https://www.pewresearch.org/politics/2021/08/12/deep-divisions-in-americans-views-of-nations-racial-history-and-how-to-address-it/

110 Chanelle Chandler, "The Biden administration revises race and ethnicity categories for the census. Here's what that means," *Yahoo! News.* March 28, 2024.

111 Ibid.

112 Hippocrates, *On Airs, Waters, and Places,* Part 24 (c. 400 BCE), translated by Francis Adams, published online by MIT Department of Classics, 1994.

113 Johann Friedrich Blumenbach, *De Generis Humani Varietate Nativai* (1795), published online for the Royal Society of London on the *InternetArchive.org.*

114 Julian Huxley, "Clines: an Auxiliary Taxonomic Principle," *Nature* (July 30, 1938), 142 (3587): 219–220.

115 Kirsten N. Morehouse, Keith Maddox, and Mahzarin R. Banaji, "All Human Social Groups Are Human, but Some Are More Human than Others: A Comprehensive Investigation of the Implicit Association of 'Human' to US Racial/Ethnic Groups," published by the *Proceedings of the National Academy of Sciences - PNAS* (2023)120, no. 22.

116 Issam Ahmed, "Harvard study finds implicit racial bias highest among white people," published online by *Phys.org*, May 22, 2023.

117 Andrew Daniller, "Majorities of Americans say there is at least some discrimination against many different societal group," Pew Research Center, Washington D.C. March 1-7, 2021, https://www.pewresearch.org/short-reads/2021/03/18/majorities-of-americans-see-at-least-some-discrimination-against-black-hispanic-and-asian-people-in-the-u-s/ft_2021-03-18_discrimination_04/

118 Aja Romano, "A history of 'wokeness.'" *Vox,* October 9, 2020.

119 W.E. B. Du Bois, *The Souls of Black Folk* (1903) (Dover Publications, 2016), 2-3

120 Ibid.

121 Sophie Mousset, *Women's Rights and the French Revolution: A Biography of Olympe de Gouges* (New Brunswick, US & London: Transaction Publishers, 2007)

122 Olympe de Gouges, *Declaration of the Rights of Woman and of the Female Citizen* [1791], Mikesch Muecke, ed. (Handcar Press, 2024).

123 Lesley Kennedy, "Reproductive Rights in the US: Timeline" History (Channel) online, updated July13, 2023.

124 Ibid.

125 Debra Michals, PhD, "Margaret Sanger" published online by the *National Women's History Museum* (2017), *WomensHistory.org*.

126 Ibid.

127 "Reproductive Rights in the US: Timeline." History online, updated July 13, 2023.

128 Katherine Kortsmit, et al., "Abortion Surveillance — United States, 2018." *Morbidity and Mortality Weekly Report*, published online by the Centers for Disease Control and Prevention, 69 (7), 1–29.

129 Rachel K. Jones, et al., "Medication Abortion Now Accounts for More Than Half of All US Abortions," published online by the Guttmacher Institute, February 24, 2022.

130 Rachel Jones and Jenna Jerman, "Abortion Is a Common Experience for US Women, Despite Dramatic Declines in Rates," published online by Guttmacher Institute, October 19, 2017..

131 Margot Sanger-Katz, Claire Cain Miller, and Quoctrung Bui, "Who Gets Abortions in America?" *The New York Times,* December 14, 2021.

132 Ibid.

133 Ibid.

134 Jamie Ballard, "Which religious groups' members are most likely to identify as pro-choice?" YouGov, May 13, 2022.

135 David Masci, "America's views on abortion, by religious group," American religious groups vary widely in their views of abortion. Pew Research Center, Washington D.C. January 22, 2018, https://www.pewresearch.org/short-reads/2018/01/22/american-religious-groups-vary-widely-in-their-views-of-abortion/

136 Domenico Montanaro, "Poll: Americans want abortion restrictions, but not as far as red states are going," article published on *Morning Edition* online, NPR, April 26, 2023.

137 Lydia Saad, "Abortion Remains a Potent Issue for Pro-Choice Voters," Gallup, June 21, 2023, https://news.gallup.com/poll/507527/abortion-remains-potent-issue-pro-choice-voters.aspx

138 Domenico Montanaro, "Poll: Americans want abortion restrictions, but not as far as red states are going," article published on *Morning Edition* online, NPR, April 26, 2023.

139 Megan Brenan, "Record-High 47% in US Think Abortion Is Morally Accept-able," Gallup, June 9, 2021, https://news.gallup.com/poll/350756/record-high-think-abortion-morally-acceptable.aspx

140 Ibid.

141 Domenico Montanaro, "Poll: Americans want abortion restrictions, but not as far as red states are going," article published on *Morning Edition* online, NPR, April 26, 2023.

142 Ibid.

143 "Deep Divisions in Americans' Views of Nation's Racial History – and How To Address It." Pew Research Center, Washington D.C. August 12, 2021, https://www.pewresearch.org/politics/2021/08/12/deep-divisions-in-americans-views-of-nations-racial-history-and-how-to-address-it/

144 Juliana Horowitz, Kiley Hurst and Dana Braga, "Support for the Black Lives Matter Movement Has Dropped Considerably From Its Peak in 2020." Pew Research Center Report, Washington D.C. June 14, 2023, https://www.pewresearch.org/social-trends/wp-content/uploads/sites/3/2023/06/ST_2023.06.14_BLM-Support_Report.pdf

145 Ibid.

146 Susan Page, "A GOP war on 'woke'? Most Americans view the term as a positive, USA TODAY/Ipsos Poll finds," *USA Today,* March 8, 2023, https://www.usatoday.com/story/news/politics/2023/03/08/gop-war-woke-most-americans-see-term-positive-ipsos-poll/11417394002/

147 Ibid.

148 "Republicans more likely that Democrats to see a lot of progress on race in the last 50 years; Democrats more likely to say a lot more needs to be done," Deep Divisions in Americans' Views of Nation's Racial History – and How To Address It. Pew Research Center Report, Washington D.C.August 12, 2021, https://www.pewresearch.org/politics/2021/08/12/deep-divisions-in-americans-views-of-nations-racial-history-and-how-to-address-it/

149 "The War Relocation Authority and The Incarceration of Japanese Americans During World War II," published online by the Truman Library, November 5, 2015.

150 Erin Blakemore, "The Thorny History of Reparations in the United States," History (Channel) online, updated September 14, 2023.

151 Audra D. S. Burch, "Nearing Her 109th Birthday, and Still Waiting for Her Day in Court," *The New York Times,* November 7, 2023.

152 Juliana Menasce Horowitz, "Most Americans say the legacy of slavery still affects black people in the US today," Pew Research Center, Washington D.C. June 17, 2019, https://www.pewresearch.org/short-reads/2019/06/17/most-americans-say-the-legacy-of-slavery-still-affects-black-people-in-the-u-s-today/

153 Carrie Blazina and Kiana Cox "Black and White Americans are far apart in their views of reparations for slavery." Pew Research Center, Washington D.C. November 28, 2022.

154 "Pro and Con: Reparations for Slavery," published online by *Encyclopedia Britannica*, January 25, 2022.

155 Carrie Blazina and Kiana Cox. "Majorities of reparation supporters think financial assistance for education, business and home would be helpful forms of repayment." Black and White Americans are far apart in their views of reparations for slavery. November 28, 2022, https://www.pewresearch.org/short-reads/2022/11/28/black-and-white-americans-are-far-apart-in-their-views-of-reparations-for-slavery/

156 Richard Fry, Jesse Bennett and Amanda Barroso, "Racial and ethnic gaps in the US persist on key demographic indicators." Pew Research Center Feature, Washington D.C. January 12, 2021, https://www.pewresearch.org/interactives/racial-and-ethnic-gaps-in-the-u-s-persist-on-key-demographic-indicators/

157 "Where Do Americans Stand on Abortion?" The Short Answer, Gallup, updated July 7, 2023, https://news.gallup.com/poll/321143/americans-stand-abortion.aspx

158 Hannah Hartig, "By more than two-to-one, Americans say medication abortion should be legal in their state," Pew Research Center, Washington D.C. April 11, 2023, https://www.pewresearch.org/short-reads/2023/04/11/by-more-than-two-to-one-americans-say-medication-abortion-should-be-legal-in-their-state/

159 Ibid.

160 Juliana Menasce Horowitz, Anna Brown and Kiana Cox, "Views of racial inequality," Race in America 2019. Pew Research Center, Washington D.C. April 9, 2019, https://www.pewresearch.org/social-trends/2019/04/09/views-of-racial-inequality/

161 Kiley Hurst, "Americans are divided on whether society overlooks racial discrimination or sees it where it doesn't exist." Pew Research Center, Washington D.C. August 26, 2023, https://www.pewresearch.org/short-reads/2023/08/25/americans-are-divided-on-whether-society-overlooks-racial-discrimination-or-sees-it-where-it-doesnt-exist/

162 "AAA Statement on Race," published online by the *American Anthropological Association*, May 17, 1998.

163 Lizzie Wade, "Genetic study reveals surprising ancestry of many Americans," published online in *Science*, December 18, 2014.

Chapter 3 – A Green and Prosperous Country

164 *Kiss the Ground*, Rebecca Tickell and Josh Tickell, director and producers, 2020, kissthegroundmovie.com.

165 *"What is Regenerative Agriculture?" The Carbon Underground and Regenerative Agriculture Initiative, published online by Regeneration International.org,* February 24, 2017.

166 Ibid.

167 "Grow Healthier Soil, Food and Profits," published online by the Soil Health Academy.org, 2024.

168 Rebecca Leppert, "Most Americans who have faced extreme weather see a link to climate change – Republicans included." Pew Research Center, Washington D.C. August 12, 2022, https://www.pewresearch.org/short-reads/2022/08/12/most-americans-who-have-faced-extreme-weather-see-a-link-to-climate-change-republicans-included/

169 Mitch Smith, "More Lead-Tainted Water in Michigan Draws Attention to Nation's Aging Pipes," *The New York Times,* Oct. 16, 2021.

170 Megan Brenan, "Water Pollution Remains Top Environmental Concern in US," Gallup, April 19, 2021, https://news.gallup.com/poll/347735/water-pollution-remains-top-environmental-concern.aspx

171 "Economy Remains the Public's Top Policy Priority; COVID-19 Concerns Decline Again." Pew Research Report, Washington D.C. February 6, 2023.

172 Ibid.

173 Ibid.

174 Alec Tyson, "On climate change, Republicans are open to some policy approaches, even as they assign the issue low priority," Pew Research Report, Washington D.C. July 23, 2021, https://www.pewresearch.org/short-reads/2023/08/09/what-the-data-says-about-americans-views-of-climate-change/

175 Jeff Berardelli, "'We've entered a new era' of public concerns about climate change, survey find," *CBS News,* January 25, 2019.

176 Anthony Leiserowitz, E. Maibach, S. Rosenthal, J. Kotcher, M. Ballew, M. Goldberg, A. Gustafson,

Climate Change in the American Mind: December 2018, published online by Yale University and George Mason University for the Yale Program on Climate Change Communication, 2018.

177 Ibid.

178 Cary Funk, "Key findings: How Americans' attitudes about climate change differ by generation, party and other factors." Pew Research Center. May 26, 2021, https://www.pewresearch.org/short-reads/2021/05/26/key-findings-how-americans-attitudes-about-climate-change-differ-by-generation-party-and-other-factors/

179 Alec Tyson, Cary Funk, and Brian Kennedy. "What the data says about Americans' views of climate change." Pew Research Report, Washington D.C. August 9, 2023, https://www.pewresearch.org/short-reads/2023/08/09/what-the-data-says-about-americans-views-of-climate-change/

180 Ibid.

181 Genesis 1: 26, published by Bible Gateway.

182 *"Aristotle's Biology," published online by the Stanford Encyclopedia of Philosophy, Stanford University.* Revised July 16, 2021.

183 Arthur O. Lovejoy, *The Great Chain of Being* (Cambridge, MA: Harvard University Press, 1964)

184 Dr Matthew Ward, review of *Creatures of Empire: How Domestic Animals Transformed Early America*, (review no. 471 in Reviews in History), date accessed: January 23, 2024.

185 Virginia DeJohn Anderson, *Creatures of Empire: How Domestic Animals Transformed Early America* (Oxford, UK: Oxford University Press, 2002), 68.

186 Ibid.

187 Hannah Ritchie, Pablo Rosado and Max Roser, "Greenhouse gas emissions," *OurWorldinData.org*, updated 2024.

188 Robert A. McLeman et al., "What we learned from the Dust Bowl: lessons in science, policy, and adaptation". *Population and Environment*, 35 (4) (June 2014), 417–440.

189 Hannah Ritchie, Veronika Samborska and Max Roser, "Plastic Pollution," published online on *OurWorldinData.org*.

190 Ibid.

191 Roland Geyer, Jenna R. Jambeck, and Kara Lavender Law, "Production, use, and fate of all plastics ever made." *Science Advances,* Vol. 3 (7), July 17, 2017.

192 "The Nobel Prize in Physiology of Medicine 1948," published online by the Nobel Prize Outreach AB. Archived from the original on May 23, 2020. Retrieved February 12, 2024.

193 *Rachel Carson: Voice of Nature,* film for American Experience, PBS & WITF, aired March 22, 2018.

194 Ralph Waldo Emerson, "Chapter 2 – Commodity, in *Nature* (1836), published online in Wikisource.

195 Amy Leinbach Marquis, «A Mountain Calling," *National Parks Magazine* (Fall 2007), archived from original on July 27, 2011. Retrieved February 15, 2024.

196   John Tallmadge, *Meeting the Tree of Life: A Teacher's Path* (Univ. of Utah Press, 1997)

197   Jeffrey P. Schaffer, *Yosemite National Park: A Natural History Guide to Yosemite and Its Trails*. (Berkeley: Wilderness Press, 1999)

198   Hannah Ritchie, "Drivers of Deforestation," *OurWorldinData.org*, February 4, 2021,

199   Ibid.

200   Megan Brenan, "Water Pollution Remains Top Environmental Concern in US," Gallup, April 19, 2021, https://news.gallup.com/poll/347735/water-pollution-remains-top-environmental-sconcern.aspx

201   Ibid.

202   Ibid.

203   "2024 State of the Air Report," published online by the American Lung Association, April 2024.

204   Alec Tyson, Cary Funk and Brian Kennedy, "Americans Largely Favor US Taking Steps To Become Carbon Neutral by 2050," Pew Research Report, Washington D.C. March 1, 2022, https://www.pewresearch.org/science/2022/03/01/americans-largely-favor-u-s-taking-steps-to-become-carbon-neutral-by-2050/

205   Alison Spencer and Cary Funk, "Americans largely support US joining international efforts to address climate change." Pew Research Center. March 9, 2022, https://www.pewresearch.org/short-reads/2022/03/09/americans-largely-support-u-s-joining-international-efforts-to-address-climate-change/

206   Alec Tyson, Cary Funk and Brian Kennedy. "Americans Largely Favor US Taking Steps To Become Carbon Neutral by 2050." Pew Research Center Report, Washington D.C. March 1, 2022, https://www.pewresearch.org/science/2022/03/01/americans-largely-favor-u-s-taking-steps-to-become-carbon-neutral-by-2050/

207   Brian Kennedy, Cary Funk and Alec Tyson, "What Americans think about an energy transition from fossil fuels to renewables," Majorities of Americans Prioritize Renewable Energy, Back Steps to Address Climate Change. Pew Research Center Report, Washington D.C. June 28, 2023, https://www.pewresearch.org/science/2023/06/28/what-americans-think-about-an-energy-transition-from-fossil-fuels-to-renewables/

208   "Majority of Americans see unexpected problems from an energy transition as at least somewhat likely." What Americans Think about an Energy Transition from Fossil Fuels to Renewables. Pew Research Center, Washington D.C. June 26, 2023, https://www.pewresearch.org/science/2023/06/28/what-americans-think-about-an-energy-transition-from-fossil-fuels-to-renewables/ps_2023-06-14_climate-change_01_03/

209 Brian Kennedy, Cary Funk and Alec Tyson. "What Americans think about an energy transition from fossil fuels to renewables." Majorities of Americans Prioritize Renewable Energy, Back Steps to Address Climate Change. Pew Research Center, Washington D.C. June 28, 2023, https://www.pewresearch.org/science/2023/06/28/what-americans-think-about-an-energy-transition-from-fossil-fuels-to-renewables/

210 James Bell, Jacob Poushter, Moira Fagan, and Christine Huang, "In Response to Climate Change, Citizens in Advanced Economies Are Willing To Alter How They Live and Work," Pew Research Center, Washington D.C., September 14, 2021, https://www.pewresearch.org/global/2021/09/14/in-response-to-climate-change-citizens-in-advanced-economies-are-willing-to-alter-how-they-live-and-work/

211 Jacob Poushter, Moira Fagan and Christine Huang, "Americans are less concerned – but more divided – on climate change than people elsewhere." Pew Research Center, Washington D.C. September 14, 2023, https://www.pewresearch.org/short-reads/2021/09/14/americans-are-less-concerned-but-more-divided-on-climate-change-than-people-elsewhere/

212 Ibid.

213 "In US, young adults are more concerned than their elders – both in the overall population and within religious groups – about climate change." Younger Evangelicals in The US Are More Concerned Than Their Elders About Climate Change. Pew Research Center, Washington D.C. December 6, 2022, https://www.pewresearch.org/short-reads/2022/12/07/younger-evangelicals-in-the-u-s-are-more-concerned-than-their-elders-about-climate-change/ft_22-12-07_agereligionclimate_01/

214 Ibid.

215 "Global Emission by Economic Sector," Global Greenhouse Gas Emissions Data, published online by The United States Environmental Protection Agency (global emissions from 2021).

216 Freightliner Trucks, https://www.freightliner.com/trucks/ecascadia/

217   Caroline Delbert, "Alice, the World's First All-Electric Passenger Jet, Just Aced Her Maiden Flight," *Popular Mechanics*, October 3, 2022.

218 "Data: Electricity generation from wind power," *OurWorldinData.org*, updated December 12, 2023.

219 Ibid.

220 *Renewable Energy Statistics 2021*, report, published online by the International Renewable Energy Agency. August 2021.

221 Ibid.

222 Stanley Reed, "A Monster Wind Turbine Is Upending an Industry," *The New York Times*, January 1, 2021.

223 Patrick Whittle, Associated Press. "US seeks new lithium sources as demand for clean energy grows." March 28, 2022, published online on *PBS News*.

224 Ibid.

225 Hannah Ritchie, "Forest Area," *OurWorldinData.org*, February 4, 2021.

226 Ibid.

227 "Aluminum: Material-Specific Data," published online by the United States Environmental Protection Agency, updated November 22, 2023.

228 "Plastics: Material-Specific Data," published online by the United States Environmental Protection Agency, updated April 21, 2023.

229 "Plastic Wars," Rick Young, Laura Sullivan, Emma Schwartz, and Fritz Kramer, producers for *FRONTLINE* (PBS), Season 20 Episode 14, May 11, 2021.

230 "The 7 Different Types of Plastic," published online by *PlasticsforChange.org*, April 6, 2021.

231 "Plastic Wars," Rick Young, Laura Sullivan, Emma Schwartz, and Fritz Kramer, producers for *FRONTLINE* (PBS), Season 20 Episode 14, May 11, 2021.

232 Peter Moore, "58 percent support mandatory recycling programs," YouGov, June 30, 2014.

233 The Recycling Partnership, *recyclingpartnership.org/*

234 "Dashboard," *TheOceanCleanup.com*, Boyan Slat, CEO & Founder.

235 Ibid.

236 Bloomberg and Leslie Kaufman, "Governments pledged to end fossil fuel subsidies. Instead, they've doubled down since 2020, hitting record $1.3 trillion," *Fortune,* July 24, 2023.

237 Elizabeth Kolbert, *The Sixth Extinction: an Unnatural History,* back cover (Picador; Reprint edition, January 6, 2015)

238 Robert Sanders, "Was first nuclear test the start of new human-dominated epoch, the Anthropocene?" *Berkeley News*, January 15, 2015.

239 Kate Blackwood, "Ahmann co-edits journal issue on 'late industrialism,'" *Newsletter* published online by the College of Arts and Sciences, Cornell University, November 30, 2020.

Chapter 4 – Gun Violence, Immigration, Law & Order

240 Benjamin Jealous, "Chapter 10 – Beyond Black and White," *Never Forget our People Were Always Free: a Parable of American Healing* (Amistad, 2023), 90-104.

241 "Partisan differences in assessments of many national problems, but both Republicans and Democrats see the ability of the parties to work together as a problem." Inflation, Health Costs, Partisan Cooperation Among the Nation's Top Problems. Pew Research Center Report, Washingtone D.C. June 21, 2023, https://www.pewresearch.org/politics/2023/06/21/inflation-health-costs-partisan-cooperation-among-the-nations-top-problems/

242 "Americans Showing Increased Concern About Immigration," Gallup, February 3, 2023, https://news.gallup.com/poll/470426/americans-showing-increased-concern-immigration.aspx

243 "For Most US Gun Owners, Protection Is the Main Reason They Own a Gun," Pew Research Center Report, Washington D.C. August 16, 2023, . https://www.pewresearch.org/politics/2023/08/16/for-most-u-s-gun-owners-protection-is-the-main-reason-they-own-a-gun/

244 Ibid.

245 J.F. Sheley and J.D. Wright, "Motivations for gun possession and carrying among serious juvenile offenders" *Behavior Science Law* 11 (1993), 375-388.

246 "Inflation, Health Costs, Partisan Cooperation Among the Nation's Top Problems," Pew Research Center Report, Washington D.C. June 21, 2023, https://www.pewresearch.org/politics/2023/06/21/inflation-health-costs-partisan-cooperation-among-the-nations-top-problems/

247 "Total violent crime reported in the United States from 1990 to 2022," published online by Statistica Research Department, *Statistica.com*, May 22, 2024

248 "Deaths by homicide per 100,000 resident population in the US from 1950 to 2019," published online by Statistica Research Department, *Statistica.com*, June, 2023.

249 "Crime and Justice," published online by *USAFacts.org*, updated March 2023.

250 Michael Pittarro, Ph.D. "Why Did Violent Crime Surge in 2021?" *Psychology Today,* January 13, 2022.

251 Jamie Ducharme, "US Suicide Rates are the Highest They have been Since WWII," *Time Magazine*, June 20, 2019.

252 Michel Foucault. *Discipline and Punish : The Birth of the Prison* (New York, NY: First Vintage Books edition, 1979), 222.

253 Thomas Hobbes. *Leviathan*, i. xiii. 9 (Penguin Classics, 2017)

254 "The English Bill of Rights," written by the British Parliament, December 16, 1689, point #7, published online on at *TeachingAmericanHistory.org*.

255 "The History of the Right to Bear Arms," Gun Control: Restricting Rights or Protecting People? *Encyclopedia.com,* February 7, 2024.

256 Matt Jancer, "Gun Control Is as Old as the Old West," *Smithsonian Magazine*, February 5, 2018.

257 Robert J. Spitzer, "For Most of US History We've Had Both Gun Rights and Gun Regulations," *Time Magazine*, June 6, 2023.

258 Ibid.

259 Ibid.

260 "US Immigration Timeline," published online by History (Channel) Editors, August 23, 2022.

261 Ibid.

262 Khaled A. Beydoun, "America banned Muslims long before Donald Trump," *The Washington Post,* August 18, 2016.

263 Ibid.

264 Martin B. Gold, *Forbidden Citizens: Chinese Exclusion and the US Congress: A Legislative History*, TheCapitol.Net, 2012)

265 Yuning Wu, "Chinese Exclusion Act," *Encyclopedia Britannica*, updated December 23, 2023.

266 David Ross, *Ireland: History of a Nation* (Geddes & Grosset, 2002)

267 Frances Mulraney, "How the Irish Came to America, from the Great Hunger to Today," published online by *IrishCentral.com*, October 27, 2022.

268 Susan Bibler Coutin, *Nation of Emigrants* (Ithaca, NY: Cornell University Press, 2007), 179.

269 Brad Plumer, "Congress tried to fix immigration back in 1986. Why did it fail?" *The Washington Post*, January 30, 2013 (Retrieved November 27, 2017)

270 Kimberly A. Clarke, Nina Thekdi, Luis E. Avila of Varnum LLP. "Senators Propose Immigration Reform," *The international Law Review*, posted January 29, 2013.

271 "US Immigration Reform Efforts Since 2013," Mass Migration as a Travel Business, published online by *Business-of-Migration.com*.

272 "A Comparison of 2020 and 2021 NIBRS Estimates," National Incident-Based Reporting System. Published online by Federal Bureau of Investigation, March 1, 2023.

273 Ames Grawert and Noah Kim, "Myths and Realities: Understanding Recent Trends in Violent Crime," published online by the Brennan Center for Justice, May 9, 2023.

274 Ibid.

275 Ibid.

276 Ibid.

277 "Violent Crimes," *USAFacts.org*, (Primary source: Federal Bureau of Investigation)

278   Maggie Davis, "After Nationwide Decline in Property Crime Rates, 62 of 100 Largest US Cities Report Increase During First Quarter of 2022," published online by *ValuePenguin.com*, July 18, 2022.

279   Erika Fortgang, "How They Got The Guns: A look at how school shooters are getting weapons so easily," *RollingStone*, June 10, 1999.

280   Jason E. Goldstick, Ph.D., Rebecca M. Cunningham, M.D., Patrick M. Carter, M.D. "Current Causes of Death in Children and Adolescents in the United States," *New England Journal of Medicine,* 386:1955-1956. April 20, 2022.

281   John Gramlich, "Violent crime is a key midterm voting issue, but what does the data say?" Pew Research Center, Washington D.C. October 31, 2022, https://www.pewresearch.org/short-reads/2022/10/31/violent-crime-is-a-key-midterm-voting-issue-but-what-does-the-data-say/

282   Ibid.

283   Stephanie Lai and Emily Cochrane, "Here's what is in the Senate's gun Bill – and what was left out," *The New York Times*, July 23, 2022.

284   "Gun Violence Widely Viewed as a Major – and Growing – National Problem." Pew Research Center Report, Washington D.C. June 28, 2023, https://www.pewresearch.org/short-reads/2022/10/31/violent-crime-is-a-key-midterm-voting-issue-but-what-does-the-data-say/

285   Ibid.

286   M. Tyler Gillett, "New Database Compiles Common Traits of US Mass Shooter," *Jurist.* February 5, 2022.

287   "Public Mass Shootings: Database Amasses Details of a Half Century of US Mass Shootings with Firearms, Generating Psychosocial Histories," published online by the National Institute of Justice. February 3, 2022.

288   Ibid.

289   Griff White, "As mass shootings rise, experts say high-capacity magazines should be the focus," *The Washington* Post, August 18, 2019.

290   "Americans' Top Policy Priority for 2024: Strengthening the Economy," Pew Research Center Report, Washington D.C. February 29, 2024, https://www.pewresearch.org/politics/2024/02/29/americans-top-policy-priority-for-2024-strengthening-the-economy

291   Ibid.

292   Ibid.

293   Maria Ramirez Uribe, Amy Sherman, "Hamas militants 'pouring' across US southern border? Donald Trump's claim is Pants on Fire!" *Politifact,* October 12, 2023.

294   David Frum. "The GOP's True Priority: The Republicans who won't take yes for an answer," *The Atlantic,* February 6, 2024.

295 "Americans' Top Policy Priority for 2024: Strengthening the Economy." Pew Research Center Report, Washington D.C. February 29, 2024, https://www.pewresearch.org/politics/2024/02/29/americans-top-policy-priority-for-2024-strengthening-the-economy/

296 Sahil Kapur, Scott Wong, Julie Tsirkin and Julia Ainsley. "Senators unveil bipartisan bill to impose tougher asylum and border laws." *NBC News* online, February 4, 2024.

297 Lisa Desjardins, "What's in the Senate's sweeping $118 billion immigration and foreign aid bill?" *PBS NewsHour*, February 6, 2024.

298 Lisa Firestone, Ph.D. "The Inner Voices Behind Violent Behavior," *Psychology Today.* March 3, 2011.

299 Ibid.

300 Ibid.

301 Patrick Sharkey and Alisabeth Marsteller, "Violence and Urban inequality" *Vital City.* March 2, 2022.

302 Ibid.

303 Paul Vercammen, "Felons turned firefighters find new lives on the front lines." CNN online, updated April 24, 2022.

304 Katherine Schaeffer, "Key Fact about Americans and Guns." Pew Research Center, Washington D.C. September 13, 2023, https://www.pewresearch.org/short-reads/2023/09/13/key-facts-about-americans-and-guns/

305 "Firearm Deaths in the US: Statistics and Trends." *USAFacts.org*

306 "Homicide Mortality Rates," published online by the National Center for Health Statistics, CDC.

307 Katherine Schaeffer, "Bipartisan support for preventing people with mental illnesses from purchasing guns, but wide differences on other policies," Key Fact about Americans and Guns. Pew Research Center, Washington D.C. September 13, 2023, https://www.pewresearch.org/short-reads/2023/09/13/key-facts-about-americans-and-guns/

308 David Correa and Nick Wilson, "Gun Violence in Rural America," published online by the Center for American Progress. September 26, 2022.

309 Lisa Stolzenberg and Stewart J. D'Alessio, "'Three Strikes and You're Out': The Impact of California's New Mandatory Sentencing Law on Serious Crime Rates," *Crime and Delinquency*, 43 (4) (1997), 457–69.

Chapter 5 – Beyond Division, Empowering Consensus

310 Dan Barry, "One Small Step for Democracy in a 'Live Free or Die' Town," *The New York Times,* updated August 10, 2022.

311 Ibid.

312 Ibid.

313 Ibid.

314 Jeffrey M. Jones, "U.S. Political Party Preferences Shifted Greatly During 2021," Gallup, https://news.gallup.com/poll/388781/political-party-preferences-shifted-greatly-during-2021.aspx

315 "The two-party system and views of differences between the Republican and Democratic parties," Pew Research Center Report, Washington D.C. August 9 , 2022, https://www.pewresearch.org/politics/2022/08/09/the-two-party-system-and-views-of-differences-between-the-republican-and-democratic-parties/

316 "As Partisan Hostility Grows, Signs of Frustration with the Two-Party System," Pew Research Report, Washington D.C. August 9, 2022, https://www.pewresearch.org/politics/2022/08/09/as-partisan-hostility-grows-signs-of-frustration-with-the-two-party-system/

317 Ibid.

318 Carroll Doherty, "Key findings on Americans' views of the US political system and democracy," Pew Research Center, Washington D.C. April 26, 2018, https://www.pewresearch.org/short-reads/2018/04/26/key-findings-on-americans-views-of-the-u-s-political-system-and-democracy/

319 "Americans' Views of Government: Decades of Distrust, Enduring Support for Its Role," Pew Research Report, Washington D.C. June 6, 2022, https://www.pewresearch.org/politics/2022/06/06/americans-views-of-government-decades-of-distrust-enduring-support-for-its-role/

320 Charles Babington, "Partisan View Affect Trust in Government," *Pew Trust Magazine,* September 9, 2021, https://www.pewtrusts.org/en/trust/archive/summer-2021/partisan-views-affect-trust-in-government

321 Carroll Doherty, "Key findings on Americans' views of the US political system and democracy," Pew Research Center, Washington D.C. April 26, 2018, https://www.pewresearch.org/short-reads/2018/04/26/key-findings-on-americans-views-of-the-u-s-political-system-and-democracy/

322 Richard Wike, Katie Simmons, Bruce Stokes and Janell Fetterolf. Globally, Broad Support for Representative and Direct Democracy," Pew Research Center, Washington D.C. October 16, 2017, https://www.pewresearch.org/global/2017/10/16/globally-broad-support-for-representative-and-direct-democracy/

323 David Graeber and David Wengrow, *The Dawn of Everything: a New History of Humanity* (Picador Paper, 2023), 341.

324 "George Washington's Farewell Address," September 17, 1796, published online by *MountVernon.org*.

325 Ibid.

326 Ezra Klein, *Why We're Polarized* (Avid Reader Press, 2021)

327 Barry Goldwater, "Goldwater's 1964 Acceptance Speeh," from the 28th Republican Convention in San Francisco, published in *The Washingon Post* archives, https://www.washingtonpost.com/wp-srv/politics/daily/may98/goldwater-speech.htmhtm

328 Jacob S. Hacker and Paul Pierson, "Opinion: Romney is the right man for America. George Romney, that is." *The Washington Post,* February 10, 2012.

329 "Americans' Top Policy Priority for 2024: Strengthening the Economy," Pew Research Report, Washingtone D.C. February 29, 2024, https://www.pewresearch.org/politics/2024/02/29/americans-top-policy-priority-for-2024-strengthening-the-economy/

330 John Paul Stevens, "Opinion of Stevens, J., Supreme Court of the United States. Citizens United, Appellant v. Federal Election Commission," Legal Information Institute published online by the Cornell University Law School, retrieved February 12, 2024.

331 William C.R. Horncastle, "The scale of US election spending explained in five graphs," *TheConversation.com* October 15, 2020.

332 "Press Release: 2022 federal midterm election cost more than $8.9 billion," published online by the *OpenSecrets.org* Staff, February 7, 2023.

333 Taylor Glomo, "How Republicans and Democrats spend their money during 2022 midterm elections," *OpenSecrets.org*, November 22, 2022.

334 Kevin Roose, "We Asked for Examples of Election Misinformation. You Delivered," *The New York Times,* November 4, 2018.

335 Max Weber, "Politics as a Vocation" lecture (1919), 27: published online by Anthropos-Lab.net.

336 John Stuart Mill, ["Introductory" chapter, *On Liberty* (Dover Publications; 1st edition, 2002), 4-5 (originally published in 1859), italics are my own.

337 Theodore Roosevelt, "The Right of the People to Rule," speech delivered March 20, 1912, at Carnegie Hall, New York, second stanza, published online by the American Rhetoric Speech Bank.

338 "Beyond Red vs. Blue: The Political Typology: Even in deep divisions both partisan coalistion," Pew Research Center Report, Washington D.C. November 9, 2021, 5: https://www.pewresearch.org/politics/wp-content/uploads/sites/4/2021/11/PP_2021.11.09_political-typology_REPORT.pdf

339 Ibid., 6.

340 Ibid., 7.

341 "Inflation, Health Costs, Partisan Cooperation Among the Nation's Top Problems," Pew Research Center Report, Washington D.C. June 21, 2023, https://www.pewresearch.org/politics/2023/06/21/inflation-health-costs-partisan-cooperation-among-the-nations-top-problems/

342 "Highly negative views of the opposing party are far more widespread than in the past," Rising partisan antipathy: widening party gap in presidential job approval, Pew Research Center, Washington D.C. August 9, 2022, https://www.pewresearch.org/politics/2022/08/09/rising-partisan-antipathy-widening-party-gap-in-presidential-job-approval/

343 "As Partisan Hostility Grows, Signs of Frustration With the Two-Party System," Rising partisan antipathy; widening party gap in presidential job approval," Pew Research Center Report, Washington D.C. August 9, 2022, https://www.pewresearch.org/politics/2022/08/09/rising-partisan-antipathy-widening-party-gap-in-presidential-job-approval/

344 Ibid.

345 Lee Rainie, Scott Keeter and Andrew Perrin, "The state of personal trust," Trust and Distrust in America, Pew Research Center Report, Washington D.C. July 22, 2019, https://www.pewresearch.org/politics/2019/07/22/the-state-of-personal-trust/

346 "Do Americans Really Care For Each Other?" by the Making Caring Common Project, published online by the Harvard Graduate School of Education, December 8, 2021.

347 Ibid.

348 Ibid.

349 Carroll Doherty, "2 – Most Americans say it would be too risky to give presidents more power," Key findings on Americans' views of the US political system and democracy, Pew Research Center, Washington D.C. April 26, 2018, https://www.pewresearch.org/short-reads/2018/04/26/key-findings-on-americans-views-of-the-u-s-political-system-and-democracy/

350 Carroll Doherty "5 – Most Americans say policymakers should heed the will of the majority even if they and their supporters differ," Key findings on Americans' views of the US political system and democracy. Pew Research Center, Washington D.C. April 26, 2018, https://www.pewresearch.org/short-reads/2018/04/26/key-findings-on-americans-views-of-the-u-s-political-system-and-democracy/

351 "Historical Reported Voting Rates" (2015), published online by the United Stated Department Census Bureau.

352 Ibid.

353 Ibid.

354 "More engage with politics digitally than by volunteering or attending rallies," The Public, the Political System and American Democracy, Pew Research Report, Washington D.C. April 26, 2018, https://www.pewresearch.org/politics/2018/04/26/10-political-engagement-knowledge-and-the-midterms/

355 Ibid.

356 Alexis De Tocqueville, *Democracy in America,* Volume 2, Book 4, 1840 (Chicago, Illinois: University of Chicago Press, 2022)

357 John Gramlich, "What makes a good citizen? Voting, paying taxes, following the law top list," Pew Research Center, Washington D.C. July 2, 2019, https://www.pewresearch.org/short-reads/2019/07/02/what-makes-a-good-citizen-voting-paying-taxes-following-the-law-top-list/

358 E.J. Dionne and Miles Rapoport, *100% Democracy: The Case for Universal Voting* (The New Press, 2022)

359 Jacob Fabina, "Despite Pandemic Challenges, 2020 Election Had Largest Increase in Voting Between Presidential Elections on Record," April 29, 2021, published online by the United Stated Census Bureau.

360 Drew DeSilver, "Turnout in US has soared in recent elections but by some measures still trails that of many other countries," Pew Research Report, Washington D.C. November 1, 2022, https://www.pewresearch.org/short-reads/2022/11/01/turnout-in-u-s-has-soared-in-recent-elections-but-by-some-measures-still-trails-that-of-many-other-countries/

361 Global Citizen, *Globalcitizen.org*

362 Susan Davis, Scott Detrow, Domenico Montanaro, Eric Deggans, & Shannon Bond, "Unlike Trump, Folks Who Don't Like Biden May Vote For Him Anyway," transcript of The NPR Politics Podcast, April 28, 2023.

363 Drew DeSilver, "Turnout in US has soared in recent elections but by some measures still trails that of many other countries," Pew Research Center, Washington D.C. November 1, 2022, https://www.pewresearch.org/short-reads/2022/11/01/turnout-in-u-s-has-soared-in-recent-elections-but-by-some-measures-still-trails-that-of-many-other-countries/

364 "Half of Youth Voted in 2020, An 11-Point Increase from 2016," published online at the Center for Information and Research on Civic Learning and Engagement at Tufts College.

365 "Bipartisan Support for Early In-Person Voting, Voter ID, Election Day National Holiday," Pew Research Report, Washington D.C. February 7, 2024, https://www.pewresearch.org/politics/2024/02/07/bipartisan-support-for-early-in-person-voting-voter-id-election-day-national-holiday/

366 "Trust in government: 1958-2015." Beyond Distrust: How Americans View Their Government, Pew Research Center Report, Washington D.C. November 23, 2015, https://www.pewresearch.org/politics/2015/11/23/1-trust-in-government-1958-2015/

367 James Devitt, "America More Liberal than 50 Years Ago—But Change Not Reflected in Its Politics," December 9, 2021, News Release published online by New York University.

368 Ibid.

369 Ibid.

370 The Lugar Center, *TheLugarCenter.org*

371 Dan Barry, "One Small Step for Democracy in a 'Live Free or Die' Town," *The New York Times,* updated August 10, 2022.

Chapter 6 – Consensus and the US Public Sphere

372 CNN Live Event/Special with John King and Jake Tapper, June 28, 2022, transcript published online at CNN.

373 Eddie Scarry, *Liberal Misery: How the Hateful Left Sucks Joy Out of Everything and Everyone* (Bombardier Books, 2022)

374 Art Swift. "Americans' Trust in Mass Media Sinks to New Low," Gallup, September 14, 2016, https://news.gallup.com/poll/195542/americans-trust-mass-media-sinks-new-low.aspx

375 Megan Brenan, "Partisans' Trust in Mass Media, 1972-2022." Americans' Trust in Media Remains Near Record Low, Gallup, October 18, 2022, https://news.gallup.com/poll/403166/americans-trust-media-remains-near-record-low.aspx

376 Pearson Institute/AP-NORC Poll, conducted by the Pearson Institute and The Associated Press-NORC Center for Public Affairs Research, published online by the Pearson Institute (Interviews September 9 to 13, 2021), https://apnorc.org/wp-content/uploads/2021/10/MisinformationTopline_Final.pdf

377 "Many Believe Misinformation ss Increasing Extreme Political Views and Behaviors," Pearson Institute/AP-NORC Poll Conducted by the Pearson Institute and The Associated Press-NORC Center for Public Affairs Research, https://apnorc.org/wp-content/uploads/2022/10/Pearson-Institute-AP-NORC-Poll-Report-on-Misinformation.pdf

378 Michael Barthel and Amy Mitchell. "Americans' Attitudes About the News Media Deeply Divided Along Partisan Lines." Pew Research Center. May 10, 2017.

379 Ibid.

380 Jeffrey Gottfried, Amy Mitchell, Mark Jurkowitz and Jacob Liedke, "Journalists Sense Turmoil in Their Industry Amid Continued Passion for Their Work," Pew Research Center, Washington D.C. June 14, 2022, https://www.pewresearch.org/journalism/2022/06/14/journalists-sense-turmoil-in-their-industry-amid-continued-passion-for-their-work/

381 Ibid.

382 Jürgen Habermas, *The Structural Transformation of the Public Sphere: An Inquiry into a Category of Bourgeois Society* (The MIT Press, 1991), 176.

383 Marshall McLuhan, *The Gutenberg Galaxy: The Making of Typographic Man* (Toronto, Canada: University of Toronto Press, 1962)

384 John Milton, *Areopagitica and Other Writings* (Penguin Classics, 2016)

385 Corey Brettschneider quoted in "Before Drafting the Bill of Rights, James Madison Argued the Constitution Was Fine Without It," by Lesley Kennedy, History (Channel) online, September 25, 2023.

386 Ibid.

387 *Glenn R. Carrol and Michael T. Hannan, "Density Dependence in the Evolution of Populations of Newspaper Organizations." American Sociological Review, 54 (4): 528 (August 1989)*

388 Arthur Meier Schlesinger, *The Rise of the City: 1878-1898* (Ohio State University Press; 1st edition, 1999), 185-87.

389 Kenneth Whyte, *The Uncrowned King: The Sensational Rise of William Randolph Hearst* (Counterpoint, 2009).

390 *Crucible of Empire: The Spanish–American War,* documentary film, Daniel A. Miller, dir. PBS (1999)

391 "1964 Democratic Party Platform" (August 24, 1964), published online by The American Presidency Project at University of California Santa Barbara.

392 John Edward Burke, *An Historical-analytical Study of the Legislative and Political Origins of the Public Broadcasting Act of 1967* (Arvo Press, 1979)

393 "'Gavel-to-Gavel': The Watergate Scandal and Public Television," published online by the American Archive of Public Broadcasting.

394 "Inquiry into Section 73.1910 of the Commission's Rules and Regulations Concerning Alternatives to the General Fairness Doctrine Obligations of Broadcast Licensees in MM Docket No. 97-26, 2 FCC Rcd 1532 (1987), Federal Communication Commission, published online by the Internet Archive, *Archive.org*

395 Ibid.

396 Robert D. Hershey Jr., "F.C.C. Votes Down Fairness Doctrine In A 4-0 Decision," *The New York* Times, August 5, 1987.

397 Ibid.

398 Ibid.

399 Nicole Hemmer, *Messengers of the Right: Conservative Media and the Transformation of American Politics* (University of Pennsylvania Press, 2008.

400 "Medieval Sourcebook: Urban II: Speech at Council of Clermont, 1095 -- according to Fulcher of Chartres," published online by the Internet History Sourcebooks Project at the History Department of Fordham University.

401 Bruce L. Smith, "Propaganda," *Encyclopædia Britannica*, retrieved 23 February 2024.

402 John Maxwell Hamilton, *Manipulating the Masses: Woodrow Wilson and the Birth of American Propaganda* (LSU Press, 2024)

403 Robert Ensor, *The New Cambridge Modern History: volume XII The Era of Violence 1890–1945*, David Thomson, ed. (Cambridge University Press,1960), 84.

404 Edward S. Herman and Noam Chomsky, *Manufacturing Consent: The Political Economy of the Mass Media.* (Pantheon, 2002)

405 Jeffrey Gottfried, Mason Walker and Amy Mitchell, "Most Americans see news organizations as opaque, particularly when it comes to their financing." Americans See Skepticism of News Media as Healthy, Say Public Trust in the Institution Can Improve, Pew Research Center Report, Washington D.C, August 31, 2020, https://www.pewresearch.org/journalism/2020/08/31/americans-see-skepticism-of-news-media-as-healthy-say-public-trust-in-the-institution-can-improve/

406 Michael M. Grynbaum, "Fox News Drops 'Fair and Balanced' Motto," *The New Yok Times*, June 14, 2017.

407 Camille Caldera, "Fact check: Fairness Doctrine only applied to broadcast licenses, not cable TV like Fox News." *USA Today,* November 28, 2020.

408 Ibid.

409 Jeffrey Gottfried, Amy Mitchell, Mark Jurkowitz and Jacob Liedke. "Journalists are far more concerned than the public about politically like-minded people clustering around the same news outlets." Journalists Sense Turmoil in Their Industry Amid Continued Passion for Their Work, June 14, 2022, https://www.pewresearch.org/journalism/2022/06/14/journalists-sense-turmoil-in-their-industry-amid-continued-passion-for-their-work/

410 Ibid.

411 Jacob Liedke and Jeffrey Gottfried. "US adults under 30 are now almost as likely to trust information on social media sites as information from national news outlets." Pew Research Center Report, Washington D.C, October 27, 2022, https://www.pewresearch.org/short-reads/2022/10/27/u-s-adults-under-30-now-trust-information-from-social-media-almost-as-much-as-from-national-news-outlets/

412 Ibid.

413 Ibid.

414 Ibid.

415 Megan Brenan, "Media Confidence in US Matches 2016 Record Low," Gallup, October 19, 2023, https://news.gallup.com/poll/512861/media-confidence-matches-2016-record-low.aspx

416   Mark Jurkowitz and Amy Mitchell, "Most say journalists should be watchdogs, but views of how well they fill this role vary by party, media diet," Pew Research Center, Washington D.C. February 26, 2020, https://www.pewresearch.org/journalism/2020/02/26/most-say-journalists-should-be-watchdogs-but-views-of-how-well-they-fill-this-role-vary-by-party-media-diet/

417   Mason Walker and Jeffrey Gottfried. "Americans blame unfair news coverage on media outlets, not the journalists who work for them." Pew Research Center, Washington D.C, October 28, 2020, https://www.pewresearch.org/short-reads/2020/10/28/americans-blame-unfair-news-coverage-on-media-outlets-not-the-journalists-who-work-for-them/

418   Ibid.

419   Elisa Shearer, Jacob Liedke, Katerina Eva Matsa, Michael Lipka and Mark Jurkowitz. "Podcasts as a Source of News and Information." Pew Research Center Report, Washington D.C. April 18, 2023, https://www.pewresearch.org/journalism/2023/04/18/podcasts-as-a-source-of-news-and-information/

420   Colleen McClain, "More so than adults, US teens value people feeling safe online over being able to speak freely." Pew Research Center, Washington D.C. August 30, 2022, https://www.pewresearch.org/short-reads/2022/08/30/more-so-than-adults-u-s-teens-value-people-feeling-safe-online-over-being-able-to-speak-freely/

421   Ibid.

422   Mark Jurkowitz and Amy Mitchell, "Most say journalists should be watchdogs, but views of how well they fill this role vary by party, media diet." Pew Research Center, Washington D.C. February 26, 2020, https://www.pewresearch.org/journalism/2020/02/26/most-say-journalists-should-be-watchdogs-but-views-of-how-well-they-fill-this-role-vary-by-party-media-diet/

423   Dominick Mastrangelo "New CNN chief: 'We are not going to be a 24/7 Trump news network,'" *The Hill*, November 17, 2022.

424   "Majorities of Americans say partisan fighting gets too much attention, while issues and policy too little." Americans' Dismal Views of the Nation's Politics, Pew Research Center, Washington D.C. September 19, 2023, https://www.pewresearch.org/politics/2023/09/19/americans-dismal-views-of-the-nations-politics/

425   "Majority of Americans say the news media intentionally ignores important stories." Trust and Distrust in America. Pew Research Center, Washington D.C. July 22, 2019, https://www.pewresearch.org/politics/2019/07/22/americans-struggles-with-truth-accuracy-and-accountability/

426   David Folkenflik, "You Literally Can't Believe the Facts Tucker Carlson Tells You. So Say Fox's Lawyers," published in Media on NPR, September 29, 2020.

427 Elisa Shearer, "Two-thirds of US adults say they've seen their own news sources report facts meant to favor one side," Pew Research Center, Washington D.C, November 2, 2020, https://www.pewresearch.org/short-reads/2020/11/02/two-thirds-of-u-s-adults-say-theyve-seen-their-own-news-sources-report-facts-meant-to-favor-one-side/

428 John Gramlich, "What makes a news story trustworthy? Americans point to the outlet that publishes it, sources cited." Pew Research Center, Washington D.C. June 9, 2021, https://www.pewresearch.org/short-reads/2021/06/09/what-makes-a-news-story-trustworthy-americans-point-to-the-outlet-that-publishes-it-sources-cited/

429 Amy Mitchell, Jeffrey Gottfried, Michael Barthel and Nami Sumida, "The ability to classify statements as factual or opinion varies widely based on political awareness, digital savviness and trust in news media," Distinguishing Between Factual and Opinion Statements in The News, Pew Research Center Report, Wshington D.C. June 18, 2018, https://www.pewresearch.org/journalism/2018/06/18/the-ability-to-classify-statements-as-factual-or-opinion-varies-widely-based-on-political-awareness-digital-savviness-and-trust-in-news-media/

430 Carmel Lobello, "Craigslist took nearly $1 billion a year away from dying newspapers," The Week, January 11, 2015.

431 Esther Addley, "Tiny newspaper in US wins Pulitzer prize for taking on big business," The Guardian, April 11, 2017

432 Linley Sanders, "Trust in Media 2023: What news outlets do Americans trust most for information?" YouGov, May 8, 2023.

433 Jeffrey Gottfried, Mason Walker and Amy Mitchell, "Americans See Skepticism of News Media as Healthy, Say Public Trust in the Institution Can Improve," Pew Research Center, Washington D.C. August 31, 2020, https://www.pewresearch.org/journalism/2020/08/31/americans-see-skepticism-of-news-media-as-healthy-say-public-trust-in-the-institution-can-improve/

434 Len Gutkin, "The Hyperbolic Style in American Academe: How paranoid accusations of 'violence' became all the rage," The Chronicle of Higher Education, February 5, 2024.

435 Ibid.

436 Jeremiah Poff, "Students who heckled Ann Coulter at Cornell event could face discipline," The Washington Examiner, November 14, 2022.

437 The World Press Freedom Index, published online by Reporters without Borders, Rsf.org.

438 Ibid.

439 Ibid.

440 Richard Wike and Katie Simmons, "Appendix A: Free Expression Index." Global Support for Principle of Free Expression, but Opposition to Some Forms of Speech, Pew Research Center Report, Washington D.C. November 15, 2015.

441 Richard Wike. "Americans more tolerant of offensive speech than others in the world." Pew Research Center. October 16, 2016, https://www.pewresearch.org/short-reads/2016/10/12/americans-more-tolerant-of-offensive-speech-than-others-in-the-world/

442 Ibid.

443 "2023 World Press Freedom Index – journalism threatened by fake content industry," published online by Reporters without Borders, *Rsf.org.*

444 J. Baxter Oliphant, "For many Americans, views of offensive speech aren't necessarily clear-cut," Pew Research Center, Washington D.C. December 14, 2021, https://www.pewresearch.org/short-reads/2021/12/14/for-many-americans-views-of-offensive-speech-arent-necessarily-clear-cut/

445 Ibid.

On These Issues We Agree – A Synopsis

446 Clare Foran, "GOP Rep. Ken Buck to leave Congress at end of next week," *CNN* online, March 12, 2024.

447 "In GOP Contest, Trump Supporters Stand Out for Dislike of Compromise," Pew Research Center Report, Washington D.C. December 14, 2023, https://www.pewresearch.org/politics/wp-content/uploads/sites/4/2023/12/PP_2023.12.14_GOP-primaries_REPORT.pdf

448 "Americans and Billionaires Survey," published online by The Harris Poll Thought Leadership Practice, August 2022, https://theharrispoll.com/wp-content/uploads/2022/08/Americans-and-Billionaires-Survey-August-2022.pdf?utm_source=Newswire&utm_medium=PR&utm_content=america-loves-and-hates-its-billionaires-but-definitely-wants-them-to-21804699

449 E. Napoletano, "Here's How Many Billionaires And Millionaires Live In The US," *Forbes Advisor,* updated October 23, 2023.

450 Ronald Wright, *A Short History of Progress* (House of Anansi Press; 2nd edition, 2020)

451 "Country Rankings by Life Evaluations in 2021-2023," published online by the WorldHappiness.Report.

452 Carter Sherman and Andrew Witherspoon, additional reporting by Jessica Glenza and Poppy Noor.,"Abortion rights across the US: we track where laws stand in every state," *The Guardian,* January 12, 2024.

453 "America's Abortion Quandary," Pew Resarch Center Report, Washington D.C. May 6, 2022, https://www.pewresearch.org/religion/2022/05/06/americas-abortion-quandary/

454   Constantine Kanakis, MD MSc, "What to know about IVF after Alabama Supreme Court ruling leaves it in limbo," *ABC News,* February 28, 2024.

455   David Crary and Hannah Fingerhut, "AP-NORC poll: Most say restrict abortion
after 1st trimester," June 25, 2021, https://apnews.com/article/only-on-ap-us-
supreme-court-abortion-religion-health-2c569aa7934233af8e00bef4520a8fa8

456   "Deep Divisions in Americans' Views of Nation's Racial History – and How
To Address It," Pew Research Center Report, Washington D.C. August 12,
2021, https://www.pewresearch.org/politics/2021/08/12/deep-divisions-in-
americans-views-of-nations-racial-history-and-how-to-address-it

457   Ibid.

458   Ibid.

459   Kiana Cox and Khadijah Edwards, "Black Americans are pessimistic about
their position in US society." Pew Research Center Report, Washington D.C.
August 30, 2022, https://www.pewresearch.org/race-ethnicity/2022/08/30/
black-americans-are-pessimistic-about-their-position-in-u-s-society/

460   Ibid.

461   Ibid.

462   Andrew Daniller, "Majorities of Americans see at least some discrimination
against Black, Hispanic and Asian people in the US," Pew Research Center
Report, Washington D.C. March 18, 2021, https://www.pewresearch.org/short-
reads/2021/03/18/majorities-of-americans-see-at-least-some-discrimination-
against-black-hispanic-and-asian-people-in-the-u-s/

463   Juliana Menasce Horowitz, Anna Brown and Kiana Cox. "Majorities who think
Blacks are at a disadvantage say racial discrimination, less access to good
schools or jobs are major obstacles for Blacks." Views of racial inequality.
April 19, 2019, https://www.pewresearch.org/race-ethnicity/2022/08/30/black-
americans-are-pessimistic-about-their-position-in-u-s-society/

464   Megan Brenan, "Water Pollution Remains Top Environmental Concern in US,"
Gallup, April 19, 2021, https://news.gallup.com/poll/347735/water-pollution-
remains-top-environmental-sconcern.aspx

465   Ibid.

466   John Gramlich, "Violent crime is a key midterm voting issue, but what does
the data say?" Pew Research Center, Washington D.C. October 31, 2022,
https://www.pewresearch.org/short-reads/2022/10/31/violent-crime-is-a-key-
midterm-voting-issue-but-what-does-the-data-say/

467   Patrick Sharkey and Alisabeth Marsteller, "Violence and Urban inequality," *Vital
City*, March 2, 2022.

468   Ibid.

469   M. Tyler Gillett, "New Database Compiles Common Traits of US Mass Shooter," *Jurist,* February 5, 2022.

470 Jeffrey M. Jones, "Immigration Surges to Top of Most Important Problem List," Gallup, February 27, 2024, https://news.gallup.com/poll/611135/immigration-surges-top-important-problem-list.aspx

471 "Americans' Top Policy Priority for 2024: Strengthening the Economy," Pew Research Center Report, Washington D.C. February 29, 2024, https://www.pewresearch.org/politics/2024/02/29/americans-top-policy-priority-for-2024-strengthening-the-economy/

472 Ibid.

473 Ibid.

474 Ibid.

475 Lisa Desjardins, "What's in the Senate's sweeping $118 billion immigration and foreign aid bill?" *PBS News Hour,* February 6, 2024.

476 "8 ways to solve the world refugee crisis," published on by Amnesty International, October 12, 2015.

477 "Inflation, Health Costs, Partisan Cooperation Among the Nation's Top Problems," Pew Research Center Report, Washington D.C. June 21, 2023, https://www.pewresearch.org/politics/2023/06/21/inflation-health-costs-partisan-cooperation-among-the-nations-top-problems/

478 "Highly negative views of the opposing party are far more widespread than in the past." Rising partisan antipathy: widening party gap in presidential job approval, Pew Research Center, Washington D.C. August 9, 2022, https://www.pewresearch.org/politics/2022/08/09/rising-partisan-antipathy-widening-party-gap-in-presidential-job-approval/

479 "Rising partisan antipathy; widening party gap in presidential job approval." As Partisan Hostility Grows, Signs of Frustration With the Two-Party System, Pew Research Center, Washington D.C. August 9, 2022, https://www.pewresearch.org/politics/2022/08/09/rising-partisan-antipathy-widening-party-gap-in-presidential-job-approval/

480 Ibid.

481 Carroll Doherty "2 – Most Americans say it would be too risky to give presidents more power." Key findings on Americans' views of the US political system and democracy, April 26, 2018, Pew Research Center, Washington D.C. https://www.pewresearch.org/short-reads/2018/04/26/key-findings-on-americans-views-of-the-u-s-political-system-and-democracy/

482 Carroll Doherty "5, Most Americans say policymakers should heed the will of the majority even if they and their supporters differ." Key findings on Americans' views of the US political system and democracy, Pew Research Center, Washington D.C. April 26, 2018, https://www.pewresearch.org/short-reads/2018/04/26/key-findings-on-americans-views-of-the-u-s-political-system-and-democracy/

483 Eric Holder quoted on *Real Time* with Bill Maher, HBO, Season 12 Episode 8, March 15, 2024.

484 Robert D. McFadden and Michael M. Grynbaum, "Rush Limbaugh Dies at 70; Turned Talk Radio Into a Right-Wing Attack Machine" *The New York Times*, February 17, 2021.

485 Dylan Byers, "Donald Trump has earned $2 billion in free media coverage, study shows." *CNN Business*, March 15, 2016.

486 "AllSides Media Bias Chart" published online by AllSides, https://www.allsides.com/media-bias/media-bias-chart

487 Linley Sanders, "Trust in Media 2022: Where Americans get their news and who they trust for information," YouGov, April 5, 2022.

488 Ezra Klein. "Steve Bannon Is On to Something." Opinion. *The New York Times.* January 9, 2022.

489 Jeanne Sahadi. "The $787.5 million settlement Fox agreed to pay is a lot. But its net cost will likely be much less." *CNN Business* online. April 20, 2023.

490 Esther Addley, "Tiny newspaper in US wins Pulitzer prize for taking on big business," *The Guardian.* April 11, 2017.

491 Tim Berners-Lee, "Marking the Web's 35th Birthday, an Open Letter," *Medium.com*, March 11, 2024.

492 Ibid.

493 Richard Wike, Laura Silver, Janell Fetterolf, Christine Huang, Sarah Austin, Laura Clancy and Sneha Gubbala, "Social Media Seen as Mostly Good for Democracy Across Many Nations, But US is a Major Outlier," Pew Research Center, Washington D.C, December 6, 2022, https://www.pewresearch.org/global/2022/12/06/social-media-seen-as-mostly-good-for-democracy-across-many-nations-but-u-s-is-a-major-outlier/

494 Reporters without Borders Press Freedom Index, *Rsf.org.*

495 Richard Wike and Janell Fetterolf, "Global Public Opinion in an Era of Democratic Anxiety," Pew Research Center, Washington D.C. December 7, 2021, https://www.pewresearch.org/global/2021/12/07/global-public-opinion-in-an-era-of-democratic-anxiety/

496 Katherine Schaeffer, "On July Fourth, how Americans see their country and their democracy," Pew Research Center, Washington D.C. June 22, 2022, https://www.pewresearch.org/short-reads/2022/06/30/how-americans-see-their-country-and-their-democracy/

497 Ibid.

www.ingramcontent.com/pod-product-compliance
Lightning Source LLC
Chambersburg PA
CBHW020523270326
41927CB00006B/426